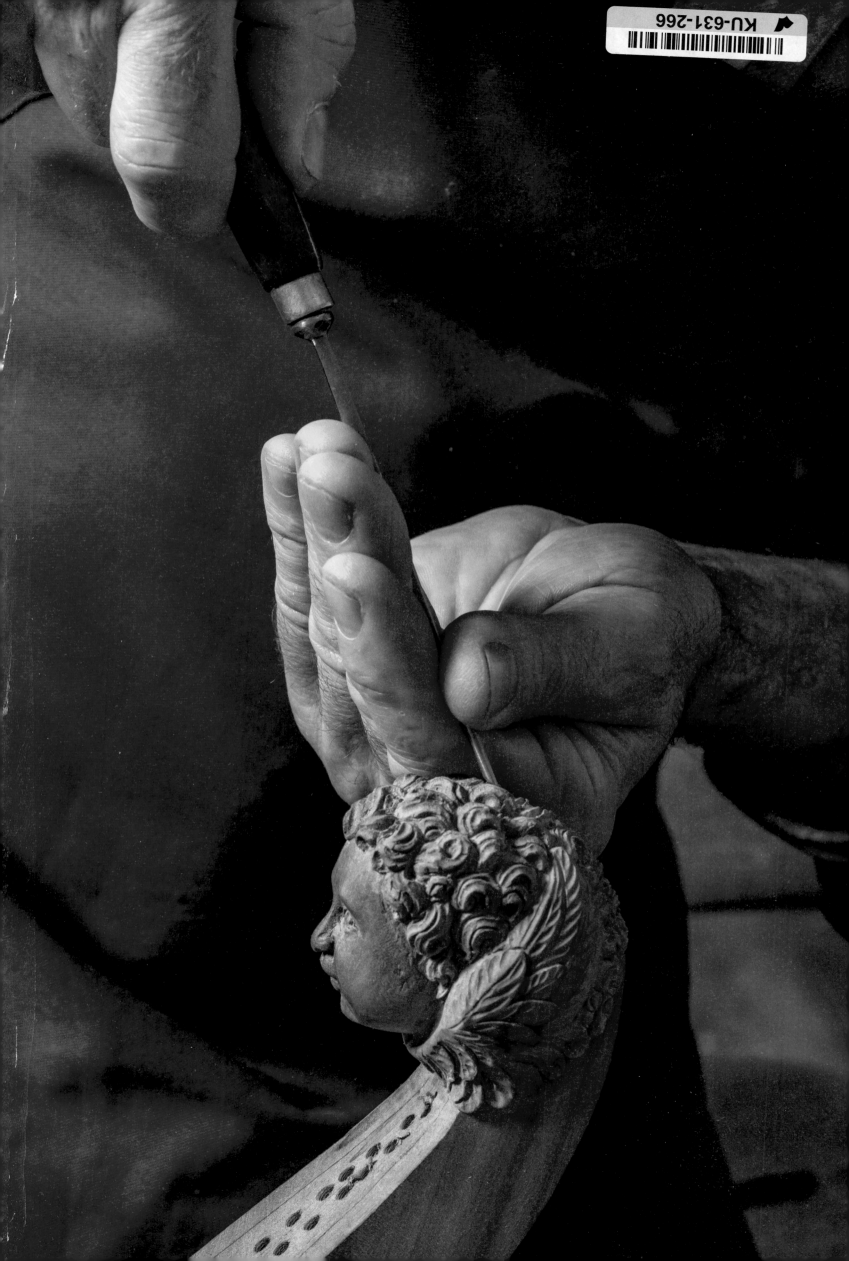

A Celebration of British Craftsmanship

Foreword by H R H The Prince of Wales

Introduction by The Earl of Snowdon

Photographed by Julian Calder

Written by Karen Bennett

Published in 2018 by Impress

Impress
Editorial Department [156]
95 Wilton Road
London, SW1V 1BZ

ISBN 978 1 9997825 8 0

www.impress-publishing.com

Designed by Prof. Phil Cleaver
and Jennifer Penny of
et al design consultants.
Typeset in Adobe Caslon Pro.
Print production by Dave Davies
of dlm creative.
Printed in England by
Geoff Neal Group on Tatami White
supplied by Fedrigoni UK.
Bound by Diamond Printing Services.

COVER
Rod Kelly *Goldsmith & Silversmith*
Manasi Depala *Silversmith*
Photographed near Rod's South House Silver
Workshop on Muckle Roe, Shetland Isles,
holding works in progress.

OPP. PAGE 1 Jennie Adamson *Bespoke Tailor*
Sewing a peacoat of red wool and alpaca
Loden cloth with a number 7 Sharps needle
and silk thread, wearing a tailor's thimble.

PAGE 1 Shem Mackey *Luthier*
Applying fine detail to the curls on a head,
carved in English wild service wood, for the
pegbox of a French, seven-string, bass viol.

PAGE 2 Rod Kelly *Goldsmith & Silversmith*
Chasing a decorative image in low relief onto
a silver beaker, supported by pitch made from
the gum of pine trees.

PAGE 3 Jacqui Carey *Braidmaker*
Holding samples of her multi-coloured
braidwork.

PAGE 4 Deborah Carré *Hand Sewn Shoemaker*
Shaping an English oak bark tanned leather
insole to the last, using a British-made,
Damascus steel knife.

PAGE 7 Kate Hetherington
Collar & Harness Maker
Filling a horse collar with rye straw.

PAGE 222 Anneliese Appleby *Printmaker*
Hand inking the lino to print the next
section in a 10-metre length of *Oak &
Acorn* wallpaper.

PAGE 237 Melissa White *Decorative Artist*
Using lamp black, size paint to outline
a *Tree of Life* design for a bespoke
wallpaper commission.

PAGE 238 Juliet Bailey
Woven Textile Designer & Maker
Preparing a strié striped linen warp for
weaving, by straightening and tensioning
the threads, before tying the yarn to the
front beam of the handloom.

OPP PAGE 240 Ruth Anthony *Hand Engraver*
Adding the finishing touches to an acanthus
scroll design on a steel plate.

Contents

It was nearly thirty years ago that Her Majesty Queen Elizabeth The Queen Mother, my beloved Grandmother, suggested to the Royal Warrant Holders Association – that distinguished body of tradesmen supplying their crafts, services and products to the Royal Households – that they should establish a charity to support and sustain Britain's cultural heritage through excellence in craftsmanship. Thus, The Queen Elizabeth Scholarship Trust was born.

Craft has always been at the heart of our country's identity, from the charm of our many thatched houses, to the magnificent stained glass of our cathedrals and to the finest weaves and fabrics that remain the world's envy. Craft is too often wrongly thought of as preserving the old when, in fact, it is the new that gives craft the relevancy and commercial viability for that continuum of tradition.

It is recognizing the opportunities that change creates which gives confidence – firing the imagination with the kind of innovation so often needed to attain the excellence that a truly gifted craftsperson will aspire to; excellence achieved through an eagerness to learn, a fearless exploration of ideas, of process, of materials and, of course, of teaching. Above all, it is important to look to the future through an intimate understanding of the past so as to maintain a living tradition…

This book celebrates the craft of just over a hundred scholars out of the nearly five hundred that The Queen Elizabeth Scholarship Trust has supported, with talent drawn from all corners of the United Kingdom.

How fortunate it is that in this country we have such a rich craft heritage to draw upon and how wonderful to see this deep vein of creative intelligence inspiring the future and enriching our very identity for years to come.

Introduction, The Earl of Snowdon

VICE PATRON

Portraiture is a craft in itself and the 100 photographs by Julian Calder in this book go far beyond capturing a likeness of the men and women they portray; they capture the soul of the craftsman. My father was a portrait photographer and I grew up assisting at sittings, so when I see Calder's work in these pages I don't just see the journey he has taken across the four corners of the United Kingdom – from a Cornish coppersmith, to a silversmith on Shetland, a willow artist in Northern Ireland, a gem carver in Norfolk and a harp maker from the Marches of Wales. What I see is an insight into their stories: their inspirations, their tools, the landscapes and studios they work in, the materials they choose and all the disciplines that define their practice, documented in this book. ¶ These pages are filled with excellence and potential. No-one spends ten thousand hours honing their skills to be a mediocre craftsman. It is by pursuing such excellence that allows great craft to triumph. The portraits presented here are full of examples of how tradition and innovation are complementary – like Oluwaseyi Sosanya who has developed 'Gravity Sketch', a tool that translates hand gestures into 3D designs as easily as drawing on a piece of paper. Decorative Artist Melissa White has brought an ancient craft up to date, by taking the experience of her apprenticeship in Elizabethan paintings and the traditions of the Tudor painter-stainers, to create scenic artwork for contemporary wallpapers and fabrics. ¶ QEST also supports people at different stages of their careers. Mila Chielman has just completed the first year of his apprenticeship in spectacle making, whilst Julian Stair is internationally recognised as one of the UK's finest potters. Many have studied abroad to acquire knowledge to enrich their practice back in the UK – travelling to Italy to study the origins of fresco and mosaic work, or to the Pilchuck Glass School in Washington State, renowned for the creative use of glass in art and design. Others are working in crafts rooted in their location, like watchmaker Craig Struthers in Birmingham's Jewellery Quarter, Andrew Swinscoe maturing Lancashire farmhouse cheeses, Gail McGarva building traditional wooden boats on the Dorset coast, and sign-writer Amy Goodwin, who grew up with travelling steam fairgrounds in the West Country. ¶ Crucially, many are passing on their skills to the next generation. Silversmith Rod Kelly has now taught seven QEST Scholars in silver chasing at his Shetland workshop and Deborah Carré is teaching her third QEST Scholar in hand sewn shoemaking. Jacqui Carey is writing books so the knowledge that she has rediscovered on English braidmaking and embroidery is not lost again. ¶ This book features only some of QEST's 467 Alumni, all of whom are very much part of one large family; often meeting to exchange ideas, to learn or to collaborate – each of them pushing boundaries, using their craft to educate, inform and innovate. ¶ Together, QEST and its Scholars sustain Britain's cultural heritage through excellence in craftsmanship, which nourishes our Islands' memories, and challenges the way we look at things; lighting the fire of ambition with the humility that working with your hands exemplifies.

Timothy Harris

GLASSMAKER

In 1973, pioneering artists Michael and Elizabeth Harris founded Isle of Wight Studio Glass. Their son Timothy Harris was drawn to the heat, fire and smoke of the studio from an early age. *By 13, I was making glass birds for pocket money.* The studio was on farmland owned by Sam Twining, ninth generation of the family tea merchants. Timothy had studied glassmaking at college and been working for 10 years when Sam told him about the Royal Warrant Holders Association's new charity for craftspeople. ¶ While his late father had worked with American makers to establish studio glass in the UK, Timothy wanted to visit eminent glass artists back in the United States. He applied to QEST and was awarded one of the inaugural Scholarships. His first stop was Penland in North Carolina, home of Harvey Littleton, a founder of the studio glass movement. Then Pilchuck Glass School in Washington State, established by Dale Chihuly to foster the creative use of glass in art and design. *I was enthralled by the scale and complexity of the installations – often thousands of components being made by perhaps 50 glassmakers.* ¶ The trip gave Timothy the confidence to experiment, emboldened his use of colour and he became more flamboyant in his designs. This experience remains vivid almost 30 years on and continues to influence his attitude to glass every day. *I go to the furnace with an idea, but allow myself the freedom to let the piece develop (although I do like to have the last word). Scale too – I always hanker to make something bigger.* ¶ Timothy's connection to the Isle of Wight endures. His decorative pieces are handmade here and sought by collectors around the world. He was proud to be commissioned by the people of the island to make a glass bowl inspired by the sea and coastlines for Her Majesty The Queen's Diamond Jubilee visit, and the Isle of Wight Museum of Glass is home to over a thousand objects that chart glassmaking by the Harris family and other studios on the island, several started by former employees. ¶ In 2012, Timothy took a year out to convert a building at Arreton Barns Craft Village into a new studio. He crated his two furnaces, the heart of any glassmaking practice, and sent them to Peter Wren Howard, a technician in Stourbridge who used his wizardry to construct a single, state-of-the-art furnace. It worked perfectly from day one, but the first time Timothy gathered the molten glass, he had a momentary doubt whether he could still do it. *Five minutes in, I realised I had started whistling.* The studio was opened in 2014 by *Antiques Road Show* expert, Mark Hill. *This coincided with our first Collectors Open Day and we invited William Walker, who developed a range with my father in the 1970s, to demonstrate.* ¶ Timothy is pictured at the glassmaker's bench where he spends most of the day, although sitting for only seconds at a time as he is constantly back and forth to the furnace a step away. He is working on an onion-shaped vase from his *Stratum* collection, striped like layers of rock. This is typical of his approach: mixing techniques, creating multiple layers of glass and incorporating precious metals to reflect the colours, textures and forms found in nature. ¶ Timothy is generous with the skills he has developed as a designer and maker of studio glass and is always interested to see how they are used by others. *Degree students often come to the studio. Running a glass course is expensive, so whilst they might have the chance to do cold work (sandblasting, carving, engraving), if like me they have a passion for the hot side, opportunities are rare.* ¶ He also enjoys seeing how different disciplines, metalsmithing to woodturning, combine with his craft, but for Timothy it will always be glass. *It can burn when it's hot and cut when it's cold, but when you've had a good day making and something magical comes out of the fire, there is nothing more wonderful.*

QEST R. Twining & Company Scholar 1991

Aurora Pettinari York

EMBROIDERER

QEST Radcliffe
Trust Scholar 2016

The hustle and bustle of working in theatrical costume design and making was not for Aurora Pettinari York. She craved a more private space and personal way to practice her needlecraft. ¶ In search of this creative sanctuary, she studied for a Diploma in Technical Hand Embroidery at the Royal School of Needlework in Hampton Court Palace. Founded in 1872, it is the international centre of excellence in its field. *I was captivated as I learned advanced appliqué, silk shading, goldwork and more in a structured way to the highest standards, but as my course was finishing, I felt I was just getting started.* ¶ Aurora had begun to specialise in bespoke embroidery for interiors (she likes to work on objects that can be touched) and wanted to explore the potential of her new stitching skills. QEST funded a series of post-Diploma technical mentoring sessions with her tutors. *These were invaluable. They guided me as I created my first pieces and helped me to approach commissions with confidence at this early stage of my career.* ¶ Aurora grew up in Italy, family members are Classics professors and archaeologist, and holidays were invariably to sites of historic interest. The effect on her work today is profound: mythology provides her narrative, raised embroidery her medium. Her use of three-dimensional stumpwork to create Greek mythology-inspired, human figures caught the eye of *Vogue Italia.* ¶ They paired Aurora with designer Mohammed Ashi to make a garment for *Crafting the Future – Stories of Craftsmanship & Innovation* at MUDEC (Museum of Cultures) in Milan. The intention was to combine craft traditions and designers trained in technological development to encourage an innovative dialogue. Applying a stumpwork and featherwork Eros to the couture gown took over 100 hours. The opening of the exhibition marked the start of Milan Fashion Week and Aurora gave live demonstrations every day. ¶ In the picture, Aurora is holding one of six roundels she made for *Rhapsody on Wheels*, a project with atelier Y A O that brought together the disciplines of art, design and architecture. *This portrait of Medusa and the surrounding decoration, based on an Egyptian tunic, began as a sketch. I then had to make the drawings jump off the page and have form.* The background is French linen and the embroidery is a 17th century English technique that Aurora pushed to achieve sculptural effects. The head and body are constructed of muslin padded with different felts, leather was applied for the garment, and opaque embroiderers' cotton used for the hair and decorative elements. The black and white circles, mosaic-like in appearance, were made by couching, where thread is laid on the surface then fastened in place with small stitches. *I like to work with a minimal colour palette, the earthy shades remind me of those in ancient ceramics.* Each piece is set in a handmade timber frame, the shape influenced by the circular embroidery frame she used to sample the figures. ¶ The simple geometries of the display structure reference the architecture of Italian Rationalism and it was designed on wheels to become a travelling installation. This harks back to Greek rhapsodes, professional performers who journeyed from town to town and whose craft was in stitching together epic poems based on well-known myths. *Rhapsody on Wheels* was exhibited at three venues during London Craft Week 2018: Kallos Gallery ('kallos' is ancient Greek for 'beauty'); Sans Pere; and the William Morris Gallery. ¶ *The approach to the project was intuitive rather than academic and I enjoyed the sense of novelty and play. I also loved being surrounded by antiquities in the galleries that extended their hospitality on our path across the city.* The ancient roundel is Aurora's chosen direction for now. *There is a lot of scope within a circle – it works for full characters, sitting figures or a simple bust – and there is a satisfying completeness to it.*

Shelley Anderson
METAL ARTIST

The glint of metal, both elemental and alloy, has always attracted Cornishman Shelley Anderson. He toyed with the scraps in his mechanic father's garage as a boy, turning them into arrowheads. It was his default material throughout art school, then he trained for City & Guilds qualifications in Silversmithing and Metal Fabrication at Falmouth University. ¶ Having thought of little else for over a decade, he spent a few years working in Spain distanced from his craft. He returned to Cornwall in 2010 as a volunteer for artist craftsman Michael Johnston at The Copper Works in Newlyn. Shelley slotted straight into the ways of the workshop and was soon happily lost again in the physical process. *I was back in the zone: slow, steady and hyper-alert to the innerving sensations of working with metal.* He was assisting on projects, but not yet skilled enough to be left to his own devices; Michael could provide the training he needed, but not a wage. ¶ QEST, acknowledging the historic significance of coppersmithing in the area, supported a two-year apprenticeship. Shelley was exposed to restoration work on copper finials, weather veins, sheet roofs and sculptures as well as making ecclesiastical pieces including holy communion trays and baptism fonts. The diversity of the jobs enabled him to learn a range of metalwork skills from jewellery making to blacksmithing techniques. *It also bought me the freedom to develop my own style; it's impossible to work in metal without having a few expensive accidents, but you learn every time.* ¶ After sitting across a bench from Michael for eight years, Shelley set up his own workshop on a farm in St Just, West Cornwall. He shifted the focus of his practice too and now works mostly in bronze to create artworks for galleries, private commissions and sculptures for outdoor public spaces. Living in the fishing port of Newlyn and working overlooking the Kenidjack valley in one direction and Atlantic Ocean in the other, it would be impossible not to be inspired by the roaming coastline and landscape. ¶ On the table are sea life bronzes that Shelley makes for the Lighthouse Gallery in Penzance and Circle One in Padstow. The crabs, spiny dogfish, common ray and plated mackerel are modelled on his free-diving and spearfishing catches. *I have developed innovative ways of taking moulds from these soft organic forms and like to play with proportions, perhaps adding giant claws to a small crab shell.* ¶ Shelley spent three years developing chemical recipes to recreate the natural forming patinas found around Newlyn harbour and along the shore. The reactions occur in a sealed atmosphere and can take several weeks to develop. *The green-blue finish on these creatures is the result of copper sulphate and heat. I usually polish back the pincers so they are gleaming.* ¶ At The Copper Works, Shelley was most gripped by shaping work using hammers with 'dished out' and 'dome' forms tailor-made for each job. *I developed an eye for pattern cutting and feel for stretching and gathering sheet metal around complex curves.* He has applied a more relaxed, freehand version of this ancient technique to a series of bronze wall sculptures, each panel reflecting an expanse of water in a different sea state. *Looking front-on is like an aerial view of the wave patterns; from the side it feels like your head is bobbing up, breaking the surface.* ¶ He starts by hammering a few broad shapes to get the swell then adds areas of pooling and ripples guided simply by what feels right until he is satisfied by the overall effect. *Sometimes I'm fighting it, sometimes it flows.* While he doesn't consciously try and replicate anything, it often ends up representing what is happening out of the window, from glassy calmness to wild and stormy. *Either way, after a day inside getting covered in dust there is nothing more invigorating than running along the cliff path and diving in for a swim.*

QEST Hedley Foundation Scholar 2011

Melissa White

DECORATIVE ARTIST

QEST Scholar 2007

Following a degree in art history and French, Melissa White was looking to add a practical aspect to her art education. She was introduced to David Cutmore, a specialist in Elizabethan interiors, and began an apprenticeship and partnership that was to last 15 years. ¶ They travelled the country researching and reproducing Elizabethan wall paintings for museums and Tudor houses. It was a daunting initiation, painting wall cloths for four rooms at Shakespeare's Birthplace Museum. In between, they worked in pubs applying paint effects popular at the time. *I'd be mixing natural pigments with rabbit skin glue one day and scumbling anaglypta in nicotine yellow the next, but the disciplines of preparation, painting from ladders, and caring for brushes applied across the board.* ¶ Melissa was absorbing historic references, but wanted to undertake focused research into the decoration of the period. Whilst grand houses in the Elizabethan era were decked with tapestries, Tudor artisans known as painter-stainers provided an eclectic range of designs for the walls and ceilings of ordinary homes. Fashions changed and many were lost, painted over by Puritans, but fragments, records, and some complete examples have survived. *I applied to QEST and began a treasure hunt.* Melissa supplemented this pursuit with workshops in pigment mixing and wattle and daub. *I was able to construct a catalogue of historic designs to underpin my work and explore ways to express my inherent love of surface pattern.* ¶ Melissa was put in touch with Zoffany via Royal Warrant holder Sanderson. *Their fabrics and wallpapers are imbued with craftsmanship and artistic integrity. I was thrilled when they invited me to collaborate on a collection.* Melissa and David created the artwork in her Hastings studio on plastered panels. Using her signature technique, 'fresco secco', the paintwork was aged and cracked to create a patina to reflect the character of the original Elizabethan wall paintings on which the designs were based. *Arden* by Melissa White for Zoffany was born, her name became a brand, and business rocketed. Her next commission was to design two wallpapers for Lewis & Wood: *Bacchus* (for an *English Ethnic* collection) and *Rococo* (inspired by Indian blocks and rococo motifs) display her scholarly approach and passion for embellishment. ¶ In 2013, Melissa was asked to paint a mural in the Summer House at Buckingham Palace for the Coronation Festival. She discovered a pair of paintings by Georgian landscape artist John Wootton in the Royal Collection, then a third. *It is likely they were conceived to hang together, so I reunited them for this commission.* She digitally stitched her interpretation of the scenes into a panorama to flow across the walls. *It took six weeks to paint, including several days of knuckle-busting canvas stretching.* ¶ Designing for Zoffany has continued, including *Peacock Garden* for the *Jaipur Collection*, displayed here in its full, eye-catching glory. *On the table is the printed velvet, in the background the wallpaper, and I couldn't resist dressing the part, so I made an apron in the fabric the night before the shoot.* This lush, Indian landscape grew from book references, temple architecture, and a verdant palette of greens and corals. ¶ Her work for Zoffany brought Melissa's style to the attention of Kit Kemp, co-owner and design director for Firmdale Hotels. Kit and Melissa are kindred spirits, their collaborations quite magical. The first two were towering treescape wallpapers incorporating Kit's *Mythical Creatures*, one for The Whitby in New York, the other for Charlotte Street Hotel in London. ¶ At a glance, Melissa's narrative, scenic artwork is whimsical, bright and contemporary, yet there is no mistaking that her characteristic flair stems from the sweeping brush strokes and florid way in which the Tudors painted and where her career began.

Jack Row

GOLDSMITH & PENMAKER

The Assay Office in Birmingham has been assuring the quality of precious metals since 1773; its anchor symbol is among the hallmarks on every Jack Row writing instrument and accessory. ¶ Jack was 15 years old when he began five years of goldsmith training at the bench of Harry Forster-Stringer (who also became a QEST Scholar in 2017) in Nottingham. He took a diploma in jewellery and silversmithing at the Birmingham Institute of Art and Design (now the University of Birmingham's School of Jewellery) before joining specialist manufacturer Weston Beamor in the Jewellery Quarter. ¶ Alongside designing products for casting, Jack had the chance to experiment with Computer Aided Design, 3D printing, and Rapid Prototyping. *I was excited by the potential of combining my traditional background with this innovative technology, so Weston Beamor sponsored me to study Design for Industry at the School of Jewellery.* ¶ Jack was looking at perfume bottles, watches and other luxury goods to inspire his final project when he came across an article about precious metal fountain pens. *Here was an object on which I could showcase all my skills and, given that I could not find any British-made pens at the quality of fine jewellery, a potential gap in the market.* ¶ Jack's concept was for a precision-engineered, immaculately crafted fountain pen based on modern British architecture. The signature of his design was silver filigree work spiralling around the barrel and studded with brilliant-cut diamonds and sapphires. He was working on a prototype of the *Architect* when a team from Harrods visited for research. *They suggested I speak to the stationery buyer. I travelled to Knightsbridge to get feedback and returned with an offer to launch and stock my first collection exclusively.* ¶ The next year was a whirlwind. Jack graduated with a first-class honours degree, his fountain pen won a British Jewellers' Association prize and Gold at the Goldsmiths' Craft & Design Council Awards, and, at the end of 2011, *The Architect Collection* of pens and cufflinks debuted in The Great Writing Room at Harrods. ¶ Jack wanted to learn advanced engraving and stone setting, but didn't want to lose momentum in his workshop. The bespoke nature of a QEST Scholarship meant that he could spend seven days, one every week or so, back with Harry focusing on the use of precision optical equipment and compressed air engraving tools. Jack used the time in between to practice and carry on with commissions. ¶ He now hand engraves patterns and deep-relief textures on one-off pieces and sets all stones in house, including the half-carat, marquise-cut gems in the clips of the *Mirage* pens he is holding: silver with pink sapphire and rose gold plate with tanzanite. In 2014, he was commissioned by the School of Jewellery and Jewellery Quarter Development Trust to make two pens from this series to present to Their Royal Highnesses The Prince of Wales and The Duchess of Cornwall on a visit to Birmingham. ¶ Their decoration is inspired by the handles of antique military officers' swords. Jack twists 20 metres of sterling silver wire into a rope that he winds around the barrel and cap by hand. *The effect is like desert sands and, when viewed from the side, as though there is a rising heat haze.* The *Mirage Collection* pens are numbered up to a limited edition of 250 and Jack stamps and signs a certificate of authentication with his fine-nibbed, tactical black version and jet black ink. ¶ Every pen, fully bespoke or from Jack's five ranges (*Architect, Mirage, Gothic, City* and *Jaali*) is made to order, so he can always customise at least one element: a meaningful gemstone, precious metal or personal engraving on the trim. Each one is an objet d'art, but Jack never forgets he is making a tool. *I know they end up in the hands of artists, writers and collectors and I love to hear about the stories they create and record when the ink starts to flow.*

'*Four Hattersley looms
are now up and running
and fully tuned in our workshop,
at the foot of the
Mourne Mountains in
Northern Ireland,
as a result of what I learned
on my QEST Scholarship.
The business was established
by my grandmother
in 1949 and it is
wonderful to hear
the busy clack of
weaving here again.*'

Mario Sierra
HANDLOOM WEAVER

Damien McKeown
HANDLOOM WEAVER

For the last four years, Mario Sierra (right) has worked to bring his family's handloom weaving workshop in County Down's Mourne Mountains in Northern Ireland back into production and train a new generation of weavers. *There is nowhere I feel more at home than in this workshop surrounded by our looms, piles of yarn and the smell of lanolin from the wool.* Mario's grandmother, Norwegian-born Gerd Hey-Edie, set up the workshop in 1949, and his mother, Karen Hay-Edie, has guided him on the looms. ¶ Mario grew up in a house full of their textile designs: rugs, blankets, cushions and curtains. *Even our dog's basket was lined with old hand woven fabrics.* Being surrounded by this rich combination of textures and colours has given him a fascination for fabrics and their structure. *I get great pleasure from a piece of cloth woven using yarns of different weights, fibres and colours to produce a balanced, vibrant surface and I love to see our traditional looms used to create contemporary designs.* ¶ He also has the warp books that detail every piece of fabric produced by Mourne Textiles over the decades: the yarns, loom settings, and who it was made for. *My mother and I have spent a lot of time trying to decipher the scribbles.* Mario is leaning on two bolts of heritage furnishing fabrics created from this archive. Another mentor and mine of information was the late John McAtasney, a master weaver with 60 years' experience. *I used to deliver warps to his weave shed an hour away and he kept the same notebook system for jobs that my grandmother had set up.* ¶ QEST supported Mario's training in yarn spinning and development from Joan Johnston and Mark Lightowlers. This improved his understanding for ordering from commercial spinners and dyers. *I learned to talk their language of fibres and twist rates.* Mario also sought training in Hattersley loom tuning, weaving and maintenance. They are powered by small motors, yet weave a tweed much like a handloom with a woven selvedge. *We had four in the studio, but no means of getting them working.* Now they are functional, the range of fabrics and products Mario can make has expanded considerably. *These looms were used recently to make a range of scarves for Margaret Howell.* ¶ Gerd's *Milano Rug* was selected by furniture designer Robin Day to be shown alongside his pieces at *La Triennale di Milano* in 1951. *It was poignant for Mario to return to Milan Design Week with these rug designs, crafted in the workshop today.* They are made on the largest handloom with linen warp for strength. Every time the weavers 'beat in' the warm woollen yarn and soft, unspun fleece, the whole workshop shakes. *We recently sent a six-metre rug to a house in the Hamptons in New York; we had to stitch four panels together to get the size.* ¶ In 2017, Damien McKeown (sitting at one of the original handlooms imported by Gerd) joined Mourne Textiles as a QEST Apprentice. *He is a drummer so has good hand-eye co-ordination and picked up the rhythm of the loom immediately.* Damien is one of the main hand weavers for the furnishing fabrics, but his apprenticeship has been designed for him to learn all aspects of the craft of weaving for interiors, furnishing and clothing and the running of the workshop. There are four full-time apprentice weavers currently and Mario is proud to have two of the original weavers, who used to work for his grandmother in the 1960s and 1970s, back at the workshop. *The crossover between the old and new is fantastic for everyone.* ¶ In 2018, Mourne Textiles was invited to represent Northern Ireland at a Downing Street reception hosted by Prime Minister Theresa May to celebrate the UK's Creative Industries on the eve of London Craft Week. *It was a special event to attend with my mother.* Looking through old newspaper clippings, Mario and Karen found a quote of Gerd's that rings equally true today: 'out of the past flows the future'.

Mario Sierra
QEST Rokill
Scholar 2016

Damien McKeown
QEST Pilgrim Trust
Apprentice 2016

Hazel Thorn

SILVERSMITH

QEST Scholar 2011 Hazel Thorn grew up in a remote part of the Scottish Highlands. *We were five miles by road, four on foot, from the nearest town; it was the middle of nowhere and I loved it.* She would disappear into the woods to play in nature, weaving grasses and making sculptures with intertwined reeds and sticks. Her step-father, a long-distance backpacker and author, bought her a multi-tool so that she could start incorporating garden wire. *Even at this basic level I found metal exciting to work with. It can seem rigid and unchangeable, but is fantastically malleable and versatile.* ¶ Her second home has been the Edinburgh College of Art since she discovered silversmithing in 2007 on the first year of a Jewellery BA course. Hazel then gained a Masters of Fine Art, supported by QEST, was an artist-in-residence for a year, and is now a visiting tutor. *During my early studies, I loved the freedom of large-scale, exuberant painting as a counterpoint to the precision of jewellery and silversmithing. It was my fervent hope to combine these approaches in my metalwork.* In the middle of her undergraduate degree, Hazel attended a course at West Dean College with Alistair McCallum, an expert in the Japanese art of 'mokume gane' (layering metals), which she used in a special project: Hazel was one of four students selected to work with Edinburgh silversmiths Hamilton & Inches on a mace for the University of the Highlands & Islands for its first graduation ceremony. ¶ *I was attracted to mokume gane as a way of using metals to create pattern and colour, but this was the only time I worked in the actual technique.* Hazel has developed a version of her own. *I think of it as a cousin to the original.* She constructs sheets from wires of precious and base metals, the method of assembly forming the design. Applying chemical patination affects the metals in different ways, which highlights the composition: silver stays white, gilding metal (a high-copper brass) turns black, and the newly created alloy between them develops into a blue-green. She keeps detailed records so that the effects of different metal alloys and chemical compounds can be recreated. ¶ Hazel forms the sheets into sculptural vessels. *The intrinsic qualities enable me to create objects that resemble a 3D snapshot of a living thing in growth, movement or decay: seemingly fragile, but actually strong and enduring.* For the shoot, she chose *Overflowing*, her largest to date, with two interlocking sheets spilling over one another. *I live near Edinburgh, so we escaped up into the nearby Pentland Hills in search of woodland and water. I thought I was going to be wading into a rushing stream, but after a long, hot summer, there was barely a trickle.* The technique by which these vessels are formed was featured in *Silver Speaks: Idea to Object* at the Victoria and Albert Museum in 2016. ¶ In 2018, Hazel was admitted into the Worshipful Company of Gold and Silver Wyre Drawers. She has pieces in the permanent collections of the Incorporation of Goldsmiths in Edinburgh and The Goldsmiths' Company in London. She is also a beneficiary of The Goldsmiths' Company's Studio Internship Graduate Award, through which she received advanced training from three masters: Adrian Hope, Rauni Higson and Mary Ann Simmons. *I worked in plain metal during these placements, partly because it is best to learn new skills without the extra complication, but also to broaden my style of work.* One of her first pieces since is *Birch Beaker*, created for *Made for the Table*, an exploration of the evolution of silverware. It has the texture of bark and branches, but is chased in silver: familiar pattern, different technique; wild, yet peaceful. ¶ *My work has a strong link to my childhood wanderings; with every new technique to work the metal, I find a different way to explore and express my admiration for the complexity, order and chaos of nature.*

Julian Stair

POTTER

Julian Stair is one of the UK's leading potters and historians of English studio ceramics. He believes it is vital to be able to talk about and contextualise work on an historical continuum, but does not dwell on the nostalgia of handmade pottery. *We engage with pots in an extraordinary number of ways, both optic and haptic, and they facilitate an incredible agency, from baptismal font to funerary jar, and sustain our eating and drinking in between. They embody what it means to be human.* ¶ Julian emerged from his undergraduate course in Ceramics at Camberwell School of Art making sculptural work. The shift to vessels came during his MA studies at the Royal College of Art. He is pictured holding a first edition of *Ceramics: an appreciation of the arts* by Philip Rawson. *This is the book that set me on my way; I still quote him often.* ¶ The sketchbook was supreme at art school, but Julian found it inadequate for his work. *To draw, you have to take into account perspective from a single point. We have binocular vision, which gives us spatial depth and the medium of clay has a huge influence on the form.* He prefers to make maquettes. By using the material, process and techniques that he is going to use eventually, there is no disjunction between the idea and the finished pot. ¶ A QEST Scholarship in 2004 enabled Julian to vastly increase the scale of his work. *I was able to conduct fundamental research in a brick factory to explore the potential of placing my traditional studio skills within industry.* It was a fascinating amalgam of the two worlds. Whilst separate disciplines with different perspectives, the common material created synergy. Learning how they made bricks, using their clay and having access to the enormous kilns led to an astonishing technical achievement. *The biggest pots, built by eye around particular harmonic proportions, took several months to complete. They were over seven feet tall when I finished throwing them and weighed just under half a tonne each.* ¶ This feat made a significant contribution to *Quietus: The vessel, death and the human body*, the culmination of a ten-year exploration into the containment of the human body after death. *Quietus* has appeared at mima, the National Museum of Wales in Cardiff, Winchester Cathedral, and Somerset House in London, assuming different forms in each venue, including cinerary jars and life size sarcophagi. The experience in the brick factory enabled Julian to bring a monumental scale to the pots shown at Winchester Cathedral. ¶ Julian's next project was based on the nourishing act of giving and taking food. *Many years ago I bought a Richard Batterham teapot, which was probably more than I could afford at the time. I think about how many mornings that pot made tea for me, which translates to surprising 'value per wear'. This is craft at its very best.* Quotidian in 2012 was a contemporary interpretation of the dinner service that enables these daily social rituals to take place. The exhibition at Corvi-Mora gallery was a table with place settings for 16 people to share a meal facilitated by the pots, each one designed and made as the perfect vessel to enjoy its contents. ¶ The continuum, from the preciousness of making to experiencing the pots in the hand, is important to Julian's practice. He has even put signs out at exhibitions saying 'please touch'. *We are physical creatures who live in a material world. Touch is innate and something we take for granted: yet it remains elusive, we have such limited vocabulary to express how something feels.* As a maker, Julian's hands operate independently of his conscious thought; they have the muscle memory to know exactly what to do. This is the subject of an experiment that Julian is undertaking with a classical guitarist and scientist at the V&A Research Institute as part of a programme to look at new ways of revealing the complexity of touch and haptical appreciation.

QEST Scholar 2004

Kerry Lemon

ARTIST

QEST Scholar 2007 Nobody Kerry Lemon knew growing up could give her any advice on how she could use her love of drawing professionally. *I always adored drawing and found it potent; if I drew a picture of beautiful shoes, to me they were as real as owning an actual pair.* She studied Fine Art at the University of Reading, gained an MA in Museum Studies and worked in the education departments of museums, galleries and with artists-in-residence at South Hill Park Arts Centre in Berkshire, but longed to be an artist. ¶ The breakthrough came when she discovered the MA in Illustration at Anglia Ruskin University Cambridge. *I was certain this would give me the chance to be the artist I had in my head, whose drawings could end up in a magazine or on the side of an aeroplane. The QEST Scholarship was a lifeline.* At the crack of dawn every Wednesday, she travelled to Cambridge with a rucksack crammed with books so she could read and sketch on the way. Circumstances meant that Kerry only completed the first year, a Postgraduate Diploma, but she was filled with optimism. ¶ She wrote a business plan that gave her three years to become a full-time artist. *I achieved this in half the time, albeit supporting a basic existence.* Initially she was paid to illustrate print articles and websites – a typewriter here, a cauliflower there - then the jobs started to grow. Kerry was asked by the Electrum Gallery in London if she could paint their window. Her first thought was 'not in a million years, everybody will be watching', but she practised drawing backwards on the windows of her flat and experimented with paints to discover which would stay on (and come off). *I didn't sleep the night before, but loved the scale and interaction. A young girl passing by was transfixed – I would have been the same.* ¶ Kerry documented everything so she could market the service if it went well. When she contacted Liberty, they happened to be looking for an artist to paint a large mural in the Beauty Hall. *I created a magnolia and peacock to adorn the new space. This felt like a passport to a new realm of work and I have a reminder in ink: a magnolia flower tattoo on my foot.* She found the nature of retail work, prominent for a couple of months then ceasing to exist, a freeing experience. *I could create something absolutely right for the moment and to the best of my ability, knowing it wouldn't be winking at me 10 years down the line looking out of place.* ¶ Kerry also wanted to work on something lasting. She contacted property developers and was invited to a meeting about a mixed-use development in London Fields. There was a glass-bottomed, rooftop pool above an atrium with a wildflower garden at ground level; the brief was a clean slate. *They placed amazing trust in me. After a period of research, I created an 18-metre by six-metre brass wall installation cut as a patch of water lilies.* The light through the pool dances across the petals and reflects onto the atrium floor. As with every other job, this put Kerry into a new bracket and she was asked to oversee the artistic elements on the redevelopment of Bracknell town centre. ¶ She is pictured at Coutts private bank on The Strand in London. *They have a beautiful rooftop garden that I wanted to bring down to the street.* As artist-in-residence, Kerry created prints for their clients and live painted four giant canvases in the window, which were auctioned for charity. *It is empowering to know I have gone out and found these jobs; I long to tell my eight-year-old self that this is how I make my living.* ¶ From designing actual versions of her imaginary plants with molecular scientists at Royal Holloway University to painting a mural of instruments for the Musashino Academia Musicae University in Tokyo, she knows she can make anything happen from a drawing on a page and that feels as powerful now as it did as a child. The title of her book says it all: *Fearless Drawing.*

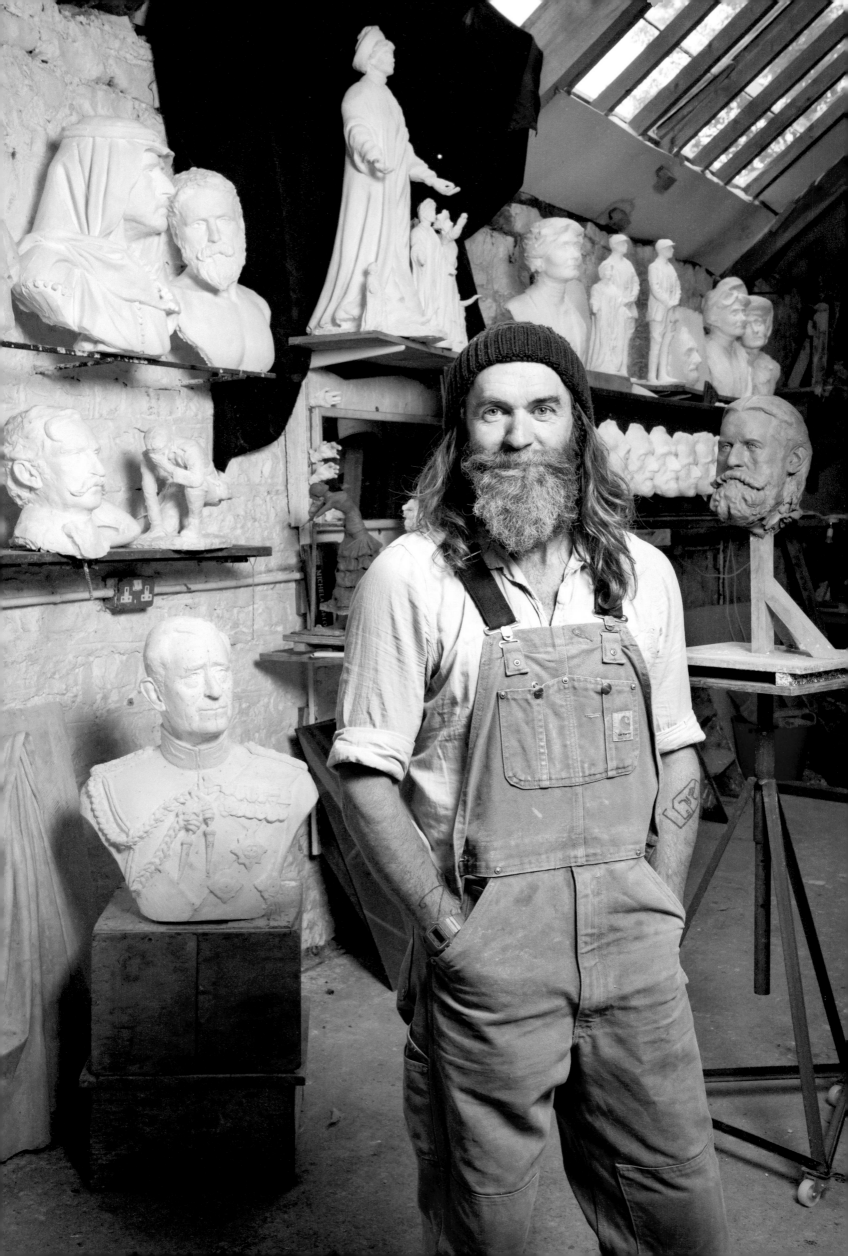

Richard Mossman

SCULPTOR

QEST Scholar 2011

Art graduate and travelling musician Richard Mossman was looking for more stability in his late 20s; he found a route through the stonemasonry course at City of Bath College. The vocational training was excellent, but Richard still felt a restlessness and need to satisfy his creative streak. He focused on the ornamental aspects and worked as a banker mason, producing bespoke architectural stonework for a few years before his mind started to wander. ¶ Boosted by a QEST Scholarship, he headed to the City & Guilds of London Art School to finesse his skills on the only Historic Carving Postgraduate Diploma in the UK. Richard specialised in portrait and figure modelling and marble busts. At the mid-point of his studies, he started to think ahead to the final show. *I had a significant marblework in mind and wrote to The Prince of Wales as an advocate of traditional craftsmanship to ask whether His Royal Highness would sit for a portrait.* ¶ Richard was thrilled when he received a call from Clarence House to arrange what turned out to be a memorable date: the 11th day of the 11th month in 2011. *I went to Highgrove. We spent two hours talking over cups of tea while I took a multitude of caliper measurements and photographs from every angle.* He also visited Clarence House to see His Royal Highness's Colonel of the Welsh Guards uniform. The tunic was placed on a tailor's dummy so he could get as accurate an impression of shape as possible. ¶ Surrounded by the pictures and references, Richard constructed the clay model. *You never want to be making big decisions during the carving; the clay is where you perfect the composition, then it is cast in plaster and replicated in the marble.* Richard used statuary marble, the best for sculptural work: pure white with delicate, grey veining. *Buying from the quarry in Italy was prohibitively expensive. I spent hours at a yard in Wiltshire and unearthed a lichen-covered slab. It cleaned up perfectly – I had found a gem.* He then set to work using a mallet and an assortment of chisels from gouge and bullnose to thinner, sharper kinds for the finer details. ¶ HM The Queen and HRH The Prince of Wales saw the finished marble at the Coronation Festival at Buckingham Palace in 2013 and he received a letter of congratulations. The bust was also on show at the Royal West of England Academy's exhibition *One Hundred Years: The RWA and Royal Patronage.* Its sale provided the means for Richard to establish a studio in the woods outside Bristol. ¶ His first foray into procurement for a public commission was the figure of Emmeline Pankhurst with outstretched arms (on the top shelf opposite). *I didn't make it through, but I learned a lot.* On the shelf below is Richard's entry for a competition in 2017. *The Descent of Man* is a series of 10 faces with eyes closed, as a counter to Jacob Bronowski's *The Ascent of Man,* to highlight the issue of male mental health. ¶ A believer in the affirmative power of sculpture, Richard runs three-day portrait courses at his studio. There is a live model and Richard talks through the rudiments of modelling a head in clay: covering the bust peg in wire to create an armature and putting the clay on, and continually referencing the model. *Everyone tends to flop at four o'clock each day, exhausted yet contented by the hours of intense concentration. I am always astonished by their application and quality of portraiture at the end.* ¶ While training in Bath, a veteran tutor told Richard that a stonemason can become a good carver of sculpture, but a sculptor does not always make a good stonemason. *He was right. The theory and skills that he drummed into me inform what I do today, I just had to learn to read anatomy.* Everything Richard makes goes from clay to plaster, then marble or bronze, and around the studio are the plaster casts that he keeps as hardcopies. *They are my extended family and I could not feel more at home.*

Eugenie Degan
VIOLIN RESTORER & LUTHIER

QEST Hedley Foundation Scholar 2007

Baroque cellist Eugenie Degan made her way from the south of France, via the Schola Cantorum and Conservatoire in Paris, across the Channel to Brighton, where she played in symphony and chamber orchestras for several years. On her quarterly visits to Peter Ratcliff, who looked after her instrument, she became curious about this aspect of the profession. ¶ Eugenie took a violin making course at London Metropolitan University and began working in well-known workshops J. P. Guivier and F. Leonhard. Her tutor Shem Mackey, a QEST alumnus, suggested applying for a QEST Scholarship so she could take up an offer of specialist training from Peter back in Brighton; this enabled her to follow the full restoration of a Thomas Urquhart violin, built in London circa 1670. ¶ In 2009, Eugenie set up her own workshop as a restorer, repairer and maker of quality instruments of the violin family. She carries out maintenance for regular clients (professionals, gifted amateurs and promising students), carving new maple bridges, ebony nuts, and spruce sound posts (the inner piece that transmits and projects the sound). Changing the length or moving this post even a fraction of a millimetre makes a noticeable difference, as does the thickness of the feet on the bridge. Eugenie makes these adjustments according to performance requirements. *You don't want to be the brash instrument standing out in an orchestra, but if you are the soloist, having the power to reach your audience is a necessity.* ¶ She also carries out minor repairs and major restorations. In the workshop is a late 19th century German cello with wide open fractures in need of slivers to close them up. The three-quarter-size French violin, in bits on the bench, came in like this having been smashed against a door in frustration. Eugenie is putting it back together like a jigsaw puzzle, piece by piece. *Nothing is beyond rescue, it is a question of knowing the provenance, recognising the value and making a judgement on the time it will take.* She repairs bows too. *They can be around 150 years old and worth up to £25,000 in their own right.* It can take an hour for a re-hair or weeks for complete restoration. ¶ The cello that has given her the most pleasure is a 1741 Louis Guersan. *It needed a little cosmetic work and new set up. I always play them before they go and this was the most exquisite I have come across.* She was a heartbeat from buying it, but sold it to a client who came from Germany to collect it. *We spent all afternoon playing it together.* ¶ In 2017, Eugenie moved her workshop to Saffron Walden. One of the first commissions through the door was a basse de violon from the Royal Collection Trust. It was bequeathed by Domenico Dragonetti, Europe's greatest double bass virtuoso and contemporary of Beethoven and Haydn, to Prince Albert (then director of the Concert of Ancient Music) after playing it in his presence in 1845. Eugenie repaired fractures on the body, pegbox and fingerboard and made a new spike and nut (the old one had low grooves, which meant the string was buzzing in contact with the fingerboard). She then completed the set up with a new bridge and sound post, and fitted custom-made gut strings to stay faithful to the original. *It was satisfying to restore it to perfect playing condition and hear world-class bassist Chi-chi Nwanoku OBE performing a piece composed by Dragonetti in 'Musical Treasures', a concert at Windsor Castle broadcast live on BBC Radio Three.* ¶ The violin to her right on the bench was made by Eugenie from scratch a few years ago. *I was given a gorgeous piece of old maple. I usually save well-seasoned wood for restorations, but this deserved to be a fine instrument.* ¶ The pigments and varnish on the shelf are for retouching repairs so they become invisible. *The better my work, the less there is to see, but I am happy as the most important result is helping people to make music.*

Ben Marks

HISTORICAL KEYBOARD INSTRUMENT CONSERVATOR

QEST Scholar 2008

Childhood piano lessons were doubly engaging for Ben Marks; he developed an ear for early music and a curiosity about the antecedents of the instrument he was learning to play. With the earnings from a teenage Saturday job, assisting an antique dealer, he bought a Georgian square piano and conserved it with the guidance of his stepfather, a period furniture restorer. *My interest and his influence came together at exactly the right time.* ¶ Whilst at college, Ben contacted specialists in historical keyboard instruments; all wrote back with advice and encouragement and he was given work experience by Lucy Coad, at her square piano restoration workshop near Bath. He chose to study History of Art with Material Studies at university, because the course had a conservation element, but it was not sufficiently practical for Ben who longed to work with his hands. After much deliberation, he decided to leave and seek a more vocational education. ¶ Fortunately, Lucy was able to offer Ben an apprenticeship. He moved to Bristol and lodged in the home of musicians Kenneth and Mary Mobbs. In place of rent, they asked Ben to assist with the maintenance of their early keyboard instruments. *Receiving one-to-one tuition from Lucy and applying my new skills as resident technician for The Mobbs Collection was an invaluable experience.* A year in, the award of a QEST Scholarship guaranteed the continuation of Ben's training and facilitated trips to meet museum curators, examine instruments and attend seminars and masterclasses across Europe. ¶ On completion of his apprenticeship, Mimi Waitzman, curator conservator of The Benton Fletcher Collection at Fenton House in London, invited Ben to become her assistant. He spent a year learning to care for the historical clavichords, harpsichords, virginals, spinets and pianos at this National Trust property before succeeding Mimi as Keeper of Musical Instruments in 2012. ¶ Ben is seated at an 18th century English bentside spinet, a form of plucked string keyboard instrument, and is holding a tuning hammer from the same period. The leather roll on the spinet case contains more antique tuning hammers, replacement strings, crow feathers for making plectra and tools for voicing and regulation. The chest on the floor holds music wire, leather and cloth that conform to historical specifications and wood, including spruce, lime, pear, holly and box, for repairs to the actions and cases of instruments. ¶ Ben also curates The Richard Burnett Collection of Early Keyboard Instruments in Kent and freelances for other heritage institutions and individuals. Christopher Nobbs, a fellow National Trust musical instrument conservator, is a significant mentor and colleague. Together they have restored a rare and important grand piano built in 1786 by John Joseph Merlin, famous inventor of mechanism. ¶ Ben is beguiled by the objects with which he works. *There is something special about rescuing an instrument from dilapidation, restoring it using historically informed techniques, and hearing it played by accomplished musicians.* ¶ There are few practitioners with the skills and experience to work at museum level and Ben feels the lack of contemporaries keenly. *My work has benefitted immeasurably from access to the craftsmanship and wisdom of the previous generation of experts. They have recovered an almost broken artisanal tradition, which makes ensuring continuity for the future all the more crucial.* Ben offers modest training opportunities at the Burnett Collection and is considering other ways to pass on what he has learned. ¶ His first piano is still in good order, he owns an 18th century example that Lucy gave him to restore as an apprentice piece, and Kenneth Mobbs bequeathed Ben a harpsichord – an extraordinary gesture that he is acknowledging in the best way possible: by continuing the legacy of his mentors through his own practice.

Natasha Mann

ZOUAQ ARTIST

QEST Radcliffe
Trust Scholar 2012

During a year in Morocco, while studying for a degree in Arabic at the University of Cambridge, a friend introduced Natasha Mann to a master of Zouaq painting. *I had always loved Islamic and North African art, influenced by family holidays to Islamic countries and memorable visits to places like the Great Mosque of Kairouan in Tunisia.* ¶ Her response to the geometry and colours of Zouaq, the Moroccan art of painting on wood, was immediate and inescapable. *It changed the focus of my attention and I spent most of the time in Fez as an apprentice learning the traditional designs and techniques.* ¶ On her return to the UK, Natasha continued to research and paint Zouaq art. QEST supported her desire to formalise this with an MA in Islamic and Traditional Arts, at The Prince's Foundation School of Traditional Arts. This is one of the few places that teaches how to create geometric designs by hand and to prepare and paint with natural pigments, a practice that has become rare even in Morocco. ¶ She graduated with distinction and was presented with the Barakat Prize for Islamic Art by HRH The Prince of Wales. She has kept a connection with the School, returning as a tutor, and four of Natasha's paintings and accompanying geometric construction drawings were selected for *Prince and Patron*, an exhibition at Buckingham Palace in 2018 to mark His Royal Highness's 70th birthday. ¶ The Radcliffe Trust helped Natasha to secure studio space at Cockpit Arts in London where she works today, interspersed with trips to Morocco to photograph ceilings, doors and furniture for inspiration. ¶ Every piece begins with either a biomorphic design or geometric pattern drawn with a pencil, compass and ruler. They are based on groupings from four-fold to repetitions of increasing complexity. The large painting by Natasha in the background of her workspace is an eight-fold design with a central rosette of sixteen petals. *Some of the geometric compositions are very intricate and time-consuming to work out from scratch. One took me a year of trial and error, then finally came together in a few days.* ¶ The drawing in front of Natasha is taken from zellige tiles in the Bu Inania Madrasa in Fes. This is part of the research for her MA on Medieval Spain & Morocco at The Courtauld Institute of Art. Studying the history of Moroccan ornament and geometric design has been invaluable in helping her to understand how the designs and techniques of Zouaq art have developed over the last 800 years. ¶ The next step is to turn the drawing into a stencil and trace the design onto primed wood (usually cedar) for a painting, decorative border or box. Natasha hand grinds the minerals and earths to make the pigments (there are jarfuls on the shelves), which she mixes with egg tempera. She tends to use four or five colours at most in a single painting. *At first I kept to Moroccan colours, but I work with a wider palette now. I've made a painting in a Moroccan design with pigments from an Icelandic volcano.* All gilding is with 24 carat gold leaf. ¶ With the scale of her work, Natasha needs long, sign-writing style brushes that she makes using Atlas cedarwood from Morocco and donkey hair. *It's soft enough to hold the paint well, but firmer than sable so I can paint a metre-long line without lifting the brush.* Natasha rarely varnishes her work. *I like the natural finishes: indigo, a plant, has a velvety texture; the earths – red and yellow ochre – are smooth; and I think grainier minerals like azurite and green malachite lose their vitality under varnish.* ¶ The Museum of Islamic Art in Malaysia has purchased a ceiling and six of her paintings and she has undertaken many commissions in private homes. ¶ With frequent research trips to Morocco, Natasha has maintained her spoken Arabic and, whilst picking up a paintbrush started as a distraction to her language studies, it has led to a fluency of hand in this striking ancient art.

Wayne Hart

LETTERCARVER, TYPOGRAPHER & SCULPTOR

Letterforms are the domain of Wayne Hart, both as a typographer and carving in stone and wood. QEST Scholar 2011 *Whereas 40 words per minute would be a good speed for typing, I am more of a 20 letters a day man.* ¶ Working carefully by hand started at the College of West Anglia in his home county of Norfolk. *The graphic design tutor made us do everything without a computer for the first few months and only in black and white; it was all about composition.* He was introduced to lettercutting while studying Typography at the University of Reading. Visiting lecturer Caroline Webb, a lettercarver, taught a class using cardboard. On self-directed study, Wayne went to Caroline's studio in Wiltshire to learn basic carving techniques on Portland stone. *I moved back to King's Lynn and worked for the local arts centre while visiting lettercarvers around the country in search of formal training.* ¶ Following work experience at the Richard Kindersley Studio, Wayne proceeded to a lettercarving apprenticeship with Pip Hall in Cumbria, through the Memorial Arts Charity (now The Lettering Arts Trust). *I could not have completed the three years without the further generosity of craft charities such as QEST.* His first job was a house sign drawn out by his mentor. The most influential experiences were a project for Sheffield City Council, carving poetry into 15 limestone benches and the adventurous task of carving six Simon Armitage poems into rock faces for *The Stanza Stones Walk* in The Pennines; each one penned in memory of water: snow, rain, mist, dew, puddle and beck (stream). *Public art can be incredibly powerful, whether in a built environment or out in the wild.* ¶ Wayne established his own studio in Manchester in 2012. Historian and funerary art specialist Dr Julian Litten, who Wayne met at a King's Lynn Arts Centre event, has been instrumental in his memorial work. *One of my earliest commissions was in celebration of C S Lewis (1898-1963) for Poets' Corner at Westminster Abbey. They wanted a fluid style of lettering to reflect the nature of his writing.* The response to this work led to Wayne being asked to carve a new headstone and ledger stone for First World War nurse Edith Cavell in the grounds of Norwich Cathedral. ¶ The Lettering Arts Trust, the UK's leading voice for the craft, has been a great support to Wayne since his apprenticeship. He has participated in recent exhibitions organised by the Trust: *Masters & Apprentices* at Snape Maltings in Suffolk and *An Elixir of Letters* at The Chelsea Physic Garden in London. The carving in the photograph, *Olive Branch*, was in response to the theme for the latter: plants used as ingredients in wines, teas, cordials, beers and herbal brews. Wayne discovered a Corsican proverb – *olive flowers in June, olives in the hand* – about an early bloom leading to a bountiful harvest. *I carved these words as flowing lines around a stone sphere, cut deeply to create a strong contrast of light and shadow.* ¶ Wayne makes research trips to Italy when he can. He has been to Naples, Pompeii and Herculaneum with Richard Kindersley, and attended a postgraduate course in epigraphy (the study of inscriptions) at the British School at Rome that focused on Trajan's Column, the basis of all Roman lettering. ¶ A winner of the *craft&design magazine* Craft Maker of the Year award, Wayne is also a trustee of the Manchester Craft & Design Centre and a Fabric Advisory Committee member (one of the youngest in the country) for St Edmundsbury Cathedral in Suffolk. His portfolio is mostly in stone, but Wayne feels a similar affinity for other materials and techniques. He has sought tuition in calligraphy, masonry, type design, sculpture and attended courses at West Dean College in woodcarving and glass engraving so he can explore new territories. *The underlying principles remain the same: strong lettering design and well-considered spacing, carved perfectly.*

Manuel Mazzotti

BOOKBINDER

QEST Worshipful
Company of
Clothworkers
Scholar 2015

As an engineer, it used to baffle me that so few books perform what I think should be their most basic mechanical function: to open and lie fully flat. An avid book collector, Manuel Mazzotti took action and signed up for bookbinding classes to understand how he could modify their structure. ¶ Not one to do things by halves, Manuel went to Switzerland to learn from some of the best bookbinders in Europe at the Centro del bel Libro. He studied the folded, origami-like structures of Hedi Kyle under school director Suzanne Schmollgruber. Hedi's background is in conservation, so her methods avoid glue (even acid-free, archival adhesive is best used sparingly for longevity). *I loved transforming a sheet of paper using only a bone folder and ingenious techniques to create a useful form.* ¶ Manuel is pictured in the studio he established in London in 2012. Hedi's famous 'blizzard binding', designed to support collections of objects, was the perfect solution for *Crags and Ravines Make a Marvellous View* (the large commission laid out on the table). Edited by Marcus Flacks and published by Rasika, this is a study of a 17th century scroll painting, *Ten Views of Lingbi Rock. We wanted to recreate the experience of handling this magnificent work.* The blizzard style of folding creates v-shaped tabs at the head and tail of the spine so the 10 paintings could be secured in place, but also removed easily for viewing by lifting the paper tabs. The prints, book of essays and a Chinese translation are housed in a clamshell box. ¶ In 2015, QEST made it possible for Manuel to receive advanced, one-to-one tuition with two masters: Kathy Abbott and Tracey Rowledge. *I learned fine binding from Kathy. It is beautiful, but time-consuming and therefore expensive. I am working on incorporating elements into a more affordable range for young collectors.* Tracey has developed a way of gold tooling that retains the intuitive feel of being drawn by hand, despite having been through the careful process of transcribing the impression and applying layers of gold leaf. *Under Tracey's mentorship I am developing a new body of work: more artistic, more focused on materials.* ¶ Manuel is inspired by working with artists and writers. *A story usually needs at least two people: one to create it, the other to present it.* The earlier someone comes to his studio, the more interesting it gets. Hormazd Narielwalla is a collage artist who works with Savile Row tailoring patterns. He first came to Manuel to print an artist's book. *We decided the best way to describe his work was to assemble the pages as Hormazd would his art, cut from different brown paper patterns.* They made 15 editions of *Anansi Tales*, each one unique. The yellow book on the table is another of their limited editions. The concertina binding opens to a three-metre length printed with the 12 artworks from Narielwalla's *Lost Gardens* exhibition. ¶ The box next to Manuel contains the result of a collaboration with Rossy Liu, a young Chinese calligrapher. *I made millboard slats on which Rossy handwrote her poem, 'Notes on Random Thoughts', inspired by a classic of Chinese literature, 'Six Records of a Floating Life'.* Manuel bound the lines to resemble a traditional bamboo scroll. *It was satisfying to find a point of connection between our differing aesthetics.* ¶ Manuel is inquisitive even when making a simple guest book. Who will the guests be? How long will it be used for? Is it for a contemporary exhibition? Or a sumptuous hotel lobby? *It is important to translate the surroundings into the book – and of course, for it to lay flat – as it is a direct point of contact for the guest.* He is now questioning another element of his craft; in partnership with Officina Corpuscoli, Manuel is working on *The Mycelium Books*, an exploration into pure fungal materials as alternatives to leather for bookbinding. *Watch this space.*

Claudia Clare

POTTER PAINTER

QEST Scholar 1998

Potter painter Claudia Clare is known for her large, slip-painted, earthenware jars that depict everyday scenes showing the impact of social change and historic events on ordinary lives. *Pots are our museum pieces and our archaeological evidence: mine are the contemporary version.* ¶Claudia learned her painting skills at Camberwell School of Art and potting through adult education classes. She was awarded a QEST Scholarship to research methods of placing her images onto a pot. The first stage was mouldmaking and screenprinting with Paul Scott, an artist known for his research into printed vitreous surfaces. Claudia used these techniques to make *Wedding Feast* 1999 while waiting for news of a friend temporarily lost to her during the Kosovo War. It was a significant work, acquired by the New Hall Art Collection, but she found the fiddly processes were too much of a distraction to maintain. *As an artist, it is as important to find out what doesn't work for you as much as what does; these complications were standing in the way of the image.* The second phase was a study tour of Hungary. Through visits to the Kovács Margit Ceramic Museum and Zsolnay Museum in Pecs, Claudia discovered a rich European tradition of potter painters. ¶Since her QEST Scholarship, Claudia has moved from grant-maintained artist to artist-scholar (she completed a PhD at the University of Westminster in 2007), to represented artist and published writer. *I chronicle real life as it is lived around me.* She uses photography for quick, visual notetaking. The stories evolve in her mind and she draws them out, but everything gets put away before work starts on the pot. *I picture where the widest point needs to be – on the shoulder, waist or hip – to take the shape of the highly fictionalised narrative that will flow around the curved surface.* ¶Claudia keeps a couple of pots that are often borrowed by museums. *Travelling West* is one of many that feature Hossein, her Kurdish muse. It tells the account of his journey to seek asylum in Britain. *It was full of all the inconvenient details that make a narrative human.* For several months, they pored over Google maps tracing the route he took on horseback over the Iranian border, searched for images of the bus he took across Turkey, and the unseaworthy craft that brought him to the Greek mainland. The form of the pot dramatises the precipitous heights and drops of the mountainous regions along the way. *Despite all his hardship, there was an audible joy when he described this landscape.* The other is *Nightwalker*, a satirical urban nighttime landscape of Hossein's view of London. ¶Claudia paints her pots when they are 'leather hard' and tends to use black, white or red for a tonal range over which she places other colours. She is working on a series of landscape studies, partly to push her use of colour: for instance, a summer landscape in the full tonal range of blue or the cooler shades of the winter scene in progress on the pot in front of her. Relatively abstract by her standards, these are also a return to the basic principle of painting on a three-dimensional form, exploring the relationship between colour, light, distance and the viewer. She recently showed others in this series at *Claudia Clare: The Wootton Pots* put on by Zuleika Gallery in her childhood home, Zions Hills in Wootton, Oxfordshire. ¶Claudia also has a line of pots about how people look at things. *I am fascinated by watching people taking photographs. Looking at a landscape and placing yourself in it is a very 18th century thing to do. At the time, you would have needed money to employ an artist; now all you need is a mobile phone.* The pots are titled *How to look at art, How to look at landscape…*but everyone refers to them as *Selfie Pots.* The half-finished one on the shelf features Claudia and Hossein watching the sunset in Margate, her favourite place to escape to from London.

Mel Howse

VITREOUS ARTIST

QEST Scholar 2008
QEST Thomas
Fattorini Award for
Excellence 2013

Sometimes you have to change your tools, your environment and your expectations to create a new, progressive view of what you do. This remark was made by Mel Howse during her guest lecture at the American Glass Guild Conference in Philadelphia 2014. ¶ She studied architectural stained glass at Swansea College of Art in the early 1990s and her work for ecclesiastical settings ranged from windows and doorways to screens, altars and fonts. *Over time, my approach became more contemporary, accelerated by advances in technology that gave me fresh ideas for architectural glass art.* ¶ QEST funded a residency at vitreous enameller A.J.Wells & Sons on the Isle of Wight so Mel could explore materials and understand manufacturing on a large scale. She combined this research with her manual decorative skills, to evolve processes that would fulfil her expanding design vision. ¶ In 2008, after the installation of a 500-square-metre, enamelled glass façade for Sainsbury's in Milton Keynes, Mel published a record of its creation. *The book was called 'Vitreous Art', as stained glass was no longer an adequate description of the technique or form of my work; I was also enamelling steel and wanted a definition to capture the common elements of the metal and glasswork in one discipline.* ¶ After working on a commission with the late Peter Collins, Mel was invited to move into his Hourglass Engineering glass factory in Hampshire. *I remember stepping through the door and being staggered by the cathedral of industry in front of me, capable of working glass in many dimensions.* It was a meeting of open minds and Peter understood her desire to remain a designer and maker. *So much would be lost without this direct input and freedom of expression through the creative application.* Mel is pictured in one of the spray booths making enamelled maquettes. Over the last decade, she has made at least 25 site-specific installations with the factory as her studio, bridging art and manufacturing by using her hand techniques alongside industrial practices. ¶ In 2015, Mel collaborated with developer Clarion and architects Conran & Partners on the redevelopment of an Art Deco cinema in Hove, West Sussex. The aim was to create a connection between the original picture house and the new building, Friese Greene House, named after William Friese Greene, a photographer and pioneer of cinematography who lived in the town. *I used the interaction of linear and curvilinear shapes to create Art Deco sensibilities in a geometric design for our time, made with toughened glass and present-day industrial techniques for performance. Succession of Light,* on the principal south-facing elevation, makes use of natural and artificial light to animate the surface from every angle, inside and out, day and night. The installation won a Building Crafts Award from the Sussex Heritage Trust. ¶ A recent project gave Mel the opportunity to unite her artistic roots, current practice and a design for the future. She was appointed by Durham Cathedral to make a stained glass window, donated by Jonathan and Jools Pilkington in memory of their daughter Sara, who was a student at Durham University. *Working on any memorial is a privilege; this was coupled with the responsibility of putting a modern work into a UNESCO World Heritage site considered to be one of Britain's most important buildings spiritually and architecturally. The Illumination Window* – full of colour and youthful energy – will be installed in the North Quire Aisle in 2019. ¶ Working in this environment again reminded Mel that traditional craft skills were once viewed as cutting-edge technology, it is just a matter of perspective. *Colour, translucency, opacity and reflection are what play the most important role in any era of glass and vitreous enamel art; it is my job to reveal these spectacular properties in the most meaningful and dramatic way I can today.*

Andrian Melka

SCULPTOR

The civil unrest that accompanied the fall of Communism in Albania in 1990 QEST Scholar 2008 coincided with Andrian Melka's studies at art school in Gjirokastra and the Academy of Fine Arts in the capital, Tirana. *Made against this volatile political backdrop, a lot of my work, and that of my contemporaries, would best be described as socialist realism.* ¶ After graduation, he spent two years carving portraits and reliefs in a marble workshop before leaving Albania during the Civil War for London on a Getty Scholarship to the Building Crafts College. He immersed himself in the traditional training and developed an interest in Classicism and Renaissance sculpture; at the end of the year he was awarded the City & Guilds Medal for Excellence. ¶ Andrian joined the workshop of renowned architectural sculptor and carver Dick Reid in York to assist on the *Golden Jubilee Fountain* for Her Majesty The Queen's Sandringham Estate. He also worked in Dick's workshop on independent projects: a stone coat of arms (the cast is pictured on the wall) for the base of an equestrian sculpture of Her Majesty by Philip Jackson in Windsor Great Park, and his relief of *Laocoön*, the centrepiece of the Statues Courtyard at the Vatican, that he installed at Highgrove Royal Gardens. ¶ In 2007, Andrian self-funded a month in Italy. His approach had always been freestyle: using a drawing of the frontal view as a template, then working by eye, finding his way inside the stone. In Pietrasanta, he learned to enlarge from a small maquette to any size of block. QEST funded a further three months of tuition for Andrian to consolidate these skills with another figure study. His own tools were mostly for limestone; marble required a new set at considerable expense. *I bought the major tools and created a smaller work than intended: a relief of Michelangelo's 'Pitti Tondo'.* He found the technique of working from model to marble somewhat repetitive, but understood the benefit, particularly for commissions requiring an exact replica. On other work, he often reverts to working directly into the stone. *It is a lengthier process and can be fraught, but creatively I find it more satisfying.* ¶ In 2011, Andrian went to California to work on the *Spirit of the Ocean Fountain*, carved in 1928 by Ettore Caldorin at the Santa Barbara Courthouse. It had lost much of its form and the stone was badly sealed in the 1980s, which had trapped moisture and blown the surface. A team from Britishstone located similar sandstone in a quarry in the surrounding mountains; blocks were cut and transported for hand carving on site. *I spent a rewarding couple of months completing the figurative work using some of the original tools.* ¶ Melka Sculpture Studio is now firmly established in Bugthorpe, East Yorkshire. Andrian has secured his next two commissions in stone: the recarving of a Romanesque frieze at Lincoln Cathedral and a First World War memorial. *It is in a coastal alcove at Bamburgh Hall in Northumberland; the limestone has been weathered and eroded by sea water; we are remaking it in a more hardwearing stone.* ¶ He is also learning bronze casting. This was initially for a solo exhibition, *Vulnerability of the Gods & Humanity*, at the Art of Protest Gallery in York in 2018. Andrian grew up near the archaeological site of Butrint and Neptune, Bacchus, Atlas and Venus were the subjects of early commissions. *I am accustomed to gods depicted as idealised human forms; I wanted to explore their darker traits too.* He portrayed these divergent themes as pairs of sculptures: one exquisitely polished representing heroism and immortality, the other battered and beaten with holes ripped through the bronze alluding to the conflicts and jealousies that blighted their relationships. *Like the gods, humanity has challenges to face and we all have our vulnerabilities. The holes, scars and tears we bare may not be as visible, but they definitely shape us.*

Mary Wing To

LEATHER ARTISAN, DESIGNER & WHIP MAKER

QEST Worshipful
Company of
Leathersellers
Scholar 2012

The final collection designed by Mary Wing To for her MA in Fashion Design & Technology at the London College of Fashion depended on her finding a skilled leatherworker to help her make the garments. During her search, she came across a telephone number for Capel Manor College saddlery lecturer Line Hansen. *We arranged to meet and she was so supportive; I went along to her classes to learn the skills I needed to make my collection.* ¶ Mary had always had an affection for horses and there was an equine influence to her designs. She fell in love with the leather craftsmanship and decided to take a two-year saddlery course so that her craft skills would never restrict her creative process. *I enjoyed working on saddles and bridles, but always had in the back of my mind how I could translate their making to fashion.* The two years flew by and Mary still wanted to refine her skills, know more, and learn from the best. ¶ *I wrote to Frances Roche, Master Saddler at the Royal Mews to ask if she would consider taking on someone who intended to use the skills in a different discipline.* Mary took her portfolio to Frances, who agreed to train her on a harness making apprenticeship. Meanwhile, Mary pursued her vision to revive British saddlery craftsmanship in design with a creation for the internationally-renowned World of WearableArt Awards in New Zealand. Her winning entry – a hand-stitched, moulded leather, couture dress with sculpted leather horse head – was a dramatic showcase for her traditional workmanship and pushed the boundaries of leather in fashion. ¶ Mary had one more specialism on her list of skills to master: whip making. *I wanted to learn intricate lacing, plaiting and braiding techniques, all of which are displayed in whips.* The difficulty was finding someone to teach this rare craft. She tracked down traditional whip maker Dennis Walmsley, who made everything from scratch (including the tools) and had a four-month waiting list for his whips. He was reluctant at first (in his entire career, no-one had asked him to teach), but said if she proved capable on a few practical tests, he would take her on. Mary was awarded a QEST Scholarship to study with Dennis and drove out to his cottage once a week for two years to learn carpentry to prepare the cane, how to plait and braid the leather around the core, and silverwork for the collar. *He was a genius and quite a character; I had to promise to bring homemade soup each time.* ¶ In 2017, Mary was asked by QEST to make a bespoke show-jumping crop that she presented to Olympic gold medallist Nick Skelton CBE when he retired formally on the final day of Royal Windsor Horse Show. *He kindly leant it to me for the shoot; it is the whip in my left hand.* Fully handcrafted, it is made on a traditional rattan cane stock, hand plaited in a 12-strand kangaroo leather lace with a saddle-stitched flapper, and decorative Turk's head knot at the end. It is finished with a silver collar engraved with the initials NS. ¶ Mary is member of The Society of Master Saddlers, qualified City & Guilds Harness Maker, Liveryman of The Worshipful Company of Cordwainers and has been awarded a City & Guilds Lion Award trophy for Creative Craftsperson of the Year. She now works for Chanel, running its UK fashion atelier, employing her full range of skills for the repair and quality control of its leather goods, costume jewellery and shoes. ¶ *It was not my intention to also make whips for a living, but when Dennis died a couple of years ago I did not want his amazing skillset to disappear.* Mary set up Whip in Hand, offering bespoke, luxury whips from her London studio to continue the legacy of this brilliant master. She also takes on her own commissions for the fashion, film and equine industries. *When you know how to handle such a distinctive, versatile material, the possibilities are limitless.*

Frances Plowden

ARTIST BLACKSMITH

Artist blacksmith Frances Plowden has produced metalwork by commission for over 30 years. Her first access to a forge was on a three-year, 3D design course at Brighton Polytechnic in the 1980s. *There was no specialist tutor for the first six months, but I learned to weld and revelled in the freedom to respond to briefs in metal.* ¶ Frances graduated knowing she wanted to be a blacksmith and needed to find a way to learn the techniques more thoroughly. She spent a year apprenticed to a master blacksmith at Kew Steam Museum before opening her own workshop in east London making candlesticks and furniture. ¶ A trip to Barcelona was a revelation. *The Gaudí architecture was amazing and metalwork is such an integral part of building design in the city.* QEST funded Frances to spend six months in Spain learning from a traditional Catalan master blacksmith. She ended up living in Barcelona and working at his forge in a nearby village for three years. ¶ Frances also spent time as a welder for a European circus group creating surreal props and vehicles from old metal and scrap materials. These outlandish creations continued back in the UK for television programme *Scrap Heap Challenge. It was a fantastic job. I got to spend a month at an enormous scrapyard with a dumper truck at my disposal, picking up any and all sorts of metal to design and build the set for filming.* ¶ On her return to London, Frances established a workshop in Brixton with the experience and inspiration to work at scale. She also volunteered at a refugee organisation teaching one evening a week. In response to the stories of the people she met, Frances made a three-metre birdcage from forged and rolled steel that she exhibited with a woman lying inside, conceivably asleep, imprisoned or dead. She then travelled to migrant camps in Calais and Dunkirk to put her metalwork skills to practical use, helping to build a communal kitchen from steel shipping containers. ¶ In 2012, Frances was on the team that created the steampunk-inspired vehicles for the Paralympic Games Closing Ceremony. A film was shown depicting people from all over the world travelling towards London before the performers entered the stadium on a procession of these trucks. *I helped to make the pirate ship with lots of railings that formed the stage and a giant fish from piles of scrap and recycled materials.* ¶ Frances has had plenty of opportunities to let her imagination run riot, but her greatest enjoyment is making something for a home. *It might be security gates, steel railings, handrails or a small front gate – even this simple change has the power to transform a threshold and make a house stand out as special as you wander down a street.* ¶ She is pictured leaning on a row of customised railings at a house in Herne Hill. *I love working on scrolls and curves. I made these at my workshop down the road then welded them onto the original posts.* The design evolved from her architectural sketches of column capitals and stonework above doors. Frances drew it true to size in chalk on the floor, traced string along the curling lines, straightened each piece to get the exact lengths of steel required, then lit the forge. *I get completely lost in shapes, adjusting in and out of the fire for as long as it takes. It's a methodical process and can be quite meditative.* ¶ Breaking down barriers and passing on three decades of experience is her next mission. She was involved in an outreach project, with immersive art group Arcadia London, in 2018. Over 150 teenagers came to experience working with metal; in an afternoon, they learned to cut and weld to make sculptures of bugs and spiders for *Metamorphosis*, a performance at Queen Elizabeth Olympic Park. She has also co-devised a pilot programme of forging and welding workshops to encourage girls into the construction industries – another example of the transformative power of Frances and her craft.

QEST Scholar 1992

' *One of the greatest*
challenges in running your own
workshop is finding the
time and capital to invest
in specialist training.
The QEST Scholarship provided
an invaluable opportunity
to refine my skills
in the endangered craft
of watch case making
and will help secure
its future for contemporary
British watchmaking. '

Craig Struthers

WATCHMAKER

Years of tinkering with classic cars and scooters gave Craig Struthers an appreciation of vintage mechanics that he rediscovered on a minute scale in the antique watches he was learning to repair at Birmingham's School of Jewellery. While studying, he met his wife Rebecca, fellow watchmaker and antiquarian horologist (the first in the UK to earn a PhD in horology). ¶ Craig and Rebecca founded Struthers Watchmakers in 2012 and their first collaboration, a rock crystal pendant watch called *Stella*, collected a design innovation award. Together they offer a *Tailor-Made* range of heritage movements, rescued from the bullion industry and remastered as modern timepieces, and bespoke watchmaking. They also restore pre-1960s mechanical timepieces. ¶ The Struthers work exclusively with 19th and 20th century hand tools, including six lathes set for different purposes. This started as an economic necessity, but has become a defining influence. *They are our workforce; we call them all by name and couldn't do it without them.* They also have an apprentice, Heather Fisher. ¶ Their Georgian workshop is in Birmingham's Jewellery Quarter. There were over 30,000 workers in the area in the early 1900s; Craig and Rebecca are among the several hundred that remain, continuing its reputation for British manufacturing excellence. In 2018, they commissioned photographer Andy Pilsbury to document the Jewellery Quarter today for an exhibition, *We're Still Here. It is important for us all that we maintain the network of specialist services on our doorstep, such as metal stamper W. Downing and hand engraver Matt Smith.* ¶ Similar concern for the vanishing trade of watch case making prompted Craig to apply for a QEST Scholarship to learn from Adam Phillips, one of the few expert makers in the UK (all are nearing retirement). Craig's expertise as a master watchmaker meant that he could grasp the techniques relatively quickly to raise a case from sheet silver, gold and platinum. *I wrote pages of notes and took hundreds of pictures of the forming, burnishing, soldering and firing out, from which I am compiling a manual to train others.* ¶ Craig is putting these skills into practice on their next venture. The Struthers are designing and machining their own in-house watch movement, the first to be created in Birmingham in over a century. This is a defining step for an independent watchmaker. *We are combining our 30 years of knowledge in this new wrist watch, working title 'Project 248': two minds, four hands and an 8mm lathe.* ¶ It is inspired by one of the first machine-made, English watch movements from 1880. Craig has translated their ideas into hand-rendered design illustrations, and a family of tools has been customised to make the movement. They have picked up where late 19th century British watchmaking left off and developed an improved English lever escapement (this pushes the balance wheel and creates the tick) that incorporates the latest material and technological advancements. The movement also reintroduces features that have been lost in modern production, including a rocking bar keyless work (that winds the watch) and parachute shock setting (Rebecca is holding a pocket watch in which they are testing their version). *We also want a domed, vitreous enamel dial, but there is no longer anywhere in the UK with the know-how, so Rebecca is working with Deakin & Francis to re-establish this skill.* Finally, the top plate will be hand engraved in traditional style with their names and address '15–17 Regent Place, B'ham'. ¶ The details of every watch made by Craig and Rebecca are recorded in a ledger and they will soon be entering the specifications of five personalised *Project 248* watches. The owners of this initial, limited production are being invited to give design input, wear prototypes, and suggest a fitting name for this significant timepiece in the chronology of Struthers Watchmakers.

QEST Johnnie Walker
Scholar 2017

Scott Benefield

GLASSBLOWER

QEST Eranda Foundation Scholar 2013

The most pleasurable part of the day for Scott Benefield is walking into his studio each morning with a sense of anticipation as he opens the kiln door to see the previous day's work that has cooled overnight. This is coupled with the inspirational potential of the equipment and material around him as he starts to make something new. ¶ Scott was born in Osaka in Japan, received an MFA from Ohio State University, and lived in Seattle for more than 20 years before he came to the UK for the first time in 2004. This was for a residency at a glass centre in Wick in the north of Scotland, where he met architectural glass artist Andrea Spencer. They married and he moved to Northern Ireland where they have studios across the courtyard from each other in Ballintoy on the North Antrim coast. *We are now waving distance apart after a six-year, transatlantic relationship.* ¶ Everything Scott makes is from the end of a four-foot blow pipe. *Glass is an unusual medium in that you cannot get your hands on it; you have to remain one step removed from its scalding heat.* Glassblowing demands immediate attention too. Once the glass is gathered, it has to be kept above 600 degrees Celsius throughout the shaping. *It is not a craft that you can put down, contemplate and come back to.* ¶ The pieces in the photograph are Scott's production range, all created with a practical role. *I like to incorporate pouring functions into the jugs and bowls so they can go from kitchen to the table.* The pattern scheme, created by an Italian technique developed in the 16th century called 'cane work', is designed to integrate the range. Instead of cold glass processes such as engraving or painting to decorate the finished objects, Scott places opaque glass rods into the ball of molten glass so that fine white lines, called 'filigrana' ('filo' is Italian for thread) are formed as the glass is blown. *You can either pull a straight cane, or twist to make a spiral design, such as the bowl I am holding.* ¶ Scott learned this skill in the United States working with Italian craftsmen, including well-known glass artist Lino Tagliapietra. In 2002, he travelled to Italy to be closer to the source of the tradition and understand the culture it came from. *It was interesting to work with teachers I had studied under on their home territory in Murano.* It has been a feature of his studio work ever since and is also the technique that he teaches, including workshops at the Penland School of Crafts, Pilchuck Glass School, Haystack Mountain School of Crafts, National College of Art and Design in Ireland and as a visiting scholar at Osaka University of the Arts. ¶ In 2013, QEST enabled Scott to study the chemistry of coloured glass on a intensive, two-week workshop at the Guadaloupe Glass Studio in New Hampshire, USA. *Each day we formulated, mixed and melted seven colours and tested them. Glassblowers usually have a more empirical approach to colour, but I was keen to understand it from a material scientist's perspective.* This was excellent preparation for Scott's residency in 2015 at the Creative Glass Centre of America (WheatonArts) in New Jersey, where he was given full access to the studio for six weeks. *This would have been far less productive without the ability to make my own coloured glass.* His cane work and colour came together in *The Tapestry Series*, which was exhibited at the Vessel Gallery in London. Scale is essential for working in coloured glass (it requires four crucibles in one furnace), but Scott is finding ways to introduce it more into his work. ¶ He is also developing innovative permutations on traditional cane profiles and discovering new applications in blown glass vessels, supported by The International Institute of Cane Technology. *I think of my work as existing in relation to the long history of glass objects and embracing a range of techniques and traditions to enliven this narrative.*

Margaret Jones

TAPESTRY WEAVER

Every time I begin a new tapestry, I start work sitting on the floor. As it advances up the frame, I have all sorts of things to perch on to be at the right height. Margaret Jones is sitting on a cushion, resting on a book, placed on a bar stool as she nears the completion of a tapestry destined for the *Istanbul Design Biennial.* ¶ Margaret has always had an interest in textiles. At 50, and having suffered a head injury that affected her considerably for a few months, she re-evaluated her priorities and decided she wanted to practice professionally. Her first step was a Foundation Diploma in Art & Design at West Dean College, built of ten short courses. *After the class in tapestry weaving I started to see and dream in warp and weft.* A year later she set out to do a Graduate Diploma at West Dean; with help from QEST, she went on to gain her Master of Fine Art, specialising in tapestry weaving. In 2016, *Gwendolyn,* the bubble tapestry on the wall made during her studies, was selected for *Scythia,* an exhibition of contemporary textile art in Ukraine featuring work from 90 artists from 28 countries. ¶ *Sitting in my tapestry room in West Sussex holding a bobbin and my brass beater, it is astonishing to think of the global community that I have joined through my craft.* Margaret plays a role in sustaining its vibrancy too. She created and organises *Heallreaf* (the Old English word for a tapestry hung on a wall in a public place), a biennial exhibition of small-format tapestry, judged by Anne Jackson, at West Dean College. In 2017, Arts Council England funded a second show of Heallreaf 2 in the Brick Lane Gallery in London. ¶ Above her head is *Pomegranate* made for *Tapestry Mischief,* an exhibition arranged by The British Tapestry Group at Gracefields Art Centre in Dumfries. The brief was to create contemporary work inspired by historic tapestry. Margaret was at West Dean College when the 14-year project to restore the medieval tapestries, *The Hunt for the Unicorn,* for Historic Scotland was completed. *Pomegranates were used widely in this series as symbols of fertility; I used cotton with silk and Tencel to create the different textures and gloss of the fruit.* ¶ The black and white tapestry on the wall features a section of a bass clarinet. It shows the progression of Margaret's technical skill. *It is finely woven with seven warp threads per centimetre (four is more usual) in cotton, wool and linen for clarity of the lines.* ¶ Back to the tapestry on the frame. Margaret applied to take part in *Google Weaving Stop-time,* a PhD project by Emelie Röndahl to connect hand weavers around the world through a shared woven assignment. *I met the two criteria: a Mediterranean link – my grandmother was Italian – and ability to tie a Turkish knot, a pile weaving technique.* On a given day, the makers had to Google the phrase 'Textile Labour Turkey' and select an image from the search results to make into a tapestry. Margaret chose the face of a boy looking over a sewing machine. It has taken around 80 hours to complete, alternating between a row of knots and a row of weaving. *Tapestry is traditionally woven on its side – he will be upright in the exhibition. The pale squares are where I decided to pixelate some of the image in reference to its digital origin.* ¶ Margaret also writes poetry, both about her tapestries and to inspire new ones. The colours of *The Fallen* (the tallest tapestry in the background), based on her poem *About Not Having Wings,* were chosen from iridescent butterfly patterns. She usually works closely to a cartoon (outline of an image), but this was much more fluid in the making, especially when it got to the red and green yarns. *They felt as though they wanted to be blended together rather than conform to the rigid structure.* She has a large-scale partner piece for *The Fallen* in mind. *If it goes to plan, I'll need a ladder and scaffold frame to reach the top.*

QEST Garfield Weston Foundation Scholar 2014

[61]

Thomas Merrett

SCULPTOR

QEST Garfield
Weston Foundation
Scholar 2014

In 2018, Thomas Merrett was invited to tell his story at *A Celebration of Craft*, QEST's annual fundrasing dinner at the Victoria and Albert Museum, a narrative retold here by the objects in his studio and sculpture at his side. Thomas completed this clay torso live at the V&A for auction, to be cast in the winning bidder's material of choice. It represents the figurative, observational nature of his training for which QEST provided the means. ¶ At 18, he enrolled at the City & Guilds of London Art School where every student gets a workspace to immerse them in practice and the physicality of materials, tools and techniques. Thomas specialised in architectural stone carving and got a job in restoration. He made figurative work in his spare time and it became increasingly apparent that this should be his principal discipline. ¶ Thomas used his QEST Scholarship to attend a sculpture workshop at the Florence Academy of Art. *I thought the training would suit my needs, but it was too big an investment to leap straight into a long course.* The summer school convinced Thomas that a full academic year would be crucial to his progress as a contemporary realist sculptor. ¶ Working from life, he spent three hours every morning drawing and sculpted every afternoon. The intensity pushed his visual acuity and ability to represent the human form; the time frames – a single pose might last five weeks – taught him sustained focus. *My next commission will take 12 months, which would have been unthinkable beforehand.* ¶ He returned from Florence in 2016 with a body of work that would otherwise have taken years, and set up a studio in Shoreditch, east London. He sketches in charcoal from life then makes sculptures from the drawings and memories of the sitting. *This creates a liberating distance from the subject, so I can focus more on the natural rhythm of a composition than exact reproduction.* ¶ There were several affirming moments during his first year of practice. *Alessandro*, on the furthest plinth, was selected for *FACE*, The Society of Portrait Sculptors Annual Open Exhibition. This was the third time Thomas's work was chosen, which resulted in an invitation to apply to become a member of the Society (he was elected in 2017). He became sculptor-in-residence at Makers House, The New Craftsmen collaboration that brought to life *Orlando* by Virginia Woolf, the inspiration behind Burberry's London Fashion Week collection (his painted cast is standing in the corner). Thomas was also awarded the biennial Founders' Sculpture Prize, a competition run by the Worshipful Company of Founders for sculptors in the first decade of their careers. He was commissioned to realise his winning design, *Flight*, of three figures moving through chaotic abstract forms seeking refuge. His mentor on the project suggested the Bronze Age Foundry, a bicycle ride from his studio, to cast his work. ¶ He visited often to learn his role in the process, such as checking the wax replica used to make a ceramic shell into which the bronze is poured, to removing seamlines, and watched as patinas were applied. *I prefer dark bronzes as the effect is closest to the original clay. I also like to leave rough texture on the surface, even fingerprints, to retain something of the hand making. This would look too busy if the finish was not monotone.* ¶ Back to the torso. The lot sold twice, once in bronze and another in resin. Thomas made a mould to cast the resin (this destroys the clay sculpture, but occasionally a feature emerges intact – he has a perfect nose and a few ears on a shelf that he can not bear to part with). For the bronze, he called again on his local foundry. ¶ He has also returned to the Historic Stone Carving and Drawing course at the City & Guilds of London Art School, this time as a tutor – a new chapter for Thomas and the next generation of QEST Scholars he is now teaching.

Gayle Cooper

ART FINISHER & WIGMAKER

When the feature film of J.K. Rowling's novel *Harry Potter & The Philosopher's* QEST Scholar 2013 *Stone* was released in 2001, Gayle Cooper watched a documentary on its making. *There was as much wizardry behind the scenes as in the story.* Nearing the end of secondary school, she applied to study model design and special effects at the University of Hertfordshire. ¶ Since graduation, Gayle has worked in the television and film industry as an art finisher specialising in prosthetic make-up and creature effects. She had made wigs for a series of animatronics during her degree and picked up basic hair skills through practice, but wanted to study traditional wigmaking as the pinnacle of the craft. ¶ A QEST scholarship funded a place on the Lace Wig & Hair Replacement course at The UK Wig School. Taught by founder and master wigmaker Ms Rosa, Gayle gained knowledge and practical skills for every stage: foundation fabrication; hair selection, preparation and blending; measuring and fitting. *I soon became proficient in the knots – single, double, under and invisible – to attach the hair to the lace and learned to accurately pattern a front hairline.* ¶ The timing could not have been better. High-definition filming was becoming increasingly common and the difference in appearance between Gayle's fully-knotted, human hair wigs and machine-made substitutes was enormous on screen. *You can even buy superfine, HD lace now. Its fragility makes it time consuming to work with, but it is almost invisible against the skin. I used it for the cap of a couple of character wigs worn in the BBC drama 'Poldark'.* ¶ Gayle has also enhanced the quality of her art finishing by incorporating more realistic facial postiche, from moustaches to bear fur. The technique is similar to making a full wig: a tiny hook is used to attach individual hairs to a fine, flesh-coloured lace, which can then be applied directly or onto prosthetics. *This is especially useful for likeness make-up, when we are trying to make an actor resemble a famous face.* She has become known for the accuracy of the eyebrows she makes in mohair and recently worked with Oscar-winning prosthetics designer Mark Coulier on a film, *Leader's Way*. ¶ With a skillset that now includes mouldmaking, casting in silicone and fibreglass, painting, wigwork, hairwork, punching and flocking, Gayle often uses a combination of techniques to achieve special effects. *To make a canine head I might punch hair directly into the silicone, knot in where the hairline will be visible, then flock around the muzzle with electrostatically charged nylon fibres to get a stubbly effect.* A bearded lizard and an alien croupier in a casino scene in *Star Wars: The Last Jedi* are the result of her handiwork and she spent several painstaking days attaching yak hair to Lycra for Chewbacca costumes. She also has a number of extra-terrestrial beings for *Doctor Who* to her credit and led the fur work on Moz, the friendly monster that starred in the John Lewis Christmas campaign in 2017. ¶ Gayle has amassed a reference library of hairstyles from different eras and cultures, books of wildlife photography, and palaeontology books too from her latest project: puppets and models for the interactive *Dinosaurs in the Wild* exhibition on the Greenwich Peninsula in London. She has also demonstrated hair knotting for students at Gorton Studio, Europe's most authentic screen prosthetics school run by internationally acclaimed prosthetics designer Neill Gorton, and makes art wigs, like the mermaid in the picture decorated with driftwood and seashells. ¶ The training in lace wigmaking has been invaluable on set, but Gayle has not forgotten that Ms Rosa, having suffered from alopecia, designed the course with an emphasis on hair replacement. *In time, quality wigs for those with medical hair loss will become an important focus for my business too.*

Peter Ting

TABLEWARE DESIGNER

QEST Thomas Goode
& Co Scholar 1997

Peter Ting is standing in a showroom at Thomas Goode, surrounded by some of the world's finest tableware, china and silverware. He is back at this emporium in the heart of Mayfair in London for the third time in his career as a designer of china and glass. ¶ Peter studied both studio and industrial ceramics and uses these skills to inform his design practice. Following an MA at Cardiff School of Art & Design and Stoke-on-Trent, he released his first collection as *Tingware*. In 1996, Thomas Goode bought Peter's business in Stoke-on-Trent. He stayed on for two years running the Thomas Goode Bone China Manufactory, responsible for over 40 patterns referencing new designs and archival re-introductions. ¶ Peter was young, ambitious, and had been working at warp speed for a decade. *It was time for a break. I took a year out and learned to cook.* A call from Rumi Verjee, then owner of Thomas Goode, enticed him back to work as an in-house designer, which culminated in a range of his tableware being acquired by the Victoria and Albert Museum. Rumi also proposed Peter for a QEST Scholarship in 3D printing, which was in its infancy at the time. ¶ In 2001, he was invited to join Asprey as head of homeware. *The history and archive were a rich source of inspiration for exclusive crystal, glassware, cutlery and silver.* Peter introduced the signature *Grafton* shape and numerous exclusive patterns. ¶ A veteran Londoner, he knows the city from east to west and has a strong understanding of retail and hospitality across Europe, the United States and East Asia. His appreciation of European and Asian food culture often overlaps with his ceramics expertise. A dialogue between Peter and teasmith Tim d'Offay of Postcard Teas about the shape of a teacup affecting the experience of flavour led to extensive research and development. Using their combined skills and knowledge, three essential forms to enhance the aromas of either green, black or fragrant teas were selected from over 40 hand-thrown prototypes and launched as *1660 LONDON*. These porcelain drinking vessels can be found in the permanent collection at the Victoria and Albert Museum and were used to illustrate epicureanism at the *What is Luxury?* exhibition in 2015. ¶ In 2016, Peter and porcelain expert Ying Jian launched Ting-Ying, a gallery concept to showcase the best of traditional and contemporary Blanc de Chine made in Dehua, Fujian Province, China. Work by three of their artists was acquired by the V&A within the first year, including *Small Paper No.1* by Su Xianzhong. *He laid fine layers of porcelain 'paper' onto a brick from the dismantled kiln of the state porcelain manufacture to symbolise the rebirth of the craft in the area. It is the most exquisite work.* The *Flower Cylinder* series, created by Peter with accomplished flower maker Zha Caiduan, and six mini teapots by exceptionally talented 22-year-old thrower Lei Aiguo featured at *COLLECT: The International Art Fair for Contemporary Objects* in London in 2018. *We are developing an invited residency programme too, on which other makers can engage with these ancient skills.* ¶ Peter also provides creative art direction for Cumbria Crystal and has been instrumental in guiding traditional French porcelain specialist LEGLE through its transformation into an international luxury brand. He contributes first-hand industry experience to the syllabus at the Royal College of Art and Central Saint Martins and has spoken at TED conferences in Shanghai on the diaspora of being a Chinese citizen in the modern world. ¶ The Crafts Council, responsible for championing the UK as the best place to make, see, collect and learn about contemporary craft, made Peter a trustee in 2009 and he has been elected to the International Academy of Ceramics. Peter's career can be encapsulated by its aims: to stimulate communication between members in 56 countries and encourage the highest quality production in all ceramic cultures.

Amelia Crowley-Roth

WOODCARVER

The daughter of luthiers, Amelia Crowley-Roth was always inclined towards arts and craft. *When I was young I assumed everybody had a workshop at home.* ¶ Painting came most naturally, so she went to study Fine Art at the City & Guilds of London Art School. Amelia immersed herself in the training, but there was a distraction: the woodcarving room. *The smells and sounds made me feel nostalgic about my parents' violin making, and eager to find my own direction working with wood.* She persuaded her tutors to let her spend a day a week at the bench. ¶ Amelia completed her degree and enrolled on the Ornamental Woodcarving & Gilding course. *It was quite a financial stretch going straight into the Postgraduate Diploma until QEST agreed to cover the second-year fees.* The curriculum focused on the range of skills required to become a professional wood carver, often through copying historic examples. *It was useful to gain an understanding of techniques, but I was determined to use my design skills and make original work.* ¶ It was 2015, the 150th anniversary of Lewis Carroll's *Alice in Wonderland*. Amelia researched the manuscripts, illustrations and photographic prints held at Christ Church, the Oxford College where Carroll was a mathematics lecturer. This inspired a fanciful collection of furniture for her final show: typical 19th century living room antiques at a glance, but as in Wonderland, everything is not as it first seems. The legs of the reclaimed mahogany table (pictured) are flamingos standing on their heads, their claws reaching up around the edge. The inlaid chessboard of holly and iron wood is a nod to *Alice Through the Looking Glass*, the sequel in which a game comes to life, and a photograph that Carroll took of his aunts playing chess. ¶ Ready to start work in earnest, Amelia established a workshop and a company, London Wood Carving. One of her most significant early commissions was from QEST trustee and bespoke furniture maker Neil Stevenson. He had been asked by the Galileo Foundation on behalf of Pope Francis to make a commemorative crozier for the Most Revd and Rt Hon Justin Welby, Archbishop of Canterbury. Amelia designed and carved the head with a serpent and ram, symbolising Jesus the Risen Lamb. This was based on the crozier presented to Saint Augustine by Saint Gregory the Great when he sent him to convert the pagan English in 597. *It was a proud moment when it was presented during an official visit to celebrate vespers at the Church of San Gregorio al Celio in Rome.* ¶ In 2016, Amelia was invited by City & Guilds to return for a part-time Fellowship in Decorative Surfaces sponsored by the Worshipful Company of Painters and Stainers. This gave her the space to explore different finishing techniques, particularly gilding, décor-marbling and the art of 'japanning' (the European imitation of lacquer). *The timing was perfect as my wood carvings were becoming more artistic.* ¶ *The Goose That Laid The Golden Egg* (pictured), Amelia's reaction to Brexit, was made during her Fellowship. *I was taught originally to make a clay model then work with measuring devices to realise the composition in wood. I always felt restricted working this way; now I like to deviate from the models, allowing changes and alterations as I go.* The result is a more natural and coherent piece. This can be seen with the knot that she uncovered in the lime when carving the wing. *Given the fate of the goose, I went with it, as it looked like a knife wound.* Below are gilded goose eggs, one intentionally broken. ¶ Amelia divides her time between London and new home in Somerset. *When we moved, a case that belonged to my great-great-grandmother containing my gilding equipment went missing; I was devastated. I probably got a little over-excited when it came to light a few months later; the name of our farm now gleams in gold on the rickety wooden gatepost.*

QEST Radcliffe Trust Scholar 2014

Aidan McEvoy

FURNITURE MAKER & DESIGNER

QEST Scholar 2006 Aidan McEvoy is sitting in a sawmill in the middle of 16 acres of Hampshire woodland where Paul Goulden sells air-dried, rough-sawn, British timbers. The pages of Aidan's design book are turned to the start of his latest project: a table and four chairs, sideboard and queen-size bed for an apartment in Paris. *I am here to buy a whole log of prime English walnut to guarantee consistency of tone, colour and grain pattern for this commission.* He has just used the box scraper (once used to remove addresses on tea chests as they were shipped from place to place) to get a closer look. ¶ Resting on Aidan's book is the maquette for the leaf motif that will appear throughout this collection, part of his ongoing body of work inspired by Aestas, Roman goddess of summer. The first piece was a table to go in the Summer House for the Coronation Festival at Buckingham Palace in 2013. Aidan spent weeks agonising over what to make. *It would have been easy to get carried away by the grandeur of the address, but this was a place to simply sit and enjoy the gardens.* The final sketch, based on the crocus flowers that bloom early in the season, came good in less than an hour. He made the tabletop from petals of English walnut set in an English cherry surround; the stems flow down through the centre to form the legs. Aidan also created a limited edition *Aestas Jewellery Box* that takes its form from a primrose: six wooden petals, each with a carved handle resembling the flower's stamen, open to reveal removable trays. ¶ *The organic nature of my designs springs from the scenery of my childhood in West Cork in Ireland.* Aidan spent several years working there before living in France and Germany to absorb other approaches to his craft. He settled in London and established his first company supplying commercial woodworking solutions. The business grew rapidly, but Aidan felt too removed from the design and making of furniture. He signed up for three months of training at The Edward Barnsley Workshop in Hampshire. *I thought this would be plenty of time, but it was like opening an encyclopaedia of furniture making and reading the preface; I had another three inches of the book to go.* A QEST Scholarship enabled Aidan to return for a year and a half. *I spent 10 hours a day, six days a week at the bench.* One of his pieces was purchased by the New Walk Museum & Art Gallery in Leicester to showcase the legacy of the Arts & Crafts movement. ¶ In 2008, Aidan set up a new workshop in Surrey. As well as making bespoke furniture, he runs short courses. These started five years ago when he was asked to mentor three cabinetmakers for *Monty Don's Real Craft*, a television series celebrating traditional crafts. *I thoroughly enjoyed the experience and requests for training followed. I now teach 150 people a year.* The most practical for an aspiring maker is the eight-day build of a *Moroubo* workbench. Designed by Aidan, it marries the rock-solid stability of the French Roubo bench with the portability of those used by Moravian carpenters in 18th century Germany. *The split top doubles as a tool holder as I like to have my saws and chisels in arm's reach when I am hand cutting joints.* The students prepare the timber – flamed beech, oak and Douglas fir – and learn joint work, hardware fitting and finishing, and at the end have a bench to practice on at home. ¶ Aidan is about to start teaching a year-long professional course. This is the first step towards opening a residential school back in Ireland with his wife Laura. *We have found a site and are planning the syllabus.* There will be visiting specialists to help mentor the students through projects such as a wood and carbon fibre stool, seat rushing and watercolour painting (this is how Aidan presents the final sketch for private commissions). *West Cork was such a nurturing environment for me, I cannot wait to welcome students from all over the world.*

Gordon W. Robertson

PEWTERER

A double-decker craft bus came to Helensborough on the west coast of Scotland one summer when Gordon Robertson was a child. *Once or twice a week we got to try different projects; they showed us how to screenprint and it caught my imagination.* He also had an inspirational art teacher who introduced him to pop art and those who shaped the movement, including Paolozzi and Warhol. ¶ At Gray's School of Art in Aberdeen, Gordon specialised in printed textiles and printmaking, treating them as fine art and working at an architectural scale. He moved to London in 1983 and found a job with Alecto Historical Editions working on *Banks's Florilegium* with the Natural History Museum, which had a profound effect on him. From 1768 to 1771, botanist Joseph Banks sailed on the Pacific voyage of the *HMS Endeavour* with Captain Cook. Botanical artist Sydney Parkinson was on board producing amazing watercolours of the plants they encountered. On their return, engravings were made for scientific research and everything was bequeathed to the British Museum. *The engravings are astonishing. Nine years were spent restoring and chroming the 874 plates, removing dried ink from the lines so they could be used again.* An edition of 100 colour prints was created, and, as one of the editioners, Gordon was given an artist's proof of each that he worked on. *These have proved to be great reference material for my work.* ¶ As a printmaker, he was amazed at how many of the metal plates were thrown away after use, so he began upcycling them. *I started by making jewellery from etching plates, which I sold with the corresponding print.* ¶ Gordon took a day-a-week course at Morley College to learn silversmithing. *It was here, learning to press forms, that I discovered my inner metalworker.* However, he soon found the confines of jewellery-making too limiting, but experimenting at a larger scale in silver was too expensive. By chance, he discovered pewter. ¶ Gordon also came across *Pewter Live*, a competition run by the Worshipful Company of Pewterers. The brief that year was to create a retail item for a public entity. He made a series of *Botanique* plates, bowls and jewellery based on his pen and ink drawings from visits to Kew Gardens. The collection won the top awards. He repeated his success in 2013 on the theme of time. *I viewed an eclipse in a tray of water and my sketches became the design for my entry: 'Il sol et la lune'.* ¶ Pewterers' Hall suggested that Gordon should apply to QEST to learn more. He arranged in-house training with Wentworth Pewter in Sheffield, which has led to an ongoing partnership. *I used to travel up there every month for two or three days, my bag packed with pieces of pewter, textiles and print to experiment with.* Gordon was in his element spinning, casting and soldering in the workshop to explore the potential of the material. *I love working in pewter. It can be quite tricky to solder if you don't lift the flame off quickly enough, but it is lead-free, does not tarnish, and it polishes and patinates beautifully.* In 2014, he was invested as a Freeman of the Pewterers' Company. ¶ Gordon now specialises in etched metal surfaces to produce tableware, furniture and jewellery. He also works on luxury interiors for companies such as Martin Kemp Design on fittings, from door handles to architraves, mostly in brass. *I was working on items for a penthouse recently and persuaded them to use pewter for a marbled glass effect. All it needs is a rub with a soft cloth; the cleaner will be delighted!* ¶ Through an introduction at *Pewter Live*, Gordon was commissioned by Sir Andrew Parmley to create the gifts for his year as Lord Mayor of London. Gordon designed a swan and vine motif that he etched into pewter with Wentworth Pewter to form into a bowl and bottle holder. *The design was applied to a silk scarf as well; a good opportunity to tie my work back to the crafts of pattern and printmaking where everything began.*

QEST Worshipful Company of Pewterers Scholar 2013

[73]

Deirdre Hawken

MILLINER

QEST Scholar 1999

Deirdre Hawken trained in theatre design at Central Saint Martins and spent many years designing sets and costumes around the UK. She worked on West End shows including *Fosse* and ballets at the Royal Opera House in Covent Garden, where she made thousands of flowers for a production of *Sleeping Beauty*. She delighted most in the hats and decided to pursue this further. ¶ Deirdre is one of four Scholars who QEST has funded to study couture millinery with Rose Corey MBE, former milliner to Queen Elizabeth The Queen Mother. She took a one-day-a-week class for nearly two years. Almost 20 years on, she has exhibited and sold internationally as a designer and maker of headpieces and jewellery that are a feast for the eyes. ¶ Much of her work springs from a playful obsession with food. A menu comes to life in Deirdre's hands. *I was taken to lunch at Mosimann's and the summer pudding was delicious, bursting with fruit and gorgeous colours. I had to make it myself.* Her handmade berries spill out of the rich, velvet casing like jewels, every bit as mouthwatering as the original. ¶ The pink chocolate box in the corner of the picture is the latest version of a hat she made for an exhibition at Fortnum & Mason. She usually tries to evolve rather than repeat, but this proved so popular she had to make four in Fortnum's signature eau de nil. When Duchy Originals commissioned a biscuit box, she couldn't resist adding a cascade of oatcakes. ¶ Wandering through food markets is another source of inspiration. A basket laden with plump, pinkish-brown borlotti beans caught her eye on a trip to Venice. On her return, a friend grew a crop to help Deirdre with her research. *My painted leather pods and beans, crisscrossed on a band (far left), look much healthier than the real ones did by the time I had finished.* This is one of the headpieces that appeared in a solo exhibition at the Halcyon Days store in The Royal Exchange in London in the run up to Royal Ascot in 2018. ¶ Glancing around Deirdre's workshop, it is almost more allotment than studio, but with a definite couture sensibility. She researches every ingredient extensively and has a detailed picture in her head before picking up her tools. *My husband, a sculptor, finds it baffling that I don't draw everything out, but I prefer to be hands on straight away, letting my work grow organically.* ¶ Each piece begins with a maquette. She makes the bases with buckram, a stiffened cloth usually woven from cotton (also used by bookbinders) then photographs every step of the model making, at this stage entirely in white. She then takes it apart to hand dye each piece of fabric and leather before final assembly. ¶ Some materials lend themselves naturally to being styled as food: silk velvet for the soft texture of apricot skin; glossy beads as redcurrants and blackcurrants; bright yellow leather for lemon skin to hold segments of fresh silk. Others are more of a challenge. *Red onions proved particularly tricky. After many iterations, thankfully no tears, I settled on a combination of leather and silk taffeta.* ¶ Deirdre avoids using glue to be environmentally friendly and to make to archival standards as many of her hats end up in public collections: a salad at the Victoria and Albert Museum, a prawn at the Kyoto Costume Institute, a cauliflower in the Metropolitan Museum of Art in New York. For many years, her work was also sold in New York at Julie: Artisans' Gallery, a showcase for clothing and jewellery as an art form, and her theatrical jewellery made an appearance on Fifth Avenue one Christmas in the Winter Palace-themed windows at Saks. ¶ A Fellow of the Society of Designer Craftsmen and Royal Society of Arts, Deirdre has an imagination as lively and colourful as her portrait: framed by hats she has made, plates spinning around, ideas popping out.

Ben Short

CHARCOAL BURNER

QEST Ernest Cook Trust Scholar 2013

Meeting a charcoal burner in a Hampshire downland copse on a school trip is etched in Ben Short's memory. *Even as an eight-year-old boy I had an intuition that it was a more beautiful way of life.* In his early teens, he was struck by the still and steady character of a man who lived and worked cutting hazel in the wood beyond the family farm. *He was practising an ancient craft (with a tamed wood mouse living up his sleeve) while the rest of society hurtled towards the madness of the 1980s.* ¶ Despite an upbringing that had conditioned him to the outdoors, Ben became an urban animal. *I made good in my career as an advertising writer, plying my trade in London, but somehow felt hollow. My only wish was to return to the country and be of practical use.* ¶ The freewheeling of his childhood – wandering rutted drove roads and climbing straw bale towers – was a distant memory; he knew it would be a long haul to regain this intimacy with the land. After a stint as a forester with the National Trust, a QEST Scholarship allowed Ben to dedicate a year to learning coppice restoration and management. He now lives in Dorset as a charcoal burner, woodsman and hedgelayer. *The materials with which I make my living couldn't be more simple: wood, earth, air and fire. I deal in elements.* ¶ He is not interested in swathes of high forest, but rather maintaining small woods and maximising their potential as ecosystems and sustainable resource for their stewards. *I like the phrase 'copse work'; it is old-fashioned and straightforward.* The original meaning is the making of coppice products within the wood, like sheep hurdles and cleft ash gates. Ben has appropriated the term for his general practice of woodland husbandry: from restoring derelict coppice to thinning parcels of woodland, removing damaged or 'wolf trees' to give selected specimens the space and light to grow. Coppicing also lets sunlight and warmth back onto the woodland floor so that bluebells and anemones, long-dormant, reappear. ¶ He finds joy in traditional hedgelaying too. *Under a hedger's billhook, the boundary is tamed, given body and form, and the laid hedges provide nesting sites for small birds – wrens seem particularly enamoured.* Being first and foremost a charcoal burner, Ben's satisfaction goes further. The hedgelaying gives him paid work in the winter; it also provides the means for a summer income as the larger trimmings are a welcome harvest from which to make charcoal. *This elegance of fit between work and seasons is most satisfying.* ¶ He has a charcoal kiln at his yard under Eggardon Hill (an Iron Age hill fort overlooking the Jurassic coast), but prefers to take the burner to the source material. The skill lies in knowing where to site the steel ring kiln (the vagaries of wind, rain and different soil qualities affect a burn), how to lay it, and when to close it down. *I spend most of the summer overnighting in the woods; I've got two kilns on the go at this camp.* ¶ A doggedness is required. It is hot, physically-exacting work, and does not pay much, but making and selling native charcoal is not only a way for people to 'feast well' (as he prints on the sacks), it helps to support a rural economy that means the woods can be managed for the long term. Ben Short Barbeque Charcoal is a blend of hazel, ash, thorn, oak, and field maple. Unlike much of the imported charcoal that proliferates the market (and notches up a significant carbon footprint in shipping), it contains no additives or binders, just carbonised English hardwood that lights easily with a twist of newspaper and match, and warms quickly for cooking. ¶ A day's work can still put a dent in him, but it is a good dent of an honest day's work out of doors rather than the exhaustion he felt from office life. When not enveloped in smoke, Ben is writing a book about his life as one of England's few remaining woodland charcoal burners.

Sophie D'Souza
STAINED GLASS ARTIST

QEST Scholar 2010 The methods used to make leaded stained glass have changed little over the past thousand years. A reclaimed front door for a house she was restoring prompted Sophie D'Souza to find out enough so she could replace the missing stained glass panels. *I was working as a carpenter at the time; soon other domestic stained glass repairs started to crop up through conversations with clients on existing jobs.* ¶ A few years later, Sophie was at a Diocese of Westminster meeting; replacement of the stained glass windows of The Roman Catholic Church of s s Peter & Paul in west London, where she is a parishioner, was on the agenda. The quotation was beyond the budget and it was sounding as though they would have to make do with imitation film and stuck-on lead. *I could not bear the thought. I reckoned I could make a good attempt at the real thing and volunteered to do the project at cost.* Her offer was accepted. ¶ It was an enormous undertaking. She made four windows either side of the nave to represent St Peter and St Paul, in the side chapel an image of Christ crowned with thorns to face a painting of the crucifixion, and opposite the Lady Chapel, is *Our Lady, Crowned with Glory.* Sophie is standing in front of the Trinity windows: *Burning Bush* (the Father), *Lamb of God* (the Son) and *Holy Spirit. These are the windows I am most proud of and have been asked to make time and again. When I do, I always change something.* The 13 stained glass windows were blessed by Archbishop Vincent Nichols at a Mass to celebrate the 50th anniversary of the Church's consecration. ¶ Sophie learned a lot through their making and decided to train professionally. With a QEST Scholarship, she completed the Postgraduate Certificate in Architectural Stained Glass at Central Saint Martins. She was in the last class to graduate the programme after over a hundred years of teaching glass artists. *Our end of year show was entitled 'Fiennale 2011'.* ¶ Stained glass art is one of the oldest forms of storytelling and Sophie's work has a strong narrative quality. Her ecclesiastical stained glass commissions are mostly for Roman Catholic churches and schools. *With my background in theology (I am a Divinity graduate), we have a shared language.* She returned to the Church of s s Peter & Paul to complete the sanctuary windows: *The Evangelists, Word of God, Bread* and *Wine.* In local schools, Sophie likes to involve the pupils. *The windows for St Benedict's School Chapel in Ealing were drawn by an 11-year-old; the colours cast a beautiful light across the bay where the tabernacle stands.* At St Joseph's School in Hanwell the stained glass features the flags of the children's countries of origin. *It is a wonderful way to celebrate the diversity of the student body.* ¶ The architecture in Roman Catholic churches is quite modern (most were started in the 1930s and 1950s), which suits Sophie's graphic styling. Due to the financial constraints of the era, they tend to have 'quarries': Crittal-steel-framed windows of clear or amber glass. *Many of the frames have degraded and churches are taking this opportunity to introduce stained glass.* Once a design is agreed, Sophie draws a full-size cartoon showing the lead lines. The glass is cut to these lines and 'stained' by painting using ground pigments with water, vinegar or oil. Each section is fired to between 560 and 680 degrees Celsius, at which point the glass begins to melt and the stain is fused to its surface. Next is leading (Sophie has regular blood tests to check her levels of the metal remain normal). She fits the glass into channels of lead, held in place with horse shoe nails temporarily for soldering, then cements with a substance that creates rigidity and weatherproofing. Blacking with graphite darkens the solder and creates a patina on the lead. *I love the dramatic contrast as the light comes through the glass and brings it to life.*

Hannah Griffiths

MOSAIC ARTIST

A fine artist by training, Hannah Griffiths has a painterly approach to her mosaics. QEST Scholar 2009 *I discovered a passion for the craft while chipping away at an adult education class. A few decorative projects at home led to jobs for family and friends, then 'proper' commissions.* ¶ Hannah was awarded a QEST Scholarship to attend a two-week Master in Mosaic course at Orsoni, the famed Venetian producer of artisanal mosaics. She learned to work with 'smalti', the richly-coloured, enamelled glass tesserae (blocks) developed during the Byzantine era. The Orsoni foundry has made them in the traditional way since 1888. In 1889, an artwork with almost 3,000 shades and tones was created for the Universal Exhibition in Paris. Spanish architect Antoni Gaudí was amazed by its beauty and decided to use Orsoni tiles in the construction of the *Sagrada Familia* in Barcelona. ¶ *Their glass is so sumptuous, it reminded me of giant sheets of glossy caramel, and being handmade, the surface and thickness are slightly irregular; this individuality adds to the charm.* The smalti are cut with a traditional hammer and hardie (chisel embedded in a tree trunk that works like an anvil). *I usually work with nippers. It took me a while to get the hang of holding the glass on the steel hardie and tapping to get the exact size and shape I wanted.* Hannah found it exhilarating soaking up the history, theory and application of mosaic art while living and working at Orsoni. *My studio is exceptionally modest in comparison, but I could not wait to get back to East Sussex with this renewed creative energy.* ¶ Most of her work is for private homes. Hannah visits to get a feel for the client's style, interior design, and intended location for the mosaic before presenting paintings of suggested designs. Subjects have included African textiles to The Crown Jewels. *I once made a table with a world map. It was for a retired geography professor, so I had to be painstakingly accurate.* Hannah is pictured making a simple splash back for her kitchen. She is using this as a chance to experiment with a new tool recommended by a stained glass maker, which has increased the variety of shapes she can create. *I love the colours and patterns of vintage china, so I am cutting stars from fragments of old porcelain cups and saucers.* ¶ Some commissions have a far wider audience. Elephant Parade is a social enterprise that runs outdoor art exhibitions around the world to raise awareness and funds for welfare and conservation projects. Hannah was invited to decorate one of the 250 life-size, baby elephant statues when the show came to London. She created *Figgy* with fig fruit mosaics on a painted tree, each falling leaf representing a lost species. In 2015, Hannah was involved in the *Synaesthesia Garden* designed by Sarah Wilson that won Gold at the RHS Hampton Court Flower Show. Set inside a dome, coloured lights swept across the garden in response to trigger words and music to recreate the unusual, multi-sensory reaction to a stimulus experienced by a synaesthete. Hannah's mirrored mosaics reflected the light to represent the electrical activity in the brain. *I also collaborated with QEST Scholar and vitreous artist Mel Howse to create a mosaic for the floor beneath the enamelled steel font that she made for St Cuthbert's Church in Portsmouth.* ¶ Fern Hill Primary School in Kingston is full of bright mosaic art thanks to Hannah and the pupils. She held two weeks of workshops involving every class. Their drawings were enlarged and mounted on boards for the children to decorate with glass tiles. *I taught some of the older ones to cut too. It was such a joyful experience for everyone.* Hannah is planning a similar project in Canterbury and is about to start a course for Mencap in Hastings. *I have met the group, adults of all ages with learning disabilities, and am sure they will love the tactile nature of the craft as much as I do.*

Rod Kelly

GOLDSMITH & SILVERSMITH

Manasi Depala

SILVERSMITH

Rod Kelly
QEST Scholar 2000

Manasi Depala
QEST Clarins
Scholar 2016

On the cover of the book, Rod Kelly is holding a dish that he is chasing for a set that will celebrate the events of a client's family history, stretching over five hundred years, from the Battle of Agincourt to the First World War. *I enjoy the collaborative process: the dialogue while working up a brief together and discussing elements to include in a design until we have built an image that they are happy with.* Rod is inspired by people, history, the countryside surrounding his Norfolk home and the beauty of the Shetland Isles (where the photograph was taken, by his workshop, looking out towards the coastline of Muckle Roe and the Atlantic beyond). ¶ For the last 14 years, Rod and his wife, enameller and jeweller Sheila McDonald, have spent up to eight months a year in Shetland, where they founded and run the purpose-built South House Silver Workshop. The landscape and climate are testing, but inspirational. *Some days when the wind blows we wonder what we were thinking, but when the sun comes out, the wildlife appears and you can see whales, porpoises and dolphins passing by, it is breathtaking.* It was a significant move, intended so they could pass on their skills honed over the last 30 years to others who will carry them on for the rest of their lives and, they hope, hand them on to the next generation. ¶ For Rod's QEST Scholarship in 2000, he worked with Alan Mudd, who taught him how to recess for gold inlay, and a trade silversmith, with whom he made a large dish so they could compare hammering and soldering techniques. Zoe Watts, due to arrive on Shetland shortly, will be the seventh QEST Scholar Rod has welcomed to South House following four in 2013 (Ryan McClean, Sophie Stamp, Elizabeth Peers and Kate Earlam) and Louise Perry and Manasi Depala in 2016. Manasi, pictured with Rod, has returned to prepare for the Goldsmiths' Fair. In this photograph, she is holding a silver chased vessel inspired by the conical-shaped Lotus Temple in Delhi; on the back cover, she is holding a box made during her training. ¶ One of Rod's most significant commissions was by The Worshipful Company of Goldsmiths to commemorate Her Majesty The Queen's Diamond Jubilee. He created *The Diamond Jubilee Rosewater Dish*: raised, 'beaten sunk' by hand, and hammered into an octagonal form with chased decoration and inlayed gold highlights. The centre is chased with the royal crown and the cipher *EIIR* against a background of flowing lines, signifying the sea. The four applied panels each present a symbol of the four nations of the United Kingdom: an English rose; Scottish thistles; daffodils for Wales; and shamrocks for Northern Ireland. The raised panels produce a cross to represent Her Majesty as Defender of the Faith. ¶ This dish is the centrepiece in a new display of contemporary pieces by modern silversmiths that is used on formal occasions at the Goldsmiths' Hall; *The Buffet Plate* highlights to guests the Company's role as a major patron of modern silver and the exceptional quality of British silverwork. Rod along with Geoffrey Munn, former Assistant at The Worshipful Company of Goldsmiths, and Rosemary Ransome Wallis, Art Director and Curator of the Company, were invited for a private audience with Her Majesty to present the piece and tell its story. ¶ One of the most poignant commissions for Rod was an alms dish for Lichfield Cathedral, as his son was christened there, and he has recently completed a pair of Altar candlesticks in walnut and chased silver for the chapel at Eton College. The design features Madonna lilies, referencing the William Morris Altar hangings and Eton's crest, which has lilies as a sign of the fidelity of the Virgin Mary. *They took 12 days of solid chasing using punches and a hammer to emboss and form the low relief patterns; I had to keep the woodstove roaring throughout to ward off the chill of February on Shetland.*

Jacqui Carey

BRAIDMAKER

Coming from a mathematical family, the teenage Jacqui Carey, who was equally QEST Scholar 2005 numerate and inquisitive, assumed she would follow a related career path. She also loved art, but it did not work with her school timetable. *The art teacher offered to fit classes into my lunch hour. Only years later did I realise he was kindly giving up his lunch hour too.* ¶ She encountered the two subjects in harmony for the first time on a weaving loom at Winchester School of Art and continued training in woven textiles at West Surrey College of Art & Design. Braiding was a small element taught in passing, but, as she needed trim for her textiles, she kept an interest. The more intricate the structures, the more Jacqui was drawn into this beautiful, formulaic world of sequence and colour. ¶ This culminated in her discovery of 'kumihimo', the Japanese art of braiding. *I found a book on the Living National Treasures of Japan – their mastery of craft was inspirational.* She decided to spend three months unravelling the mysteries of kumihimo. That was in the 1980s; she is still going. ¶ Jacqui is sitting at an 'Ō-marudai' (Japanese for 'big round stand'). The smaller version on the left is used for making simple braids where the colours run throughout. This larger frame has an extra set of arms that allows her to create more complicated designs, interworking two layers using teams of weighted bobbins (she has over 50 on the go here) so she can choose where the colours are visible along the braid. ¶ The surface of the marudai is called a 'kagami' (mirror) as the braid that forms here reflects the maker. *This is uncannily true, a lot of my work expresses how I feel and my surroundings.* There are phases when she works in creams and whites, then explosions of colour like the jacket she is wearing, and in the height of summer her braids often take on the pale green hues of parched terrain. ¶ Kumihimo is an active craft in Japan, but English braidmaking died out in the Industrial Revolution. In 2005, Jacqui undertook an analysis, enabled by QEST, to figure out potential techniques by which extant examples could have been made. Working on 16th and 17th century pieces, she also jotted down details of embroidery stitches she saw; it turned out that almost two-thirds were long forgotten. She published *Sweet Bags* to share her findings and in recognition became the first beneficiary of a Wellcome Trust Research Bursary. ¶ She studied an exquisite 15th century embroidered cover, the earliest of its kind to survive intact, of an English folding almanac produced for medical practitioners to gather astrological information. This led to a book, *MS.8932*, named after the object's Wellcome Collection library number. *It was a privilege to unlock and reveal its secrets as it is too fragile to be on public display.* ¶ Jacqui is conscious that she has a lot of rediscovered knowledge that is not recorded anywhere. *I enjoy teaching for its individuality – I taught a kendo expert to make a braid for his sword and in the same class a student wanted to make braids for corsets – but through writing I can reach the greatest number of people, so I make more time for that now.* ¶ While researching and writing, Jacqui still likes to make at least one braid a day. *It is good for me – and some days I make many more.* Her most unusual commission was to make a braid for a pair of forceps for the Royal College of Obstetricians and Gynaecologists, based on the earliest original pair of functioning forceps they have, made in the 1700s. ¶ *It is a wonderful subject: humble, accessible, present in every culture, every era. It is just string, albeit fancy string, and in one sense very ordinary, but dive in and you'll find history, mathematics and anthropology interlaced.* It's all in the name: 'kumi' means 'coming together' and 'himo' means 'threads', and through kumihimo Jacqui has brought together the strands of her life: textile maker, teacher, researcher and author.

' The traditional City &
Guilds education we received
in classical drawing,
sculpture, portraiture and
stone carving techniques
through QEST has proved
extremely valuable.
We use these skills
every day, on the architectural
and sculptural stonework
we undertake,
at our London Stone
Carving workshops. '

Tom Brown
STONE CARVER

Tom Nicholls
STONE CARVER

Tom Brown
QEST Scholar 2009

Tom Nicholls
QEST Scholar 2011

Carving stone demands more than a mastery of the craft. The carver must supplement their skills with knowledge of period style, ornament and construction techniques to interpret designs and produce work for any context: traditional, classical or contemporary. This statement underpins the work of London Stone Carving, a collective of four stone carvers, sculptors and masons: Tom Brown (on the stool), Tom Nicholls (standing), Josh Locksmith and Sam Lee. Brown and Nicholls met on a stonemasonry course at Weymouth College. Independently, they received QEST Scholarships to study for the Postgraduate Diploma in Historic Carving at the City & Guilds of London Art School. ¶ *Our training enables us to carry out sensitive restoration and conservation work on the thousands of listed public and private buildings and monuments that we are fortunate to have in the UK.* They also fabricate stone works for artists and take on private and public sculptural commissions. Brown and Nicholls recently completed rose panels and two ornamental roundels in Portland stone for Sir John Soane's Pitzhanger Manor in London. *They gave us artistic licence to interpret original designs and we elevated the stone in the studio to carve from a similar perspective as visitors will have now they are in position.* Brown and Nicholls each maintain a private practice from the London Stone Carving workshop. ¶ Tom Brown, a member of the Master Carvers Association, began his career in the time-honoured tradition of travelling around Europe to gain experience on high-profile commissions. He graduated from the City & Guilds course with a first-class Diploma (the *Canova Lion* in the picture was his final piece), following which he worked at Horace Walpole's Strawberry Hill House, a fine example of Gothic Revival architecture in London. Brown created ornate chimney pieces and his heraldic carving is installed above the main entrance. ¶ Other restoration projects include the Renaissance Galleries at the Victoria and Albert Museum and St George's Chapel in Windsor. *It is always fascinating to be up close to the architectural stone work adorning buildings like these.* ¶ The two clay models (above the lion) are for Tom's latest commission, *Bittern Finials*. They are ready to be cast in plaster and carved in Portland stone for the gateposts at a private residence. *I will need to add a few strategic stone reeds to support the bodies, and the beaks and necks are going to be nerve-wracking to carve.* ¶ Tom Nicholls was awarded Carver of the Year from the Master Carvers Association and the Worshipful Company of Masons for his City & Guilds final show. The piece next to him on the banker (workbench) was a college study to establish his ability to capture equine anatomy. *Horses are one of the main subjects for my own work; I find their physicality, power and grace exciting from a sculptural point of view.* ¶ In 2015, he was selected from a nationwide competition to create a gargoyle for Ripon Cathedral to replace one that was eroded beyond repair. His design was based on the features of a Daubenton's bat, an endangered species from the area, the Gothic architecture, and surrounding gargoyles. It took five weeks to carve from a one-tonne block of Highmoor Magnesian Limestone. ¶ *I have found public memorial works to be especially rewarding.* Nicholls designed and carved a two-metre high, Portland stone sculpture depicting a pair of hands releasing a symbolic cockney sparrow as a tribute to the 513 Barnardo's children buried in unmarked graves in Tower Hamlets Cemetery. It was unveiled by David Barnardo, nephew of the charity's founder. ¶ London Stone Carving courses run throughout the year for people to come and try any aspect that interests them, from letter cutting for a sign to conceptual stone sculpture. *They are also a chance for us to pass on skills we've been taught and our enthusiasm for the craft.*

Amy Goodwin

SIGNWRITER & FAIRGROUND ARTIST

QEST Scholar 2016

Summers spent travelling the West Country with a steam fairground gave Amy Goodwin an appreciation for its heritage, traditions and visual language. This influences the style of her commissions and own practice in traditional signwriting and lining, fairground art and design. *I love the elaborate and visual typography, flamboyant colours and meticulous lines.* ¶Amy was taught by Joby Carter and adheres to traditional methods: by hand, no tape, nor digital assistance. She was photographed during preparations for the summer season of Giffords Circus. *I answered an advertisement four years ago when they were looking for a signwriter who could work in the style of Victorian lunar parks.* The first year was signwriting and lining on a single wagon; the following year was creating a Western-themed set design. *Giffords is a very theatrical circus, they really care about the aesthetic of their set.* This year, Amy spent four weeks on a complete overhaul of their wagons. ¶*I like to keep my hand in with the steam fairground way of life; my father owns an engine so I lend a hand.* The steam engines are the providers in every way: power, visual appeal, hot water, heat for cooking, and they move the fair from place to place. It is an early start, cleaning and putting the coals in a couple of hours before they are needed for the rides. *You have to be methodical, which has instilled a work ethic in me.* ¶In 2012, Amy began a two-year, part-time Masters in Illustration through Authorial Practice at Falmouth University. *It was designed to foster an approach that stems from personal experience.* Amy focused her narrative on a Victorian travelling fairground with an assortment of factual and fictional characters, and created a book, but the main output was a series of hand painted signs. *It made me realise how much I enjoyed in-depth research, which marked the beginning of my PhD proposal.* ¶Amy is at the midway point of a practice-based PhD supported by QEST to unearth the rich history of fairground people and their art through the identities of five fairground females. There is a National Fairground & Circus Archive in Sheffield, but fairground women are not catalogued: present in photographs, but absent in the records. *World's Fair*, a newspaper for fairgrounds, has been published weekly since 1906. Amy read every issue until 1953 (mostly on microfilm) to trace the stories of her characters. She has combined this analysis with oral history through interviews with descendants. ¶Amy concluded the first phase by consolidating the research to contain their identities. With QEST Scholar Emily Juniper, she printed 150 A1 sheets of newspaper articles, archival photographs and oral history anecdotes compiled on each of the five subjects. These were folded into a hanging system and coloured threads were used to connect moments of coincidence between them and bring to life the depth and complexity of Amy's findings for an exhibition at Dingles Fairground Heritage Centre in Devon. Their lives will be stored in colour-coded, archival boxes. *Sophie's fairground burned down in Plymouth in 1913 and there was evidence to suggest it was the Suffragettes. I discovered that rival fairground owner Martha had lit the fire and tried to use them as cover. Martha's box is yellow, the colour of the Suffragette rose.* ¶One of the others, Lizzie, worked for a fairground and travelling menagerie. She was called away for essential work during World War I; when she returned, it had been sold. *Lizzie is one of the reasons I hesitate between females and women when I am describing the five: she is an elephant. It may sound extraordinary; however, all the same principles and issues apply.* ¶Amy's studio is now set for phase two, telling their stories through authentic, crafted signs. *I have a fantastic list of their sayings to work through, but I think this should probably be the first: 'system is the secret of all good work'.*

Mark Angelo-Gizzi

LEATHERWORKER

Hand cut, hand stitch, hand finish. This has been the steady rhythm in Mark Angelo-Gizzi's Hertfordshire workshop since he traded a thirty-year career as a graphic artist for earning his living as a leatherworker in 2014. ¶ Mark had been working a four-day week for many years, originally for time with his young children, when he discovered an introductory leatherworking course at Capel Manor College in London that fell on his day off. He is pictured at the bench in the saddlery and leatherwork room where he sat every Monday for five months and his fixation with the craft took hold. *I was totally engrossed in the beauty and utility of everything we made.* The next few years were mostly book learning, which became harder and slower as the skills increased in difficulty. ¶ *I overcame this plateau with a* QEST *Scholarship for a three-stage programme of tuition from some of the finest leathercraft teachers in the country.* The first was five days in Suffolk to get an insight into factory practices with Peter Wall, who had worked in leather goods manufacture for his entire career. *This was a useful exercise in specifications and tolerances that I applied on a recent project to design an elegant case from a single piece of leather for Parker Pens to manufacture.* He then took a class in cartridge bag making with Mark Romain at The Saddlery Training Centre in Salisbury. Finally, a creative leatherworking course with MacGregor & Michael in Tetbury, Gloucestershire. *The Leatherworking Handbook* by Valerie Michael was the most thumbed manual in Mark's collection. *It made such a difference to experience in person how she and Neil MacGregor design, plan and make their range of leather goods, and they oversaw me working on my largest project to date: a wooden-framed travel trunk.* ¶ The next thing Mark constructed was a workshop in his garden, now the home of Gizzi Leather. He makes bespoke leather bags and satchels by hand using high-quality vegetable tanned leather from British and Italian tanneries. Following design and material selection, he sketches the components then marks, cuts and shapes for assembly and finishing. Before stitching, he runs the linen thread over a block of beeswax for waterproofing, durability and to give it an attractive gloss. *I work with an awl (very sharp to pierce the leather), cork and needle, keeping to seven stitches per inch, which I think looks best. There is no one stage more important than another, but accurate marking and cutting makes the rest more straightforward.* ¶ He has designed and made a bag for a law professor in Finland who has to carry two awkwardly-shaped legal books. A sales agent in North Carolina requested a bag to fit his sample books and match the rest of his luggage; Mark tracked down co-ordinating leather and together they worked out made-to-measure compartments with a hard-wearing, turned and stitched top edge on the dividing panel. ¶ Mark makes handles to suit each case and sit comfortably in the hand. The dark green music case at the far end of the bench has a rolled leather handle with a solid brass securing bar that ensures that the bag stays closed when carried. Behind that, the pink briefcase has an attaché-style handle made from thirteen pieces of leather. *I carve the leather under a coverpiece, building up the layers by folding, gluing and stitching. It is covered with a cut of finishing leather that is stitched through and shaped while damp. The raw edges visible on one side look beautiful when polished.* ¶ In the foreground is Mark's dark brown journal case that he takes with him everywhere. Made as a prototype, the part-book jacket, part-envelope design holds his notebook of commissions, has a large slip pocket and a place for bank cards. As with every piece of Gizzi Leather, it is moulding perfectly with use, deepening in colour and richness, and, with a little care, will last a lifetime.

QEST Worshipful Company of Leathersellers Scholar 2013

Cameron Short

BLOCK-PRINTER

QEST Scholar 2011 Bonfield Block-Printers is the home of artists Cameron Short and Janet Tristram. Their workshop in west Dorset retains the frontage of the Thorncombe village store that once occupied the premises. Janet, originally from New Zealand, trained in printmaking at the Whanganui School of Art. Cameron had spent two decades in London as an advertising copywriter and art director when they met, but was ready for a change. ¶ *I was captivated by an article in 'World of Interiors' about the pre-eminent block-printer of wallpaper, Marthe Armitage.* When Cameron and Janet moved to Dorset, he bought a press on eBay, carved blocks at the kitchen table in the evenings, and worked as a labourer on building sites during the day. After two years, Cameron sent a speculative email to Marthe via The Art Workers' Guild in Bloomsbury. *To my surprise, I received a reply to say she would be happy to talk to me.* Marthe agreed to mentor Cameron for a year; the award of a QEST Scholarship enabled him to spend a couple of days each month in Marthe's studio. ¶ *I took sketches, designs and carved blocks for Marthe to scrutinise. She would tell me what worked well, what didn't, and what I could do to achieve a better result.* It was a wonderful way to experience and learn the craft, from prosaic considerations such as ink and temperature to creating tonal values in a monochromatic print. Cameron started to make wallpaper on his hand-cranked proofing press. *I have to remove the block and re-ink with every strike. Creating a 10-metre roll of wallpaper requires considerable effort and it proved difficult to sell at a price that reflects the time spent.* ¶ Cameron continues to carve blocks in artist's linoleum, but uses them to print textiles for lampshades, cushions and upholstering one-off pieces of antique furniture, as well as limited edition prints on archival paper. Bonfield's imagery is rooted in Cameron and Janet's love of the countryside and the sea, bygone rural life and the folklore of trees, plants and animals. ¶ The 1930s machinists chair in the photograph is covered in *Lyme Bay* on the seat and back. *This geometric print took over 55,000 individual cuts to create a woven effect on the natural linen.* Resting on the chair is a cushion in *Azook!* (Cornish for 'All together'): reminiscent of an old Isles of Scilly map, it shows the mile-wide starting line of the St Agnes to St Mary's pilot gig race (which Cameron rows every April in a gig made by QEST Scholar Gail McGarva). On the wall is a block print of *Ode to the Ash*: a collection of stories related to the tree in response to the ash dieback crisis. Alongside this, a fox peers out from a bank of foxgloves licking her lips. *This is a reminder of the beauty and brutality of nature, inspired by Tennyson's famous line: nature, red in tooth and claw.* The poacher's coat draped over Cameron's arm is a recent addition. It is beautifully patterned, drafted and sewn by Janet and lined with block-printed, life size, trompe l'oeil pheasant, eel and hare. ¶ Memories of Cameron's upbringing on a farm in the Wessex countryside feature in their work too. *Nightjars* is based on a true story. Cameron and his twin brother (charcoal burner and QEST alumnus Ben Short) used to help their uncle in the fields loading hay bales. Of an evening, Ernie, an old farm hand, used to pass the time by hanging his lamp in a hawthorn tree and watching the moths dance in the light. The Bonfield design features this scene with the nightjars that used to appear in June sweeping in open-mouthed. ¶ Cameron and Janet also create motifs and identities for rural businesses, and their own Bonfield Block-Printers logo, a magpie with a ring in her beak from their *Treasure Tree* block, is about to change. *We are working on a simple monochrome design with 'BBP' in a geometric shape, inspired by the previous owner of the workshop and infamous local character fondly known as 'Black Diamond', Albert Bonfield.*

Alex Pengelly
TEXTILE DESIGNER

Alex Pengelly grew up in Northern Ireland and was taught to knit by her grandmother, a beautiful Aran knitter. *Traditional Irish knitting is quite sculptural and her heirloom pieces have always guided me; the longevity of these handmade garments appeals too.* ¶ On the Fashion Knitwear BA course at Winchester School of Art, form interested Alex more than colour and pattern. She studied Elizabethan Royal Court dress and armour and found beauty in the structure and detailing. Keen to develop these themes and explore how the skill and stitches of hand knitting could be adapted beyond domestic practice, she applied to do a two-year MA in Knitted Textiles at the Royal College of Art, supported by QEST. ¶ Alex became a frequent visitor to The Wallace Collection, home to the most important collection of armour in the UK. *As I sat sketching, I began to consider the suits of armour as protective shells, juxtaposed with the feminine dress and corsetry.* Her drawings evolved into preparatory illustrations for a knitwear collection. ¶ The three-quarter suit of German armour from around 1540 (on the right) was the direct inspiration for the two jumpers in the picture. She took design cues from the alternate bombé (rounded) and slashed bands (slashed dress was in vogue in the early 16th century as a fanciful illusion to the cuts received in battle). The arm detailing and articulation informed the pattern and technical craft, and the wrapping techniques came from the accompanying undergarments. ¶ Alex had won a hand knitting competition in her first year; the prize was for her final collection to be sponsored by Zegna Baruffa, world leader in the production of fine yarns. *I went to the mill in Italy and chose noble yarns such as merino and cashmere.* Combining these natural fibres with technical performance yarns allowed her to introduce functionality such as water resistance and breathability while retaining the luxurious hand feel. The collection was made with a combination of digital and manual knitting machines and hand manipulation. This considerable investment of skill and time in the making was undertaken with the aim of creating future heirlooms which, like the armour, would work with the body. ¶ The grey jumper won the Worshipful Company of Haberdashers Award. It was knitted by hand to shape (a zero-waste method of construction, an important consideration for Alex) using merino wool and a silk and steel yarn on a Dubied industrial machine. The cream jumper was knitted on a 1980s, domestic machine using British merino from John Arbon's mill in Devon and a special laceweight wool that she selected on a trip to meet a hand knitting association in Iceland. *They do not allow their sheep stock to interbreed, so it is a pure line with an unusually long fibre.* The surface embellishment was created by an inlay technique, hand wrapping yarns onto the needles while the jumper is being made. *The front took a week to knit, and that was the less complicated side.* ¶ Alex also won a prize to design beachwear for Monsoon based on modernising traditional Indian crafts. She travelled to Jaipur and Delhi to work with masters of block-printing. Together they developed a technique to create a watercolour effect with the hand cut, wooden blocks and the fabrics were decorated with local beading and braiding. ¶ *Getting to know the craftspeople who produced fabric, fibre and yarn during my Masters was fascinating and improved me as a designer.* Alex was selected to show at Texprint (now TexSelect), which promotes the UK's most talented, newly graduated textile designers to the commercial world. She was spotted by Nike, where she has worked for the last three years as a material designer specialising in *Flyknit* footwear: strong, lightweight strands of yarn knitted into a one-piece upper for support and flexibility – an impressive leap, from ancient armour to crafted running shoes.

QEST Iliffe Family Charitable Trust Scholar 2013

[97]

Shem Mackey

LUTHIER

QEST Scholar 1998
QEST Thomas Fattorini Award for Excellence 2014

I was a late starter, 27 years old when I went to college, but the timing was perfect for my interests in woodwork and music to come together. Shem Mackey grew up in County Kilkenny in Ireland. When he first visited the London College of Furniture, he was only considering the possibility of training as a furniture maker. A friend's brother was studying there and Shem popped into the early fretted instrument workshop to say hello. *That was it, I knew what I wanted to do, but all the places were taken for that year.* ¶John Clark, his mentor in Ireland, introduced him to a Steiner community in Switzerland. Shem worked in the musical instrument workshop and on returning to Ireland, he set up his own business. Two years later, in 1985, he was accepted onto the National Diploma course in Musical Instrument Technology, and specialised in early fretted instruments, particularly the viola da gamba. Shem completed the Higher Diploma in 1989; it was a tough economic climate, which ruled out his intended path of working on repairs and restoration in a violin shop. *I had undertaken a few commissions in my final year at college and the Crafts Council offered maintenance and equipment grants at the time, which were useful in establishing my own workshop to make early violins and viols.* ¶After six years, Shem wanted to add repair and restoration skills to his repertoire and applied for a QEST Scholarship to spend a year in the workshop of Marc Soubeyran in Dalston, London. Soon afterwards, Shem decided to phase out violin making and concentrate solely on the viol, a bowed string instrument that first appeared in Europe in the late 15th century. ¶The viol ceased to be made in England around 1720. Arnold Dolmetsch reignited interest in early music again in the late 19th century, but with many of the methods lost, techniques for viol construction were borrowed from violin making. This approach had carried through to current teaching. *I started to feel dissatisfied; it was impossible to achieve the finish and idiosyncrasies of the original instruments the way I had been taught.* ¶Shem returned to the primary evidence. He examined instruments for makers' marks: some were heavily restored, but a few remain untouched. Shem admired the clever use of tools in finishing and could spot the quick use of a knife or gouge. *I felt as though I was looking over the shoulders of the 17th century makers and came to adore the work of Frenchman Michel Collichon and Henry Smith from London.* ¶While studying an instrument from 1683 in the Musée de la Musique, Shem noticed that the wood was different from the official description and set out to show that three Collichon viols were in fact made of cedrela odorata (commonly known as Spanish cedar); his proof was accepted. There are only eight extant Collichon viols and he made another significant discovery recently. *I was in the laboratory of a major European collection when I spotted a viol with familiar characteristics on the bench next to me and thought it merited a closer inspection.* It turned out to be an original Collichon that had been misattributed to another maker. ¶Commissions for Shem's viols, made in the true early style, come from all around the world. *I am at the bench in my Ramsgate workshop carving a lion head in maple for a tenor viol, the second instrument for this customer.* The design is inspired by the viol in Raphael's *St Cecilia* (known as a patron of music largely because of this painting). With the change of construction method, Shem can provide a fully bespoke service. *It is like measuring someone for a suit.* He is also inspiring and informing a new generation of makers with his interpretation of historic construction as a tutor at West Dean College. ¶Shem loves going to early music concerts at Wigmore Hall and churches around the country. *There is nothing quite like a consort of viols, it is such a beautiful, blended sound.*

Harry Forster-Stringer

GOLDSMITH & ENAMELLER

Nottingham goldsmith Harry Forster-Stringer was born in London and spent his childhood in Pakistan. He has a vivid memory of going to Kathmandu for Christmas when he was seven years old. His father wanted to commission a ring for his mother; Harry went along too. *Sitting on the floor picking out the topaz stone while someone was working away in the corner is seared in my memory. I don't think it would be an exaggeration to say that I wanted to be a jeweller from that moment on.* ¶ At 16, he started an apprenticeship in Birmingham's Jewellery Quarter covering all aspects of goldsmithing from civic and masonic regalia to diamond rings, engraving and small-scale enamelling. Harry remained with the company for another decade before setting up his own workshop in Nottingham in 1994, where he has specialised in fine jewellery ever since. ¶ While teaching at Birmingham's School of Jewellery, Harry watched a demonstration of enamelling by the late Rachel Gogerly, former chairman of the Guild of Enamellers. It rekindled his love of the process and its many effects. He spent six or seven years putting money aside for specialist training, but it was still just beyond his reach. *I heard about QEST through Jack Row, who had been apprenticed to me and returned through QEST to refine his engraving and stone setting skills.* Harry applied and was awarded a QEST Scholarship for a total of three weeks of one-to-one tuition, with an emphasis on the complexities of enamelling at scale. ¶ *The time this gave me with second-generation enameller Phil Barnes saved me years of trial and error and quadrupled the scale at which I could work.* It is a methodical craft. Harry learned to spend longer on the preparation of enamels, including triple the time on grinding the glass with a pestle and mortar before even thinking about the metal. This is extremely labour intensive, especially as a design might require 15 colours (and they do not keep – once the glass is ground it starts to oxidise and change colour), but worth it for the perfect finish. *Phil is a man of few words and a master of understatement. I was over the moon when I got my first 'that's good' for a green enamelled pot I made to hold Bendicks mints, inspired by the colour and design of the foil covering.* ¶ Phil encouraged Harry to be more adventurous with colour and explore advanced techniques. The lid of the Bendicks pot is blended through five shades from green to yellow. Alongside it on the bench are a mustard yellow cigar holder and a 'sleep pot' decorated with stars and planets. *It has a tilting bowl inside for drops of lavender oil.* The geometric background patterns are created by engraving the silver before laying on the enamel with a quill, in the same way the Egyptians would have done. ¶ Enamels cannot be mixed. Colours have to be built up one after another, in and out of the kiln each time. This can be fraught: silver is always trying to return to its original shape and the metal contracts at a different rate to the glass as it cools. *It is so upsetting if a beautiful enamel that has taken an age to create pings off its base. As Phil told me, you need to have your angel on your shoulder. All you can do is be in the right frame of mind and watch it like a hawk in the kiln.* Going back and forth to Phil in Suffolk over several months and practising in between was ideal. *Otherwise, if everything goes well the first time you do something, you do not ask enough questions as you don't know there are any.* ¶ The enamelling skills are already proving valuable as Harry is turning his hand to making larger precious metal objects that incorporate the disciplines he has mastered during his 30-year career. *I now have the skills to complete every element of my commissions in house; the only other mark that gets made on my work is by The Assay Office in Edinburgh to guarantee its metal fineness and provenance.*

QEST Bendicks Scholar 2017

Lai Symes

MILLINER

QEST Scholar 2000 A tape measure around her neck has become Lai Symes' most worn accessory since receiving a QEST Scholarship to retrain from teacher to couture milliner in 2000. Equipped with steel pins and needles, scissors and a thimble, she travelled from Suffolk to London every week for four years to study with Rose Cory MBE. *Her students came from all walks of life: people learning to make for Vivienne Westwood to local pensioners making a hat for church. Rose was so egalitarian and generous with her teaching.* ¶ Lai now lives in the grounds of Eastbourne College in East Sussex where her husband is Second Master. Her workroom is a five-minute stroll from the South Downs National Park, the same in the other direction to the beach where she starts every day walking her border terrier. *Hats are optional for Speech Day here, but I am trying to resurrect the tradition; I think they make a special occasion even more so.* Last year, she made a navy straw, pillbox hat for the new headmaster's wife. *I added a white straw conch shell on the side as a nod to the seaside location.* ¶ Her favourite references are the elegant creations of mid-20th century designers: Madame Agnès who had a store on rue Saint-Honoré in Paris; Lilly Daché in New York, best known for her draped turbans; and couturier Cristóbal Balenciaga, who unusually had two dedicated millinery rooms at his Paris atelier where he worked with Wladzio d'Attainville and Ramón Esparza. *Their hats were daring and original, but also practical and wearable.* ¶ Lai's main work is with bespoke customers, often by referral from dress designers. *I love these collaborations, seeing the exquisite detail of how an outfit is made and designing a hat to complete the look and complement the style of the wearer.* This usually takes three meetings and making over several weeks. *One of my most enjoyable projects was with Chrissi Bradbury of CiBi Couture for two of her clients, a bride and bridesmaid both in their seventies.* For the bride, Lai made a 1920s-style, eau de nil, silk-covered cocktail hat with vintage silk veiling, all hand dyed to get an exact colour match. She picked up the motif of the dress with hand shaped petals and a spray of beadwork on one side. ¶ Lai has also created a series of couture ladies winter hats for Farlows, suppliers of fishing tackle, shooting and country clothing. This sprang from a conversation with her father-in-law, a farmer and keen fisherman, about his collection of hand-tied fishing flies. Lured by their beauty and evocative names, she rummaged through the antiquarian and secondhand titles at Camilla's Bookshop in Eastbourne in search of illustrated descriptions of their making. ¶ There are five hats in the *Fishing Fly* collection, including *Grouse & Claret* and *Green Highlander*. The bases are all unstiffened velour felt made from rabbit fur and each one is trimmed with a selection of feathers inspired by the dressing of the fly: pheasant from her father-in-law's farm, dyed goose and turkey biots, peacock feathers and fronds, and sustainably farmed ostrich quills. *With summer in Scotland in mind, I stitched a few midges onto the brim edge of 'Pale Evening Dun'.* ¶ Printed silks are another passion; even a tiny piece of fabric can spark an idea and become a beautiful hat. *The one I am wearing began as a sample of kimono silk, a gift from my sister when she was living in Japan.* This delicate material also influenced the design of the asymmetric hat on the mannequin and the pared down aesthetic of the surrounding collection. ¶ Having established a business making classic headpieces to be worn at English country weddings to cowboy hats for Spanish ranches (Lai delivered a pair to artists Sam Orlando Miller and Helen Underwood Miller to wear while working horses on their farm in Matarraña), Lai will be forever indebted to her teacher. *Rose is my mentor, a great friend, and middle name of one of my daughters.*

James Adair

SADDLER

QEST Worshipful Company of Saddlers Scholar 2014

I started working in leather a very long time ago, aged 13, repairing collars and leads for the 70 or so greyhounds at a family friend's kennels. Throughout his teens, James Adair pestered anyone he knew who could teach him the rudiments of saddlery. He picked up a few skills here and there, but, with no imminent prospect of an apprenticeship, he joined the Northern Ireland Civil Service. ¶ James was living in Cloughey, on the Ards Peninsula, when another family friend, Joe Garvey, returned to the area after 20 years in the Household Cavalry. *He had been a saddler in the Blues and Royals; I couldn't have found a better mentor.* James spent 12 years as a civil servant by day and saddler in his spare time, at first with Joe, then in nearby Newtownards with Brian McCully, who suggested he should work towards formal qualifications. ¶ During time off, James made his way over to The Saddlery Training Centre in Salisbury to study with Mark Romain. *Self-funding was a challenge, but Brian encouraged me to push through; we continued working together until he died a few years ago.* In 2007, he returned to learn how to refurbish a side saddle with Richard Godden, the only remaining tutor, and again three years later for an advanced bridle-making course with Master Saddler Frances Roche. ¶ James felt that the workmanship displayed in side saddles was in the upper echelons of the trade. Emulating this became the focus in his workshop, where he now worked full time. With seven years of restoration experience, he applied to QEST to support further training with Richard, by then semi-retired, in the manufacture of side saddles. ¶ Within two years James won three awards in the Society of Master Saddlers National Saddlery Competition – first place and Premium Award in the Side Saddle class and the Side Saddle Association Trophy – and has been awarded major prizes in the Royal Dublin Society Craft Competition over four consecutive years. He also uses his skills to make bespoke bridles and a range of leather accessories. *This is more lucrative, but when a saddle comes in, that's me gone – I'm engrossed.* ¶ James moved his workshop to Newry five years ago as there were no other saddlers in the area (the last closed in 1962) and, being close to the border, it is within reach of customers from across the island. Safety is always his priority. *The horse comes first so I am certain they are comfortable under saddle, then rider, as they are able to tell me their requirements.* Clients have included Lady Jane Alexander Gillespie, an equine therapist and accomplished exponent of side saddle riding, and her friend Lucinda Blakiston-Houston, who had lost her lower leg, but wanted to continue riding. *Lucinda is a wonder. I levelled the seat of her husband's grandmother's side saddle and she was out on it straight away.* ¶ On the bench is a side saddle in progress for a client in Kentucky (word of mouth travels far in the equestrian community). This is his third from scratch using traditional materials: wool serge, linen and pig skin stitched with Irish linen threads and a hemp thread that James makes himself. Restorations are more usual; he has eight in the workshop and another three on the way. ¶ *I have met a lot of wonderful craftspeople through QEST, including alumnus Bob Johnston, who lives in Bangor and works in willow.* James had a client with a disabled child who thought a side saddle may be of use for their son to enjoy an hour of freedom during a riding lesson. James assessed his needs and suggested a basket saddle, then explained the situation to Bob and described what would be required. Bob made a bespoke, woven basket seat to the shape of the horse and James completed the saddle so that it would be comfortable and safe for rider and horse. *The client and her son were so pleased, and to see the smile on the boy's face was praise enough for this collaboration.*

Adam Nash
THATCHER

Paul Fallows
APPRENTICE THATCHER

Adam Nash
QEST Scholar 2005

Paul Fallows
QEST Pilgrim Trust
Apprentice 2017

British Army training – physically demanding and being exposed to the elements whatever the weather – was good preparation for life as a thatcher for former major, Adam Nash. He served 17 years as a Light Infantry officer, including tours of duty in Northern Ireland, Cyprus, Belize, Jordan and Iraq, before his penultimate posting at the Defence Academy of the United Kingdom in Shrivenham, near Swindon. On his drive to work, he spotted a row of almshouses being re-thatched and followed the progress with growing interest. ¶ With the end of his military career in sight, Adam was contemplating jobs that would keep him active and outdoors. He decided to try thatching on a few days' leave. *I was fit and strong, but the muscles in my hands, forearms and shoulders had quite a shock.* It is a hard craft: up and down ladders, preparing straw, and twisting spars (lengths of hazel that secure the straw or reed). Lots of heavy lifting too – during a full re-thatch up to six tonnes of straw are carried up to the roof. The tools have changed little over the centuries and there is no machinery, so keeping alive one of the UK's oldest rural traditions requires strength and determination. ¶ Adam negotiated a two-and-a-half-year contract with a master thatcher in Wiltshire who agreed to teach him how to thatch and establish and run a business on the condition that he did not work on his patch afterwards. *It was for no pay, but at 38 this was the quickest and best way to get up and running in the trade.* Adam mapped out training and business plans and took them to QEST, who agreed to provide financial support through this transition. ¶ He adapted quickly and found it to be a rewarding endeavour, especially stepping back at the end of a job and seeing the completed thatch ready to protect a home (warm, humid conditions in the West Country mean the main body of a roof needs replacing every 20 years, the ridge every decade). Adam qualified, moved to Salisbury where there is a high proportion of thatch to keep him occupied, and is now an accredited member of The National Society of Master Thatchers with more than 100 roofs to his name. ¶ Adam's diary is booked with jobs up to a year ahead. He orders the straw a roof at a time, as each one fills his barn. Most of the buildings he works on are listed, so by law he must replace the thatch like for like. *I also think this is important to maintain the integrity of the building.* Combed wheat reed is the most common – combed and stripped by the farmer to get rid of the grain and leaves, then clipped by the thatcher. ¶ He is pictured with Paul Fallows, a former personal fitness trainer on a QEST Pilgrim Trust Apprenticeship with Adam. They are replacing the front section of a roof that has deteriorated due to damp created by overhanging trees (the steep angle and sunshine on the back of the house will keep that going for a few years yet). They are working with water reed, the most durable material, usually grown in marshy estuaries. *This was a useful project for Paul as he had not worked with water reed before. It is laid and dressed in place and getting 150 bundles onto the roof every day was definitely a two-person job.* ¶ Generally, it is a six-stage process: replacing the eaves course; dressing and strapping the old coatwork and laying the new thatch in 'stalches' (columns of straw); feature work (around windows, for example); creating a ridge by laying 'skirt and reverse', a layer of thatch that acts as a central fixing and for further protection; cutting the eaves with shears; and finally, dressing the roof again with a leggett (the tool Adam is holding). This is where the thatcher uses his skill to create a uniform surface and curves to reduce the effect of weathering. Then, as with any housework, out comes a stiff broom for a final sweep.

Alastair Barford

ARTIST

Baroque artist Gian Lorenzo Bernini said that three things are needed for success in painting and sculpture: to see beauty when young and accustom oneself to it, to work hard, and to obtain good advice. Alastair Barford was given these opportunities by a QEST Scholarship to study portrait drawing and painting at Charles H. Cecil Studios, which occupies the most historic Florentine atelier in active use. ¶ *Shortly after my mother died I produced a portrait of her from a photograph. I was disappointed by the image as it conveyed nothing of our relationship.* This was Alastair's primary motivation for learning to paint from life, so he would have this ability if he attempted again to paint someone he loved. During the three-year course, Alastair was trained exclusively in the sight-size technique, which has its origins in the practice of Titian, Van Dyck and Velázquez, and was used extensively by John Singer Sargent. It is a visual approach by which the artist compares subject and representation directly, making proportional, tonal and aesthetic judgements by eye. Charles Cecil follows each student's progress closely from cast and figure drawings to advanced portraiture in oils. ¶ Alastair also learned to grind his own paints and prepare a medium based on that used by Rubens: Canada balsam, sun-thickened linseed oil and turpentine. He continues to work with the traditional palette of ivory black, yellow ochre, vermillion and lead white on oil-primed canvas using hog and sable brushes. *I discovered an interest in sculpture too and was fortunate to study with experienced practitioners in clay, bronze and marble; I loved the sustained endeavour of carving in stone.* His spare time was spent sketching. *The galleries in Florence house some of the world's finest collections of Renaissance art, there are fantastic paintings in every church, a fresco on every street corner, and sculpture in every piazza.* ¶ Alastair's work came to the attention of the nation in 2015 when he was asked by *Illustrated London News* to paint a portrait of Her Majesty The Queen for a book, *The Record Reign.* This was Alastair's first portrait commission. R.H. Ives Gammell, Charles Cecil's tutor, had a dictum: make a masterpiece in nature and paint it. This is how Alastair was accustomed to working: setting the pose and designing an image over perhaps 40 hours with the subject in the studio. The final portrait is an assimilation of the expressions, gestures and postural changes during these sittings. He had ten minutes to observe Her Majesty at the Order of the Garter service at Windsor Castle, during which he gathered as much information as he could for the composition. *The challenge was to convey character and depth based on these fleeting glances and photographs.* ¶ One of the first official portraits of The Queen after the Coronation was by the Florentine artist Annigoni. By painting at a similar three-quarter view, again in Garter Robes, Alastair hoped to suggest that, despite social and economic changes over more than 60 years, the monarchy endures. *Looking off to the distance, Her Majesty could be surveying the decades passed, but I prefer to interpret this as looking to the years ahead.* It was a celebratory image, so Alastair used more colour than he would typically. He also made a sketch in charcoal (on the easel in the picture) as a companion to a portrait of Queen Victoria by Amédée Forestier. ¶ Alastair was photographed at Sarum Studio (with Smudge, the aptly named studio spaniel) in the tranquil environs of Salisbury Cathedral Close. This independent school of fine art was established by Nicholas Beer, a former instructor at Charles H. Cecil Studios, in a similar atelier tradition. *It is an intimate, inspiring environment in which to work on my portrait and figure projects and assist Nicholas in supervising students and continuing the tradition of working from life under natural light.*

Jennie Adamson

BESPOKE TAILOR

QEST Johnnie Walker
Scholar 2016

Jennie Adamson was taught to use a sewing machine by her mother. She began making clothes and considered studying fashion design, but was more curious about pattern cutting and fine hand sewing. *I read in a local Manchester newspaper about a couturier lamenting the lack of traditional training today. I got in touch for advice and she suggested Savile Row.* ¶ Jennie researched each of the tailoring houses and a week later was on a train to London for an interview with the Savile Row Academy at Maurice Sedwell; within a month, she made the move. After three years learning the basics of cutting and making bespoke garments, Jennie reached the final of the Golden Shears Award for young tailors with the first outfit she had created from start to finish. ¶ An in-house position arose in the workshop at Gieves & Hawkes, No. 1 Savile Row. *My coat-making skills evolved tremendously sitting alongside such experienced tailors.* She also worked with the head cutter on special projects: a driving jacket for Bentley Motors, alpine jacket for London Craft Week, and tailcoats for an Olympic showjumping champion. *These encouraged me to think more creatively and made me realise I wanted to be hands-on with the entire process of cutting, fitting and making.* ¶ Jennie established a studio at Cockpit Arts, a mile or so away in Holborn, to bridge the worlds of bespoke tailoring, design and couture. Luxury fashion houses often look to Savile Row for the quality of handwork and garment construction; this canvassing of jacket foreparts, sewing buttonholes, attaching sleeves and felling linings entirely by hand was second nature by now. Jennie's next step was to apply for a place on the Innovative Pattern Cutting for Graduates and Professionals course at Central Saint Martins. QEST backed her ambition by covering the fees. *We had eight tutors teaching a variety of skills from creative draping on a stand to technical pattern making for production.* Her final piece was the recreation of a floor-length skirt and structured jacket by John Galliano for Christian Dior couture from 1997. *I created a crinoline structure and used corsetry boning to support the peplum hem that extended from the jacket. It was incredibly complex, but the chance to experiment was equally freeing.* ¶ On a trip to Paris to see a Dior exhibition, Jennie visited a cloth merchant in the hope of finding something unusual. Their books were almost all English cloths that she knew, but they also had a selection of vintage remnants. She found a 1.8-metre length of wool crepe with faint Prince of Wales check from which she made the half-lined, double-breasted jacket she is wearing. *It was just enough; I had to be so precise with my cutting as I only had a fraction of an inch to spare.* ¶ Jennie now takes on her own bespoke customers. The designs develop through conversations about the functionality and style of the garment and she creates each piece using traditional Savile Row techniques, enhanced by her training in couture pattern cutting. ¶ On her right is a man's suit jacket she made in silk with raised seams and double front darts, a military-inspired detail, top-stitched by hand. To her left is a single-breasted jacket in a wool bouclé cloth. *I love the texture, and it was interesting working with so much movement.* Jennie recently sourced a beautiful tweed, green with a burnt orange and red windowpane check, from the Islay Woollen Mill to make a jacket for a customer with a close connection to the island through its whisky. *He always has a book on the go, so we added a pocket to fit a paperback.* ¶ Much of the handwork lies beneath the surface; the joy for a bespoke customer is that they get to see the hidden layers of stitching as the garment advances through the fittings. The progress of Jennie Adamson's bespoke tailoring is visible behind the scenes too, by the lengthening row of paper patterns hanging in her studio.

Anneliese Appleby

PRINTMAKER

QEST Scholar 2012

Working with a mouse, keyboard and screen in a graphic design studio was too clinical for Anneliese Appleby. *I wanted to get my hands messy.* She went back to the classroom, qualified as a teacher and became the fine art printmaking tutor at Malvern College. *I devoured every book I could find on the subject, attended workshops, and studied for an MA in Multi-Disciplinary Printmaking so I could provide my pupils with the best education.* ¶ After a decade in post, Anneliese decided it was time to make her own mark. She approached Martin Clark, proprietor of Tilley Printing, established in the Herefordshire market town of Ledbury in 1875. He agreed to teach her the principles of traditional letterpress printing and QEST granted Anneliese a Scholarship to cover the cost. *Manually setting and inking metal and wooden type was absolutely my kind of graphic design.* ¶ If Martin needed an illustration for a print, Anneliese willingly did the line drawings and cut them into artist's linoleum. *I loved the process of making these blocks and the character of the image they produced.* A couple of years into her training, they became the spark for a business idea: designing and printing wallpaper by hand. ¶ She created a Twitter account to follow people who might know about presses on the market; one alerted her to an offset lithographic printing press built in Japan around 1950 that was listed on eBay. *The seller kindly drove it from Melton Mowbray to Ross-on-Wye, unloaded it into my home studio, and handed me a box of bits and pieces that had puzzled him when he assembled it for delivery.* It turns out he had dismantled it at some point and taken photographs at every stage, but lost them. Her neighbour, a retired engineer, spent weeks rebuilding it and made adaptations so paper could be fed more easily between the beds of the press. ¶ Anneliese ventures into the countryside to make botanical drawings in the open air, which she brings back to refine and develop into full-scale, repeating patterns that run from one drop of wallpaper to the next. These are transferred into the linoleum by carving, often over several weeks. She has seven designs cut for printing in bespoke inks, mixed to complement each customer's colour scheme. ¶ *Oak & Acorns*, on the press in crimson, was the first to go on a wall other than her own and remains the most popular. Rolled in the glass jar is a length of *Strawberry Fields*, which she created one June from the plants in her garden. The flower and fruit are naturally present at the same time, so the design is a motif of a five-petalled blossom, the berries and leaves. *My strawberries were too small though, so I bought some to sketch; it took about a dozen punnets as they kept ending up in summer puddings and glasses of Pimm's!* ¶ During the winter when the woods, meadows and hedgerows lie dormant under the cover of winter, Anneliese looks to museums for references. *I had an inspirational morning in the Prints & Drawings Study Room at the Victoria and Albert Museum viewing boxes of pre-1900 wallpaper fragments.* From this research, she is working on a pastoral scene based on an early 17th century image of a farmer and his horse. *It is just a snippet, so I am extending the design to make a full sheet. I am also playing with drawings from the V&A Museum of Childhood for a whimsical nursery wallpaper.* ¶ Anneliese has been exploring other ways to make the most of her designs. *Oak & Acorn* in mossy green and *Strawberry Fields* in soft pink have become crisp, cotton tea towels, and pegged across the doorway is a range of prints to be framed. *I appreciate the faithfulness of reproduction using lino blocks, but have also enjoyed the element of serendipity in making these limited editions with multiple layers of colour and pattern.* ¶ Whatever she prints, the physical investment that Anneliese missed so much in the early days is palpable wall to wall.

Daniel Harrison

FURNITURE MAKER

QEST Howdens
Scholar 2016

I remember the excitement of entering a workshop for the first time: the aromas of freshly machined timber, curled wood shavings drifting across the floor, tools ordered neatly on the benches and walls – I had found my place. This was Daniel Harrison's discovery on starting a joinery apprenticeship in staircase making. ¶ He has a deep respect for the raw material too. *There is something spiritual about the nature of trees: majestic giants in harmony with their surroundings, supporting life, and providing wood that we have used creatively since the dawn of humankind.* Daniel's training connected him to this tradition; the gift of a copy of *Makepeace: A Spirit of Adventure in Craft & Design* from the vicar at his local church in Swansea made him realise he could use these skills to voice his own ideas. ¶ He took a furniture design and making course at the City of Oxford College's Rycotewood Furniture Centre and joined the Oxfordshire workshop of Philip Koomen Furniture to improve his hand and production skills. QEST supported this journeyman stage of Daniel's career, funding 100 hours of supervised making with Philip, a master craftsman and chair specialist. ¶ Daniel also learned about sustainable forestry practices and has embraced Philip's ethos of making furniture with a regional identity. *I am standing in front of his wood store, all sourced within a thirty-mile radius, taken to a nearby sawmill, then brought here for drying.* The local woodlands haven't been cultivated for commercial production, but the knots, cracks and irregular grains of their timbers can be worked to create unique character in bespoke pieces. ¶ All of Daniel's projects begin as sketches then technical drawings before progressing to scale models. He keeps these around him to glance at and consider for a while, then turns them into full-size prototypes to assess form and proportions. ¶ The stool on the table is from a Rycotewood brief to redesign an Ercol classic. Next along is his *Serpentine Bench*, inspired by William Wordsworth's poem *Yew-Trees*. *I have always admired this ancient tree and his description of each trunk as intertwisted fibres serpentine and up-coiling resonated with me.* Daniel cycled to the churchyard of St Mary's Iffley to sketch and photograph the yews and sat among the furniture in the Ashmolean Museum in Oxford to visualise this design. ¶ The shoal of minnow letter openers on the tray originated from the scrap bin. *A random shape caught my attention when I was emptying it one day. I refined the outline and now sculpt these on a band saw from off-cuts of walnut, yew, olive ash, sycamore and oak.* The burr walnut surface pattern of the tray is created by four-way book-matching the veneer, turning the leaves like pages so the grain is continuous and symmetrical. ¶ For production pieces, Daniel invests time in devising templates and jigs for ease and accuracy of repetition. *The hexagonal box I am holding is from the second batch of this design; I have streamlined elements of its making and made subtle improvements to the wooden petals that divide the compartments.* ¶ After three years at Philip's workshop, Daniel is moving on with a body of commissioned and speculative work in a range of techniques. The centrepiece of his next show at the *Celebration of Craftsmanship & Design* in Cheltenham will be *On The Points*, a curiosity cabinet inspired by a 1928 pen and watercolour drawing by abstract artist Vasily Kandinsky. It was highly commended at a Young Furniture Makers Exhibition at Furniture Makers' Hall and Daniel has filled the shelves with objects to inspire future projects. ¶ *There is magic in opening a log, revealing grain often hidden for centuries, and transforming it into a new form for another generation. I hope the furniture I make, with a guarantee of workmanship instilled by my QEST sponsor Howdens Joinery, will bring joy and do justice to the tree from which it came.*

Oluwaseyi Sosanya

CRAFT ENGINEER

The early years of Oluwaseyi Sosanya's career in craft were in traditional making: QEST Scholar 2013
carpentry for timber-framed housing in Oregon in the United States followed
by an apprenticeship with Ken Tomita, a Japanese furniture maker in the city of
Portland. Oluwaseyi is a mechanical engineer by training with a broad interest in
physical manufacturing. While learning the hand skills for working in wood, he
considered that developments for small batch furniture production were largely
tool based. *I knew we could make 10 pieces, almost identical yet with the individual
beauty of fine craft details, but what could 50,000 look like? I wanted to find out if there
were any possibilities to incorporate the presence of the human hand at scale.* ¶ From a
two-man band, he went to work for a year at a computer manufacturer employing
thousands of people at a factory in Taiwan. *It was a picture of efficiency and I was
certain that there were elements of making these everyday items that could pollinate
traditional craftsmanship to enable scale.* Aside from the duality of what could be
carried out by hand or machine, Oluwaseyi felt that improvements could be made
prior to manufacturing: a designer might come up with a great proposal and force
it through production, but this could be better made by collaborating with the
makers who understand every nuance of their material. ¶ Oluwaseyi's next move
was to London. *The UK has a strong foothold in the space where craft and industry
overlap and it is an exciting place to create solutions that benefit both.* The Masters
course in Innovation Design Engineering run jointly by the Royal College of Art
and Imperial College London provided the perfect platform. QEST provided the
funding for Oluwaseyi's final year. Rather than continue in wood, he decided to
take on a fresh challenge and work in a soft material. *I wanted to create a process to
weave in three dimensions that had the qualities of hand weaving, but pushed further
through the hand that built the machine and the creative brain that programmed it.*
The *3D Weaver* is an entirely new loom with technology and software that can
be manipulated to drive almost any conceivable mixed-media creation. Structures explored so far – including a strong, compressive Honeycomb weave and a
light, flexible ZigZag – have many potential applications in medical, architectural,
vehicle, aerospace and sportswear industries. ¶ Inspired by the increasing sophis-
tication of virtual reality technology, Oluwaseyi is the co-founder of a group of
entrepreneurial Innovation Design Engineering alumni looking at the future of
digital craft supported by Innovation RCA and the James Dyson Foundation
among others. *Craftspeople have always been innovators, yet the title is often used to
represent a nostalgic view of making rather than capturing this spirit that remains in
us all today.* Their first groundbreaking invention is a tool that brings human touch
to digital creation. *Gravity Sketch* is composed of a pen and pad for sketching in
real space through augmented reality glasses; each stroke instantaneously creates
3D geometry as easily as drawing on a piece of paper. These designs can then be
3D-printed to create real objects. *This is a democratic tool: it can be used by beginner
to professional designers and the extremely talented craftspeople I have met through the
Royal College of Art and QEST to unlock an idea in an intuitive way, while the software takes care of all the rigid, mathematical requirements.* ¶ They have been trading
for a year and have two major automotive clients, both intent on retaining craft in
their highly-engineered environments. Bruce Beazley, a pioneering fine art sculptor, is another early adopter, and they have co-organised 3D creation nights at the
V&A and Tate Britain. *It is my hope and belief that Gravity Sketch will become as
commonplace as drawing on a napkin or the back of an envelope.*

'*We started here in Bristol*
with two looms
and lots of creative ambition.
Our QEST Scholarships
were instrumental
in providing the knowledge
and network with which
we have set up our
own weaving mill
and created our
international business
in textile design.'

Juliet Bailey & Franki Brewer   Libby Kates

WOVEN TEXTILE DESIGNERS & MAKERS   TEXTILE DESIGNER

In 2009, Juliet Bailey (centre) and Franki Brewer (right) combined their hand weaving and industrial experience to form Dash + Miller, a studio specialising in the design, development and production of woven fabrics for fashion and interiors. *Our name comes from a contraction of haberdashery and the craft of the weaving mill.* ¶ Their shelves are stacked with traditional and experimental yarns that they draw on for their designs, every one of which is created on a handloom. *There is no substitute for the understanding and ideas that come from handling materials and placing the yarns manually.* Mastery of their equipment, from salvaged textile machinery to a digital Jacquard loom, is important to achieve the complexity and originality they strive for. Each weave structure, yarn and colour combination is accompanied by technical information for mills to enable larger-scale production. *This portfolio is seasonal to some extent, but it bubbles away more like a sourdough starter: we feed and edit to keep it vital.* ¶ *Our QEST Scholarships gave us the time and money to research all aspects of UK textile manufacture.* They visited 19 specialist facilities, spinning, dyeing and weaving their way around the West Country and Wales and up to the Scottish Highlands. They were introduced to fleece grading at Fernhill, an eco-farm in the Mendip Hills, and their eyes were opened to the breadth of finishing processes at W.T. Johnson & Sons in Huddersfield. *We had worked with Stephen Walters & Sons, the oldest surviving silk weavers in Britain, for six years; learning more about their machinery at the factory revitalised our creativity.* Having looked at all the processes individually, Johnstons of Elgin was the perfect final stop. *It was a vertical mill with everything under one historic roof; we were so enamoured, we went back with our entire team.* ¶ Before the trips, it had not occurred to Juliet and Franki that they could make their own cloth. *There was a moment at Herbert Parkinson, a mill owned by the John Lewis Partnership, when we caught sight of a woman operating a massive warping machine, and we thought, just maybe...* In 2015, with investment from the West of England Growth Fund, they took delivery of a Dobby power loom to start their own small-scale production as the Bristol Weaving Mill. They use wool from Fernhill Farm for *The Bristol Cloth*, the result of a competition run by the Bristol Textile Quarter and Botanical Inks and won by Falmouth University weave teacher Wendy Kotenko. Her design is based on the region's basket weaving heritage and the yarn is dyed naturally with onion skins discarded by the city's restaurants. ¶ The linen and lambswool blanket in the picture is prototyped and produced by the Bristol Weaving Mill for Heal's. It is resting on Franki's original handloom on which they founded their company; the one behind Juliet is their eighth, and another production loom is due soon. Standing with them is Libby Kates, who joined Dash + Miller as a QEST Apprentice and is now head of design. Together both businesses have grown to employ eight people, with a ninth about to join the Bristol Weaving Mill on the Worshipful Company of Weavers entry to work scheme. ¶ Juliet and Franki thrive on variety, from the closed-loop, sustainable production of woven goods for small-holding farmers, using their own alpaca fleece, to working with *WGSN*, the trend authority for fashion, to develop samples for its reports ahead of each retail season. Having established a market in Europe, they now visit New York six times a year and have an agent in China. ¶ Back in Bristol, things are no less international. There are projects on the go for global brands and the wonderful example of the Manx Loaghtan sheep: yarn from the fleece of this native Isle of Man flock arrives in the studio and leaves as blankets, throws and scarves destined for high-end stores in Japan.

Juliet Bailey &
Franki Brewer
QEST Scholars 2013
QEST Thomas
Fattorini Award for
Excellence 2016

Libby Kates
QEST Worshipful
Company of Drapers
Apprentice 2015

Ruth Anthony

HAND ENGRAVER

QEST Scholar 2008 Hand engraver Ruth Anthony began her training at Cape Technikon in South Africa. After graduating with a Diploma in Jewellery, she moved to the UK and started work at the bench, making and repairing jewellery for a goldsmith in Oxfordshire. She continued part-time studies, during which she discovered engraving. ¶ Ruth contacted R.H. Wilkins in London, the engraver of choice for some of the world's most iconic sporting trophies including Wimbledon and the Ryder Cup, who offered her work experience; she stayed on to complete a full apprenticeship designing and engraving cyphers, monograms and heraldry. ¶ In 2007, Ruth set up a studio in London's jewellery quarter, Hatton Garden, and built a customer base in the trade for her work in silver, gold, platinum, brass and pewter. Looking for a new challenge, she applied to QEST to spend a day a week learning from the gun engravers at Holland & Holland and James Purdey & Sons. *I learned to design and engrave complex scrollwork; given its hardness, you can get far more detail into steel.* ¶ The practice plates from both sets of training are in the picture: jewellery engraving in copper, steel from her time at Holland & Holland and Purdey. *Having experience in both has improved my technique all round and I approach commissions with a lot more flexibility.* Following her QEST Scholarship, Ruth was invited to work for acclaimed designer engraver Malcolm Appleby MBE, who discovered gun engraving at art school and has spent decades applying his decorative skills to jewellery and metal forms. ¶ Her current studio is near Elephant & Castle in London. *My world is usually reduced to what I can see on the bench through my Optivisor magnifier.* Engraving tools are slotted into a turntable in the corner for ease of access. Ruth likes the variety in scale and type of jobs from lettering to large decorative panels and the challenge of constantly adapting to somebody else's aesthetic. ¶ She receives work from several clock restorers, including Laurence Harvey and Howard Walwyn Fine Antique Clocks. While they focus on getting the mechanisms back in order, Ruth is sent the pieces they have had to re-make or original parts that need re-engraving. *The front plates of 17th and 18th century London clockmakers Benj Gray & Just Vulliamy, Daniel Quare and Daniel Delander have all passed across my bench. The style often harks back to the scroll designs I learned from the gun engravers.* Ruth has also engraved back plates and dials for contemporary watchmakers Craig and Rebecca Struthers. ¶ Another specialism is seal engraving, which requires deep carving into the metal, like a relief sculpture, in reverse. Progress is checked constantly by making an impression in wax. This technique is used for signet rings and Ruth engraves seals for jeweller and designer Jessica De Lotz among others. *I made a pair of silver desk seals with the initials of a customer's daughters. Commissions like this elicit nostalgia for a time when they would have been in daily use on handwritten letters.* ¶ Ruth's goldsmith training gives her a useful level of understanding on jewellery commissions. *I was asked to engrave a set of hammered silver bangles for a gift. Under magnification the surface looked like a landscape of hills and valleys, which required constant adjustment to create an even cut.* In 2017, Ruth engraved the numbers on a limited edition of 65 vitreous enamelled pendants by Fiona Rae to mark HM The Queen's Sapphire Jubilee and raise funds for QEST. She also works closely with jewellers such as Laura Lee, Becca and Dominic Walmsley to interpret their concepts and designs into carved and engraved finished pieces. ¶ Ruth is a member of the Hand Engravers Association and committed to her craft. *Hand engraving gives life and character to cherished objects. I love to think of my work making a lasting contribution to people's celebrations and memories.*

Jamie Coreth

PAINTER

The Archaeology and Anthropology course at the University of Oxford offers a broad perspective on human societies and the richness and diversity of cultural experience. Jamie Coreth focused his degree studies on the origins of art through cave paintings and the rock art of South African bushmen. *It turned out to be a formative decision.* ¶ Jamie had grown up in an artistic environment. He used to mix plaster for his father, sculptor Mark Coreth, and was always drawing, but he had not considered a creative career. His introduction to painting came by virtue of a neighbour, Susan Crawford, one of the world's leading equestrian artists. *I also took a summer course in Florence, which made me realise how much time I would need to invest to improve my skills as a painter.* ¶ QEST funded Jamie's training at the London Atelier of Representational Art, established in 2008 in response to the scarcity of rigorous, representational art education in the UK. The course was entirely in drawing and painting from life. *The postmodernism of the late 20th century, for all its merits, broke this tradition for a couple of generations. The classes taught me the craft of seeing in a different way and how to dissect this visual information to be able to paint what I saw.* ¶ In 2013, Jamie returned to Florence where he studied at Charles H. Cecil Studios and the Florence Academy of Art. Alongside his own studies, he worked as a lecturer in art history and assistant tutor. Jamie was awarded the prize for best painting in his final year. Intensive training from three art schools has provided him with an extensive set of representational skills. *Florence was a bubble of grand traditions; London developed my painting in a broad context.* This was his stepping off point as a professional artist. ¶ Jamie was photographed in the natural light under which he paints. *My concentration is best in the morning.* He works in historically-proven colours – white, yellow ochre, red and black – which are always placed in the same order on his palette (designed by Nicholas Beer at Sarum Studios). *The flash of blue at the top is cobalt teal, which I use for adding reflected light to reduce the darkness of shadows.* ¶ The first meeting with a subject is usually spent trying different poses. *I start thinking about who they are and what we want to convey, but the true personality comes through as we get used to each other over a course of sittings.* Jamie covers the canvas as quickly as he can then evolves the painting as a whole. *I try to remain open to painting in fleeting effects and will often repaint the head until the impression is a balance of breadth and accuracy.* In the background is Jamie's portrait of a United States federal judge. *I am trying to show her empathy without being too symbolic. She is wearing white, but there is not a single brushstroke of harsh white paint in her clothing: instead many soft colours achieve the effect.* ¶ In 2018, Jamie had a painting selected for the BP Portrait Award at the National Portrait Gallery. *Mark Jackson: Broken Bodies* is a portrait of his friend Jacko, a sculptor who was in the Parachute Regiment before he shattered his pelvis in an accident. Jamie painted him sitting in his studio in Wiltshire. *I noticed that one of Jacko's sculptures had a fracture across the hips and thought this would make an apposite composition.* In the shadows lurks an indication of a sculpture of Cain and Abel, a work that Jacko wants to make for its allusions to the origins of conflict. ¶ This was his second success in the competition. A couple of years ago Jamie and his father made portraits of one another at the same time. The painting, *Dad Sculpting Me,* was one of 53 portraits chosen for the 2016 exhibition and Jamie was announced as the winner of the BP Young Artist Award. *I am extremely grateful to my father for forming me as an artist: figuratively and paternally.*

QEST Garfield Weston Foundation Scholar 2012

Kayo Saito

GOLDSMITH

QEST Scholar 2016

Jewellery is an art form that we can all relate to physically and psychologically. Once the pieces I have made are worn, their essence passes to the wearer and becomes part of their identity and feelings. Goldsmith Kayo Saito began her training in craft design and metalwork at Musashino Art University, one of the leading creative institutes in Japan. During her BA in Silversmithing, Jewellery & Allied Crafts at London Guildhall University she experimented with paper as her principal medium to push the limits of light, delicate jewellery. ¶ She developed this aspect of her craft further during a Masters at the Royal College of Art in 1999. *I was seeking a meeting point between fragility and realistic wearability, which I reached by using plastic with a paper-like quality, coated with fibres of handmade paper.* In 2007, Kayo was chosen for the *Rising Stars* exhibition at Goldsmiths' Hall. This provided an opportunity to expand her practice into working with metals. She created a series of gold and silver brooches, a direction which led to her work being acquired by private and institutional collections. ¶ Her inspiration throughout has been the natural world, particularly plants and trees: form and texture; rustling sounds and swaying movements, and their seasonal changes. *I like the vital energy of buds about to open, the full glory of petals, leaves unfurling, and the interesting structures of seed pods. However, I am not making copies. I try to capture their essence and translate into my own language.* ¶ Kayo's jewellery is exquisite. She makes mostly in gold and silver. The simple, tactile *Petal Necklace* she is holding is her signature design; the textured finish of the gold retains the link with her original paper work. Pinned on the bust is a brooch made by micro-welding individual stems of elderflower buds, some with baby Akoya (Japanese cultivated pearls) to appear as if they are opening. The piece on the neck is a variation of Kayo's *Blossom Necklace.* ¶ In 1926, The Goldsmiths' Company began a collection of modern silver to improve design and craftsmanship in the industry. By naming the silversmiths, the Company also aimed to raise the profile of the makers and the collectability of their work. The Modern Collection numbers over a thousand pieces today, with up to 10 items added annually. In 2018, Kayo delivered *The Blossom Necklace*, accompanied by its drawing. It is designed to give the impression of a chain of flowers about to bloom. *I applied layers of hammering to create an irregular surface and rippled edge on each delicately-veined petal.* Typical of her work, the metal appears soft and organic. ¶ Kayo occasionally incorporates ready-cut stones. In 2016, she applied for a QEST Scholarship to learn to work with the natural form of the stones themselves. *I wanted to find out how to cut, carve and polish precious and non-precious stones so I could make them integral to the structure of my designs.* The first course was with Charlotte De Syllas, an early QEST Scholar. *I admire Charlotte as an artist; she spends an enormous amount of time creating one-of-a-kind pieces.* Kayo also spent time with Mike and Sandra Walford to get an understanding of commercial lapidary methods. *Their life is shaped by stones; they are completely dedicated to them and their knowledge and expertise are outstanding.* ¶ Kayo is acquiring the tools to adapt her workshop to handle both metal and stone. *They are opposite processes. I am used to shaping and soldering metal to create a design; with stone, I need to remove material to get to the desired form.* She is also sourcing rough stones suitable for the themes she is developing. The experiences with Charlotte, Mike and Sandra were invaluable, but it will be a while until she is ready to show her first range. *I have to work with the material myself until I find a way that sits comfortably with my ephemeral aesthetic.*

Gail McGarva

TRADITIONAL WOODEN BOATBUILDER

The River Thames rises in the Cotswold Hills in Gloucestershire. Gail McGarva QEST Scholar 2009 had lived on boats for years when she decided to journey to its source from her home on the River Avon near Bristol. *I was a sign language interpreter, but after this trip I had a yearning to put boats at the core of my working life too.* ¶ A magazine in her local library mentioned the Lyme Regis Boat Building Academy. She got in touch and asked to visit; a train ride and hitched lift later, she entered the workshop. *It felt like a homecoming. I think the sense of rightness came from the boats themselves; skeletal and sculptural, they have a life force that pulls you in.* Gail applied for a City & Guilds bursary and was accepted to study at the Academy. ¶ *I read about the 'Gardie' boat of 1882, the oldest at the Unst Boat Haven on the most northerly of the Shetland Isles. I longed to build a replica for my final project, but was conscious that I was an outsider.* Gail wrote to Willie Mouat, last of this boat building line, and he agreed to be her mentor. She set off from Dorset to Aberdeen for a 14-hour crossing then two more ferries to Unst. *I thought I was used to the cold, but it really bites there in December.* Gail met Willie and he showed her the *Gardie. She was captivating: a rugged working boat with a beautiful sheerline and scooping ends.* Elated, Gail headed home, but not before a visit to the chandlery to fill her rucksack with every size of the traditional rosehead copper nails. ¶ Gail and Willie spent hours on the telephone. *He would tell me that the second plank is critical and that I had to push it out a wee bit. I asked if he meant an inch; he told me I would just know.* Then there was the hurdle of the parts being named in a Shetland dialect with old Norse terminology. *I was surprised when Willie rattled off instructions about the 'humlabaund', 'stammeron' and 'kaeb', but we got there.* ¶ Gail thought it would be fitting to launch from the same slipway as the original. She towed *Georgie McDonald* (named after her Scottish grandmothers) north. The ferry company gave her free passage and the port workers, mostly Shetlanders, knew from the shape what was under the tarpaulin. Willie was overjoyed. Gail had saved a few finishing touches that they did together; then, with an oar each, they rowed her into Shetland waters. *He made me promise that I would let someone else take her out that day so I could stand on the shore and take it all in visually and emotionally.* ¶ This was the first of Gail's 'daughterboats' from old working stock. *I am preserving the art of boatbuilding by eye – there are rarely any drawn plans – to create a new generation. It is quite a moment when a finished boat, static and braced, is released to leap on the waves.* ¶ In 2007, the Lyme Regis Gig Club asked Gail to make a Cornish Pilot Gig. She worked with the late Ralph Bird, who had championed their revival for racing, from an 1838 boat called *Treffry*. Gail held a 'Knees-up Fortnight' for people to make the brackets (known as 'knees') and each one was punched with their name or a message. *I always involve the community as wooden boats need caring for and they will be the custodians.* The Club now has three of these 32-foot, six-oared rowing boats. ¶ Her QEST Scholarship in 2009 gave rise to a new Dorset Lerret, its wide beam designed to cope with working the Chesil Beach shoreline in the 1800s. Roy Gollop guided her, based on one of the two intact examples. With the build complete, Gail turned the original, *Vera*, into *The Story Boat*, an oral maritime history recording and museum space. ¶ Gail is rowing a Cornish Sea Skiff, named *Gale Force* by the townsfolk, that she made for the junior members of the Lyme Regis Gig Club modelled on one of the oldest surviving examples. *It is wonderful to see them out in her starting to feel a connection with the sea and the thrill of propelling themselves under oar.*

Bob Johnston

WILLOW SCULPTOR

QEST Scholar 2004
QEST Thomas
Fattorini Award for
Excellence 2017

Bob Johnston creates traditional and contemporary willow baskets, sculptures and living structures in his garden workshop in the coastal town of Bangor, Northern Ireland. ¶ He trained as a textile weaver, but soon after college saw an exhibition of basketwork by David Drew and was hooked. Bob searched for a course, but little structured learning remains in the field and there are few apprenticed master craftsmen. Megan McManus at the Ulster Folk Museum suggested QEST and Bob was granted a Scholarship. *I learned traditional skills from the best basketmakers at workshops in Armagh and Galway and a cave (the cool, damp conditions are ideal for keeping willow pliable) in Villaines-les-Rochers, the basketmaking capital of France.* ¶ He was soon able to manipulate a basic willow rod into a thing of beauty through the set patterns of basketry. This was a satisfying start, but too tame for Bob as he developed a feel for the raw material and its artistic potential. He began to 'sketch' with the rods, drawing them into dense, random weaves to create a series of flowing, animated forms. ¶ He applied this technique to mummers' masks, head disguises once made from straw for an ancient local tradition of plays and house visiting. The designer of a sensory garden for a special needs school in Belfast saw his work and asked Bob to make four life-size sculptures. He made the pig, sheep, cat and peacock to be particularly tactile and sensors buried in pathways triggered animal noises as the children approached. Publicity from the garden resulted in a request for an animal trophy head and everything grew from there. ¶ Bob still makes the occasional basket (in the foreground of the picture is an old Irish 'skib' that would have been used three times a day to strain and serve potatoes), but animal sculptures are the focus of his practice. Peering out from the hedge is *Elvis*, a Highland Cow head mount. *This was my first design and is still the most popular request, I think because the sinous nature of willow lends itself so perfectly to the long, wavy coat.* The horns are made of stripped willow that will mellow to a deeper cream over time. ¶ Bob works with over 40 varieties of willow and cultivates as many as possible himself, but also looks to growers in England, Wales, France and Belgium for the finest available. *I adore the diversity in the natural colour palette and am always searching for something a little different that will help with the finish.* The rods need to be free of blemishes and side shoots. Working quality is important too – the more flexible, the better. Bob harvests in winter when the plant is dormant after a season's growth. Cutting close to the ground, it is cold, slow, back-breaking work, but also exciting. *The feel of the rods and the variety of hues are inspirational – I often spend this time thinking about what I can make.* ¶ He studies images and gathers accurate measurements to make every commission as convincing as possible. Waiting patiently in the photograph is *Rollie the Labradoodle. I am halfway through, about to add colour to his frame, which will probably take another week.* Bob loves the sense of movement that he can weave into sculptures through the muscle structure and tries to fill his work with personality so it looks like it could burst into life at any moment. *One customer was thrilled with the ferocious jaws of his 'Great White Shark', although it gave his children quite a fright.* ¶ Bob's animals have travelled to ski lodges in Switzerland, museums and galleries from the Ulster Museum and Royal Dublin Society to the Smithsonian Center for Folklife & Cultural Heritage in Washington D.C, and even appeared in *Game of Thrones*. He regularly creates sculptures to raise funds for QEST, including a free-standing *Irish Moiled Bull* auctioned at *Where Craft Meets Art* at Christie's. *A little Corgi I made for Her Majesty The Queen tops them all though.*

Anne Petters

MULTI-MEDIA ARTIST

Born in Dresden in 1978, Anne Petters grew up in the German Democratic Republic. Living through the political change in her country created a lingering sense of displacement. *This is manifest in my artistic practice as an interest in controlling and displaying moments of our fleeting, vulnerable existence, which led me to the metaphoric use of glass.* ¶ Anne has a Diploma from the Institute of Ceramic and Glass Art in Germany and a Master of Fine Arts degree from Alfred University, New York. She is a conceptual artist with a cerebral approach that focuses on technique and the ephemeral aesthetic of her work. *I rarely draw my ideas; I prefer working directly through the material. My table is my sketchbook.* ¶ She had been working with glass for ten years when she spent a year as a visiting artist at Edinburgh College of Art. *I discovered a vivid scene in the UK, where I have now settled.* A QEST Scholarship enabled Anne to create a new body of work at the renowned Pilchuck Glass School in the United States. *It was amazing to have seven weeks of experimental time, looking for inspiration without the pressure of a show.* Pilchuck is on a former tree farm and the accommodation is log cabins (glass studios are often found in forests as the furnaces were once wood-fired); Anne was overwhelmed by the nature surrounding her. *There were so many precious things I wanted to hold on to.* She captured raindrops in glass and cast leaves with glass powder using traditional 'pâte de verre' (glass paste kiln casting) that she developed into a method with new sculptural possibilities. ¶ Back in her studio in London, Anne is holding a piece from a series she makes with this technique. Her glass *Books of Disquiet* are inspired by a literary work of the same name. Portuguese author Fernando Pessoa died leaving hundreds of unedited, open-ended fragments of prose. With no obvious beginning, end or indication of sequence, there are different interpretations of his story; each version is published as *The Book of Disquiet*. ¶ Anne's process starts with carving into a plaster silica mould. *I have to write in reverse, which comes naturally, perhaps from playing around writing left-handed or mirror writing as a child.* She tries to stay as unconscious as possible as she gives form to the thoughts and lines of poetry running through her mind, mostly in English, sometimes in German. *I am interested in the graphic quality of the text: the image of thinking is more important than the meaning of the words.* ¶ Anne sifts fine glass powder then clear frit (a little coarser) onto the inscribed pages. *This is my printing process, similar to inking a copperplate etching.* This glass melds into her drawings during the first firing. When she has a dozen flat sheets, she builds them into a stack, alternating with high-fire kiln paper. This is positioned to allow the spine of the book to bind, but stop the pages fusing into a block. Anne wears a pair of Kevlar gauntlets to kiln-form the book in a second firing. She opens the cover and places a piece of heat-resistant Fibrefrax onto which she turns the first page, allowing it to slump and settle. This process is repeated until the entire book has been positioned. *It is not a rational thing; when it is right, it just feels that way.* ¶ Anne is a glass technician at the City & Guilds of London Art School, works and teaches internationally and shows in glass museums and art institutions in Europe and the USA. *Glass has the magic I need, but I am not wedded to it.* On a residency in upstate New York she preserved snowflakes in a modified freezer and made a shooting star machine: dust particles caught in a beam of light are filmed and projected in real time onto blue fabric where they appear as these natural phenomena in the night sky. *This closed-circuit installation pulls us in and creates a powerful sense of our place in space and time.*

QEST Garfield Weston Foundation Scholar 2014

Effie Burns

GLASS ARTIST

QEST Scholar 2012

The National Trust Museum of Childhood in Sudbury Hall, Derbyshire, was Effie Burn's home growing up (her father was the live-in curator). *It was a showpiece for 17th century craftsmanship; the lavish interior and collections fostered my wish to make objects and curiosity about how they are displayed.* ¶ She studied for a degree in Glass & Ceramics then an Art in Context MA at the University of Sunderland, which has a long tradition of glassmaking. There were engraving lathes in the workshop, but no specialist tutors. *I was intrigued by the potential of engraving to transform the surface texture of glass and applied to QEST to learn this disappearing craft at Bild-Werk Frauenau in Germany from Katharine Coleman MBE.* ¶ A few years later, Effie was reunited with Katharine as her mentor on an ArtWorks Fellowship at the National Glass Centre in Sunderland (based at the University). *Katharine set up the two lathes for me to experiment on and create a new body of work using an amalgam of traditional engraving skills with digital technology.* ¶ She was interested in the medium of glass not only for decorative purposes, but for its expressive qualities too. *Glass, from slippers to mirrors, plays an important part in the lore of enchantment in fairytales.* Effie explored a blend of these motifs and feminism through the changing depictions of female roles, from the dark stories of the Brothers Grimm to the feistiness of Roald Dahl's characters. ¶ She also likes to create a stage or platform where her narrative can play out. *I took a cast of my left hand, a symbol of emotion and the unconscious side of our minds, on which to place this series of sculptures.* Deer, made of cast glass combined with lamp worked glass and engraved detail with spots polished to reflect the light, was purchased by the National Glass Centre for its permanent Collections Gallery. ¶ Effie also travelled to the Czech Republic with glass artist Angela Thwaites to visit the studios of Pavlína Čambalová, who she knew from her time in Germany, and Lucie Pejchová. *They told me where to source specialist materials and showed me how to engrave with copper wheels and other techniques best learned in practice rather than from books. We keep in touch via Instagram now as it is so pictorial.* ¶ Effie is holding *Briar Rose*, an evolution of the work during her Fellowship. The sculpture is based on the German tale of *Little Briar Rose* and represents both the title character (also known as Sleeping Beauty) and the plant, which in some versions surrounds the castle to shield Briar Rose from the outside world. *I enjoy bringing together different techniques and creating work that the viewer can make multiple connections with. It looks beautiful, but also has nasty thorns.* The flowers were created in 'pâte de verre' (glass paste) using the lost wax kiln casting process: a plaster mould is taken of the carved wax rose, which is steamed away and the space packed with glass frit (powder) and fired at 740 degrees Celsius. *This relatively low temperature gives the roses their opaque appearance.* To make the leaves, she fused two sheets of clear glass. *The textured surface traps air between the layers; this forms bubbles that catch the light when the underside of the final piece is silvered.* At the National Glass Centre, her drawings were converted to a digital file that guided a water jet to cut the silhouette. *With the stone wheel on the lathe, I crosshatched lines to animate the surface of the glass and reference David Hockney's illustrations of six Brothers Grimm fairy tales.* ¶ *Briar Rose* has a personal note too: the white rose it was modelled on was picked by Effie as the emblem of her new home county of Yorkshire (Whitby Abbey can be seen in the background). Also growing at the end of her garden is the brickwork for a glass studio complete with kiln, flatbed, lots of tools and, at last, her own engraving lathe.

Zoë Harding

GOLDSMITH & JEWELLERY DESIGNER

The first collection by aspiring goldsmith Zoë Harding was snipped and sculpted from her mother's aluminium foil baking trays. *This was for an A-level project on wearable sculpture. Thanks to my inspiring art teachers, I went on to study for a BA in Metalwork & Jewellery.* ¶ For one assignment, Zoë encased a sliver of fabric between two bands of sheet silver, cut with fretwork to reveal the material, then shaped to create a rigid bangle. This was the first incarnation of her signature piece: a hand-pierced, triple-layer cuff (its evolution can be seen on the table). *It is such a versatile form: I can vary the width, choice of precious metal, design detail, background and embellish with pearls and precious stones.* ¶ During her degree, Zoë found that her ideas were usually sparked by a specific technique. She had a good foundation, but wanted further practical training so she could enter the profession with a more complete range of skills for inspiration. QEST provided the funding for five intensive courses at an academy in Hatton Garden, London's jewellery quarter and centre of the UK's diamond trade. ¶ In small classes with expert visiting tutors, Zoë learned mount making, gem setting, wax carving, working in platinum and engraving. *It was transformational being taught by people who were current in the industry. They also shared nuggets of information like where to buy specialist materials and the odd trick such as grinding nails to make a burnishing tool that fits into tiny gaps.* This all-round experience in making enhanced her design capability, through which she became a jewellery designer at Vivienne Westwood. ¶ Today, Zoë makes bespoke fine jewellery under her own name, provides creative and technical design services to other companies, and teaches. ¶ For private commissions, nearly every piece is handcrafted by Zoë from forming and carving to polishing. *My QEST Scholarship gave me huge respect for specialist skills, so I also know when it is best to outsource a task, such as setting a particularly delicate stone, to somebody who does it every day.* This works seamlessly as they can trust each other's accuracy in working to fine tolerances. ¶ Zoë's cuff has been the foundation of ranges for Fortnum & Mason and Holland & Holland, and she continues to experiment with wrapping different materials: textiles, leather, peacock feathers and vintage snakeskin. It would be quicker to cut the metal by laser now, but she prefers to continue her method. *I did try with technology, but the more intricate the design, the more difficult it is to get a file into the corners for finishing; I get a better result piercing by hand.* ¶ In 2013, with her design consultancy on the ascendancy, Zoe invested time developing her 2D skills and entered the Goldsmiths' Craft & Design Council Competition. Her drawing for *Bud Pendant* in platinum and black diamond won Gold. In new territory, she responded to the brief to 'look outside the circle for a contemporary medal'. *Conserving our Arctic Habitat,* a double-sided design featuring a polar bear, whale and icebergs also received Gold, and the premier accolade, The Goldsmiths' Company Award. This is given at the discretion of the Council for exceptional and outstanding work, and only when an entry achieves the highest standards of design and originality. *This started as an exercise to keep me on my toes; I was taken aback at the result, and delighted to be invited back to join the judging panel for medals in 2018.* ¶ As a commercial designer, Zoë is known for her versatility. She works with well-known brands across Europe and the USA, designing costume, high-end fashion and fine jewellery collections, and with Swarovski crystals continuing the founder's vision to create a 'diamond for everyone'. ¶ Zoë was made a Freeman of the Worshipful Company of Goldsmiths in 2016 and is proud to uphold its almost 700 years of tradition in support of her craft.

QEST Scholar 2004

Jon Letcher

HARP & DULCIMER MAKER

QEST Scholar 2001 *The Silver Spear* is one of Jon Letcher's favourite Irish reels to play and the name under which he makes fine harps and dulcimers in the Welsh Marches, where the harp especially has been part of the cultural landscape for centuries. ¶ Suffolk-born, he has a lifelong passion for all things East Anglian. Years ago, he came across an old record of music from the region on a market stall in Cambridge. *One of the musicians was playing a Norfolk dulcimer; I had never heard of it, but was captivated by its sound.* The dulcimer is trapezoid in shape, has about 70 strings tuned in groups called 'courses', and is played with a pair of sticks. The sound is sustained, so it can be built up gradually and a melody played over the top. Nobody was making them and those being played were 100 years old; eventually, Jon found a wreck of one in a junk shop. A trained boat builder, he used his woodworking skills to repair it and began to play. *I learned by ear; rhythmic Scottish and Irish pipe and drum tunes and slow airs work wonderfully.* He made his first dulcimer from scratch in his spare time at the first boatyard he worked in at Beccles in Suffolk, then kept on going, selling each one to afford the materials for the next. ¶ In 2000, Jon spent three months in Hungary, China and Iran (where the dulcimer originated) on a Winston Churchill Fellowship. He worked with other makers and musicians on projects to highlight connections between the different cultures, a theme that resonates strongly with Jon. When harpist and engineer Andy Lowings wanted to build the first authentic reproduction of the 4,700-year-old *Golden Lyre of Ur* (found smashed and stripped of its gold inlays after looting at the National Museum of Iraq in Baghdad in 2003), he volunteered straight away. All the labour and materials were donated, including the magnificent bull's head, sculpted in wood and covered in gold and lapis lazuli, made by students at West Dean College. Jon made the lyre itself, partly from Cedar of Lebanon given by Arab Aid in Baghdad and flown to Britain by the RAF. Afterwards, Andy commissioned Jon to make a lyre to take with him on a journey around the Middle East and Africa. *I love that a lyre inspired by an instrument I saw in The Museum of Egyptian Antiquities in Cairo, while working there with archaeologists, and made in my workshop ended up being played by, among others, an Arab camel-drover on top of Mount Sinai.* ¶ A QEST Scholarship in 2001 gave Jon the opportunity to refine his craft at London Guildhall University. *I was given access to whichever lectures I thought would be useful and could take in my designs and finished instruments for expert critique.* The academic experience was especially useful in advancing his knowledge of harps, which he had been making since 1995 to enable instrument-making to become his profession. ¶ Jon is playing a harp he made in cherry, popular for its mellow sound. There are two distinct parts: the frame that holds the strings up and the soundbox where the notes are created and amplified. *When you connect the two, the harp starts to come alive; even before the strings are put on, it vibrates in response to any noise in the workshop.* A harp that means a lot to Jon was for a school 20 miles from where he lives. They had an old, unplayable harp and tried to raise funds for a new one. They came to Jon with what they had: some way short, but he was glad to do it. *They had a special assembly and a Welsh harp teacher came along to play. It was very moving.* ¶ The dulcimer that Jon played at his QEST interview (in the picture) travels with him everywhere, including the few weeks he spends each year working on classic boats in Crinan on the west coast of Scotland. There are a few musicians at the boatyard and they sometimes play together in the evenings. *We have to send the Highland piper to the end of the corridor though, otherwise he drowns us out!*

Clare Barnett

SADDLER & SADDLE FITTER

Clare Barnett had barely started to walk when she wanted to ride horses. Growing up in Birmingham, this wasn't easy; it was a daily, 40-mile round trip to the stables with her parents. A move to the New Forest was a relief to all. Betty Skelton, doyenne of the side saddle world, lived nearby and Clare visited for a 'have a go' clinic. *I adored it and carried on with lessons.* ¶ Life moved on and Clare worked as a nurse before a motorbike accident put pay to being on her feet all day. *It felt natural to return to my love of horses, but with young children, a traditional apprenticeship was impossible.* She learned leatherwork first at MacGregor & Michael in Tetbury, then onto Mark Romain in Salisbury to begin saddle making. ¶ With family commitments and self-funding, Clare took 10 years to complete her apprenticeship (it usually takes three). Her determination continued and she qualified to become a Master Saddler. *You have to be in the trade for eight years – four training, four 'out on your tools' – before you can take your body of work and competition results to the Society of Master Saddlers committee.* ¶ Following her injuries, Clare's riding had to change too. She tried carriage driving, then, while fitting a side saddle on a fell pony, her teenage passion was reignited and it dawned on her this could be the solution. *With no sideways strength in one leg and two slipped discs, I could no longer ride astride. It turns out that riding aside is not only possible, it is brilliant for my back – even my chiropractor agrees.* ¶ QEST supported Clare to train with Richard Godden, the last remaining Master Saddler specialising in side saddles. It takes a week to make an astride saddle, but three months for a side saddle as very little can be done by machine. *A side saddle feels elegant, secure and thrilling to ride and I felt a similar exhilaration in making them.* ¶ During the course, Clare refurbished a Champion & Wilton side saddle that now gets regular outings on one of her horses. In the photograph (taken at Royal Windsor Horse Show), she is holding another of her rebuilt Victorian saddles. The rider, Chloe Gunn, has an Owen saddle that Clare fixed, checks twice a year, and adjusts for seasonal changes (the glorious red habit that Chloe is wearing is made by Clare's elder daughter Alexandra). ¶ Clare has now made five side saddles from scratch (one took first prize in a national competition), restored five and has seven in waiting. The new ones are sold, but the refurbished ones are for hire only. *They look beautiful, but the tree (wooden frame) they are based on is around 100 years old. People love to ride them and they have their place, but I am an advocate of new builds.* ¶ She begins with a laminate beech tree then combines traditional and modern materials so the appearance is the same, but rather than cope with indentations moulded by others over decades, her saddles let each rider develop a sweet spot that suits their style, and the shape recovers between rides. Fitting is equally skilled. *We have a duty of care. It can take a couple of hours from taking a template of the horse's back to checking the rider is balanced and confident from walk to canter.* ¶ Bearhouse Saddlery, established by Clare in 1998, sustains the livelihoods of her husband Peter (now a Master Saddler too), their younger daughter Victoria (a recently Qualified Saddler) and QEST Alborada Trust Apprentice Joanna Murphy. Situated on the Hampshire, Wiltshire, Dorset borders they work mainly in these counties, but do make forays down to Somerset where they can also visit tanneries. *We look for strong hides for saddles and doe skin for seats, but we'll also call in at Pittards for its soft, colourful leathers, and Midgley to see bridle leather butts, as they are perfect for our bespoke sporting accessories.* ¶ It has been a long road, but Clare and her Bearhouse family are keeping this graceful art of riding alive and creating tomorrow's heirlooms.

QEST Worshipful Company of Saddlers Scholar 2013

Nina Thomas

FARRIER

QEST Radcliffe
Trust Scholar 2012

Going to Bristol University to study Equine Science led to Nina Thomas discovering her perfect career, but not in the lecture theatre or laboratory. ¶ At home in Devon she had worked at local stables before and after school, and dawn to dusk in the holidays, anything to be able to ride. Eventually she got a horse of her own. *I found a livery yard and took Lester to Bristol with me. The visiting farrier had an apprentice; it was the first time I had seen anyone my own age in the trade.* Out in the countryside making and fitting shoes for horses to perform at their best was her ideal way of life. Nina left university and committed to finding a farriery apprenticeship. It took letters to 150 Approved Training Farriers to receive an offer of work experience. *It was back in Devon shadowing Steve Luxton stable to stable; it felt the most natural job in the world.* ¶ It was early 2001 and an apprentice had to be qualified by 26 years old to be eligible for a grant; for Nina this meant starting by March 2002 at the latest. She saw a notice in *Forge Magazine* from Stuart Craig, a farrier looking for apprentices in Buckinghamshire. *The race was on; I had to follow any chance, no matter where.* Nina drove up for a trial. *The tasks were blisteringly hard; my hands were so raw by the end of the first day that I could barely move my fingers the next.* She was taken on as a polo groom with a conditional offer of an apprenticeship a year later, in the nick of time. *For every hour I worked, I could spend an hour in the forge to get to the starting standard.* ¶ A farriery apprenticeship takes four years and two months. The first eight weeks are probationary, after which the trainee presents a set of forged pieces to demonstrate their aptitude. The next four years are spent working with the master, with a couple of weeks every six months on college release for theory and practical assessments. Nina was awarded the Worshipful Company of Farriers Diploma in Farriery with distinction. ¶ She moved back to Devon and set up as a farrier making shoes to suit all horses and working conditions. To make her rounds, Nina converted a truck into a mobile workshop with gas-fired forge, anvil, welding equipment, drawers of tools and 45 pairs of shoes of various sizes and styles, front and hind, to heat, shape and fit. *After such rigorous training, I thought I knew everything, but there is no such thing as a textbook limb. The more horses I saw, the more I knew there was still much to learn.* ¶ In 2011, Nina was accepted onto a Foundation Degree in Farriery Science, including advanced study of the equine musculoskeletal system and gait analysis, at Myerscough College, University of Central Lancashire. QEST paid the fees and Nina retained her clients in Devon, as the course was distance learning, with two days a month at College. *The facilities were amazing: three workshops with 32 coke forges and anvils; more than 50 horses of various sizes, breeds and standards; and a pony stud. It was worth every hour of the 600-mile round trip.* Nina again passed with distinction and a greater understanding of the biomechanical effects of farriery interventions. ¶ She works with driving ponies and horses ridden for dressage, eventing, showjumping and pleasure, including this Connemara mare Tilly, pictured standing in a local yard. They are shod every five to eight weeks, which keeps Nina going at a rate of one hundred shoes a week. *The frequency is important to maintain correct balance as their feet are affected by everything in their routine: exercise, diet, weather and bedding.* She also does remedial work with veterinary practices to help horses regain soundness disrupted by injury or illness; these shoes are usually crafted from scratch. *¶ I hope to take on apprentices one day, but for now it is me and my two spaniels: 10-year-old veteran Henry and young Hamish – he's only one, so still learning stableyard etiquette.*

Anna Kettle

PARGETER & PLASTER CONSERVATOR

QEST Scholar 2001

Three instances collided to give Norfolk-born Anna Kettle the final push to leave the office job that was sapping her energy: catching a glimpse of the marvellous Jacobean ceiling covered in fleur-de-lys and dragons in a Suffolk pub; getting to grips with a plastering trowel on her kitchen walls; and her looming 40th birthday. *I signed up to a City & Guilds course to retrain as a plasterer and had the good fortune to be taught by a former building conservator.* One day he brought in traditional lime plaster for Anna to try. *Modern alternatives paled into the background for me; I didn't hesitate when he told me to contact St Blaise, a conservation company in Somerset.* They were looking for a team of plasterers and Anna was soon on her way to Edinburgh to cast moulds for an ornamental ceiling. *The variety of jobs around the country was a great way to understand more about the material, but I was always repairing other people's work.* ¶ Anna wanted to learn freehand modelling in lime plaster, known as pargeting, but there was nowhere to study in the UK. The craft was at its height from 1660 to 1780. Its origins lie in the Italian art of 'stucco', brought to England by gentlemen returning from their 'Grand Tours' of Europe who wanted to decorate their ceilings and overmantles. Pargeting is the rural form that was particularly popular in Suffolk and Essex. ¶ Anna traced this history and found a building conservation course in Venice for which QEST agreed a Scholarship. She focused on 'marmorino Veneziano' in which plaster made from crushed marble and lime putty is used to create marble effects: similar material and the same techniques as those adopted by pargeters. *It was an edifying three months. I came back and moved to Suffolk, where pargeting is still a live trade.* Her conservation experience and pargeting skills means that a full-time business is feasible: the repair of historic plasterwork accounts for half of her time, the rest is spent on original work. ¶ The outdoor season runs from April to October (to avoid risk of frost damage). Anna follows closely behind flatwork plasterers, mounting the paper pattern onto the wet plaster and using her fingers and a spatula to create the shapes. She can also parget onto a set surface: marking the design in pencil then cutting away the old plaster and adding fresh layers to create the new profile. Either way, scaffold is in place when she starts work, so the planning must be spot on. *It is best to finish with a lime wash, particularly externally; painting and repainting in this way protects and prolongs everything I make.* ¶ Most parget is in low relief and can be as simple as a panel filled with a basket weave or wool skein pattern. Anna has also taught herself to model in high relief. Her test piece was an *Adam & Eve* overmantle in her own home. *I have since bought and renovated a farmhouse and am sitting in the porch working on roses to surround the front door.* Commissions come through word of mouth, but she has also had enquiries from people who have passed by something she has made. *It seems my exterior work also acts as pleasingly picturesque advertising!* ¶ Anna demonstrated her craft during a visit by TRH The Prince of Wales and The Duchess of Cornwall to the Suffolk Preservation Society. As a result, she was commissioned to create a parget on the ceiling of the painting room at Birkhall on the Balmoral Estate in Scotland. ¶ She often looks at wood carvings in local churches for inspiration and encourages people to connect a design to the history of their house and family. *I have made a panel of Lincoln Longwool sheep in the old wool town of Coggeshall in Essex, and a border of wheat on a house that was once a bakery.* Anna also added a medieval baker carrying a loaf of bread and a kettle: a complete anachronism as he would have boiled water in a cauldron, but an intentional choice of motif given the pargeter's surname.

Sarah Hocombe

MURALIST & FRESCO PAINTER

QEST Scholar 1999

The design course that Sarah Hocombe took at Chelsea School of Arts in 1986 focused on stained glass, architectural ceramics and mural painting. The technical education in the first two subjects was comprehensive, but the mural painting focused only on the use of acrylic paints, intended for public art projects. Sarah's interest was more towards fresco painting (traditional pigments applied onto wet lime plaster – 'fresco' is Italian for 'fresh') for private commissions. She set about researching the craft independently. ¶Frescos were once as commonplace as the use of lime plaster, but are mainly associated with the Italian Renaissance. Sarah travelled around northern Italy on a QEST Scholarship to study the best-preserved examples. *It was like holding a magnifying glass to the books I had been reading; I could see every brushstroke, crack and overpainting.* ¶In the simplest instances, buildings were faced with a local stone to a certain height with the upper storeys lime plastered and painted in a similar colour, often etched to resemble blocks from a distance; others were more elaborately decorated. *Historically, this was to protect bricks of modest quality as it was easier to repair or replace this sacrificial layer than the structural fabric.* ¶Sarah studied façades in Turin, Florence and around the Veneto to see if the techniques for these repairs could be useful in her practice. She discovered that in extreme cases, if a wall was crumbling and there was an artwork deemed worth saving, a fresco was 'peeled off' while the wall was repaired. *This made me think: if a fresco could be removed and replaced, I could paint a panel in my studio and fasten it to a client's wall rather than repoint their brickwork with lime and work on site.* Around half of her commissions are created in this way. ¶She also learned that an old fresco is the best support for a new fresco. *They used to score over the original, add a fresh layer of plaster, and paint the next design.* However, if there was water ingress, over time parts would fall away and the multiple stories, separated by time and layers of plaster, would be visible, jumbled together. *I thought that recreating this effect might appeal to my clients in the UK, as a lot of our painted past has receded or vanished.* ¶The fresco in Sarah's studio is a sample piece using this technique. She started by drawing the pictures on tracing paper then made pinholes to dust the pigment onto the damp plaster to get an outline. The foundation layer is inspired by Visscher's 1616 *Panorama of London* (this engraving is one of the few representations of the city before the Great Fire) and there is a glimpse of St Paul's Cathedral today with a helicopter flying by. *Lettering works well as a complementary decorative feature; written on the surface are places that poet John Keats lived and visited in London, inspired by Andrew Motion's biography.* ¶There was one other major consequence of Sarah's Italian tour: observing church ceilings in every town became a masterclass in the subtleties of painting the heavens. She developed extensive knowledge of celestial formations and how colours are reflected and refracted. Sarah's cloudscapes have earned her a reputation as 'queen of the skies' in architectural and interior design circles. In 2013, Sarah painted an early summer evening sky, with swifts and swallows returning from their migration, on the ceiling of the Summer House at Buckingham Palace for the Coronation Festival. There is an undoubted romance, but so precise is her work that she is regularly commissioned by jet pilots. ¶Sarah prefers to work with natural pigments as they sit well in or on any building, minimal or richly decorated. The only tradition that she has dispensed with is painting from a wooden palette. *When I am up a ladder with a brush in one hand, it is useful having the other free; as you can see in the photograph, I have created a wearable version: my apron.*

Kate Hetherington

COLLAR & HARNESS MAKER

Kate Hetherington makes traditional horse collars with a leather outer and straw QEST Scholar 2007 filling. She started training at 16 years old as an apprentice to master harness maker John McDonald. Her first job was with a saddle maker, but lack of work due to foot and mouth in 2001 forced Kate to set up on her own. *I discovered an unmet demand for collars and applied for a QEST Scholarship to return to John and learn the skills: one week gig collar making, one week heavy collar, then hame (the metal part outside the collar that John and I still make in traditional steel and brass plate).* ¶ Learning to make collars was the catalyst for business success. Kate can make everything for the show ring and traditional carriage driving harness, and her made-to-measure collars ensure comfort and strength. Now working together, Kate and John make 40 to 70 a year at their premises in Somerset. ¶ Collar making happens away from the main workshop – there is no avoiding it being a messy trade. *The photograph illustrates the process well. The collar I'm making has its body, but no sides yet. I'm lacing in the straw with threads I make myself.* They get tightened and loosened throughout construction, so they must be very strong and long – Kate uses hemp, twisted with lots of wax for waterproofing. ¶ The straw is rye. *We buy from a farm in Hereford, cut early so it is green and less brittle, and before the heads have grown. If the weather isn't right when it's time for our harvest, it gets left for thatchers, but when it works out well, we buy as much as we can; a barnful keeps us going for years.* ¶ To one side of Kate is a collar on a block for sizing and shaping; at her feet is the block she uses when beating the leather. The mallets are made of old bowling balls, levelled on one side – ideal as they are made of such hard wood. *I buy them second hand as they feel so much better to work with.* The collar Kate is holding is upside down, as the stitching always begins at the base. ¶ The contents of the shelves in the background complete the material story. The oak bark tanned leather comes from J. & F.J. Baker & Co. in Devon, which Kate says cannot be beaten for its tensile strength. There is work in progress too: a collar for a Hackney Horse Society show and saddle straps for The King's Troop, Royal Horse Artillery. ¶ The publication of the Heritage Crafts Association Radcliffe Red List of Endangered Crafts in 2017 came as a shock. *Demand for our craft is strong and I am extremely busy, but I realise now I have been working in a cocoon. With our leather coming from Britain's last oak bark tannery and a lot of our work from coachbuilders and wagon makers, it was alarming to see us all listed as critically endangered.* ¶ There is work to sustain six makers in the UK. Two of the four current practitioners will retire soon and John only works for half of the year. Kate, a member of the Society of Master Saddlers and winner of a Worshipful Company of Coachmakers & Coach Harness Makers award, feels the responsibility to act for the future. *I will take on John's courses when he retires. Interest in initial training is good, but people need to invest money, time and effort to keep collar making alive as it requires a lot of practice to get a good eye for fit and make accordingly.* ¶ Further afield, Kate has worked on World Horse Welfare projects to develop equipment for working horses in Lesotho, Romania and Cambodia and taught a community in Honduras to make a basic collar and harness from local materials. *I hope this will be the start of a network across Latin America. The Honduran group has already helped to train others in Nicaragua, where around 400,000 horses provide vital income and services.* ¶ From answering the rallying cry for her craft in the UK to the sustainable making of affordable harnesses overseas, the equine world is enriched by Kate's talent and commitment.

Ben Laughton Smith

ARTIST

QEST Sir Siegmund Warburg's Voluntary Settlement Scholar 2016

After ten years as a lawyer, Ben Laughton Smith's first day at the London Atelier of Representational Art (LARA) in 2014 felt like a shift of monumental proportions. His family background, at least, suggested he would feel at home. ¶ Ben has a postcard from his grandfather, artist and teacher Robert Ball, that he received at school. Printed on the front is a watercolour of a marrow plant painted by Ball, aged 14. It won a competition for young artists and was bought by the Birmingham Museum and Art Gallery. On the reverse is his advice to Ben for an art examination: measure cross-section, structure, pattern; start from the inside; plot the veins of the leaves. *He was always supportive, but not keen for me to pursue an art education; he felt that the manual for teaching representational painting had been torn up and thrown away.* ¶ In recent years, there has been a revival in the UK. Ben's first figure painting was made during a month-long summer school at Sarum Studio, the atelier of fine art in Salisbury. He returned two years later to reconnect with the good practice instilled here before starting his four-year Diploma in Fine Art at LARA. In the context of representational painting, the two extremes of style are the 'licked finish' characteristic of French academic art and the visible 'bravura' brushstrokes of one of Ben's favourite painters, Swedish painter Anders Zorn. *I love the energy and freedom of his brushwork and the brilliant luminosity it gives his canvases.* Both require remarkable dexterity and razor-sharp observation, which was Ben's motivation for wanting to study from life in the tradition of the European academies. ¶ *It was gymnastics for the eyes to begin with: squinting and defocusing, flicking back and forth between subject and drawing, and isolating patches of value by creating tunnel vision with my hands.* One of the lines penned by his grandfather – 'don't speak and give it 100 per cent of your concentration' – resonated during the 50 hours he spent on the study of a cast taken from Michelangelo's *David* (the source of the features on the studio wall behind Ben) to explore how light over form can be used to convey depth. ¶ This figure on the easel was completed, over two weeks, in charcoal and white chalk on hand toned paper. These are the materials through which the transition from drawing to painting is accomplished: creating shape and proportion without the distraction of fluid and colour. *There was a single light source for this pose; I love how it flows, particularly the subtle gradations where it travels down the face, arms and abdomen.* ¶ Another preparatory technique is cast painting. Ben found this to be a good exercise in understanding how to create soft transitions in paint using a mixture of optical blending (placing subtly gradated tones side by side on the canvas) and physical blending (where adjoining areas of tone are mixed on the canvas surface). *The practical setting, with tutors doing their rounds offering critique on our individual projects, and the collective spirit of the students has been a remarkable experience that has given me the skills and confidence to pursue my new direction.* ¶ A recent highlight was producing a posthumous portrait of David Ritchie, former Professor of Surgery at Royal London Hospital and Dean of the Medical School. The challenge was reimagining the colours from a faded 1950s photographic slide to depict Professor Ritchie in his younger years while working at the Mayo Clinic in Minnesota. *I was commissioned by his son, Andrew Ritchie QC; it was touching to deliver the final painting to be hung on the main staircase at the Medical School.* ¶ Ben's aspiration is to combine technical virtuosity with a sense of liveliness and intelligence. He has also taken his grandfather's early words to heart. *'Silence and Slow Time' was the title of my first solo exhibition at Horsham Museum and Art Gallery.*

Annemarie O'Sullivan

BASKETMAKER

Former Irish champion swimmer Annemarie O'Sullivan felt an immediate familiarity with the movements as she made her first basket. *The fluidity, the repetition, building momentum – I experienced the same feelings of intensity and freedom as I do swimming.* This one-day basketmaking course awakened an obsession. Five years of part-time study at the City Lit College in London followed and, as her pieces began to sell, the realisation that a viable business could emerge. ¶ In the early days, Annemarie sourced willow from the Somerset Levels, one of the few remaining growing regions (there used to be osier beds – where willow is planted and coppiced – in every town, significant enough to be marked on Ordnance Survey maps). True to basketmaker tradition, she now grows her own near home in the Sussex countryside. The cuttings are planted closely together to promote the growth of slim, straight rods suited to weaving. *Waxy bark is good too. I like subtle shades of green and grey, and there's a willow called 'packing twine' from Ireland that has rich, darker tones.* ¶ Harvesting at the start of the year is a community effort with local friends coming to lend a hand. The willow is sorted, bundled and tied to dry for up to a year before it is ready to be unleashed into whichever form Annemarie has in mind. ¶ This is when her creativity flows. *The natural resilience and lines of the willow guide selection: the most pliable for tight twists and turns; innate toughness for structural support; and the grand, sweeping specimens for large sculptures.* The elegance of Annemarie's work is rooted in physical strength; the power and dexterity in her wrists and hands is immense. She becomes deeply absorbed in each piece, soaking the willow for around a day per foot to regain its suppleness before splitting, trimming then weaving, changing deftly between bodkin (which separates the weave) and rapping iron (for tapping down and levelling). ¶ There is a six-month waiting list for Annmarie's work, each piece made by hand to order. As a collection, they conjure up a bountiful, nourishing way of life: foraging baskets, sweet chestnut trays, and feasting centrepieces for the table. Annemarie weaves her magic into everyday domestic items too, from kindling, log and laundry baskets to willow brushes and carpet beaters. ¶ As an artist, Annemarie thrives on collaboration. She worked for a year with ceramic artist Elaine Bolt on *Making Ground*, experimenting with willow and clay at a disused brickworks in East Sussex. In nearby Battle, for *Revolution and Resonance 2017* she helped to transform drawings by Felicity Truscott into a woven oak floating sculpture anchored on the surface of a lake at Ashburnham Place. ¶ Annemarie is also lead willow tutor for City Lit Basketry. *A sense of responsibility to ensure that the knowledge and skills I pass on are accurate led me to QEST*. She visited workshops in Ireland, Wales, France and Italy to study with some of the best makers in Europe. They taught her advanced techniques such as 'scalloming' and 'fitching' (the most open style of weave pictured here) and regional styles including the *Ulster Potato Basket* (in Annemarie's left hand), *Cyntell* Welsh frame basket, and *Périgord*, an agricultural basket that originated in the Dordogne. *Mastering my craft has given me a sense of belonging; I can now engage with people through it wherever I go.* ¶ Teaching is close to home too. The courses she runs at her wooden studio are full of rural charm. Alongside willow skills and basketry, there is a day based on the iconic Japanese catalogue *How to wrap five eggs*, using rush and a simple weave (the chicken at her feet visits every morning, but is yet to contribute a single one), and a garden project to make a spiralling weave to support climbing plants. And even closer to home, Annemarie's new full-time partner in her creative endeavours…her husband Tom McWalter.

QEST D'Oyly Carte Charitable Trust Scholar 2016

Mia Sabel

SADDLER & LEATHER DESIGNER

QEST Scholar 2010 Sitting at her 17th-floor desk in London's Canary Wharf, Mia Sabel could not think of an answer to her own question: how did I end up here? *Nor could I think of a reason to stay.* She had run away to the theatre as a stage manager for her first job, returned to sit A-levels, gained a degree in Graphic Design from Central Saint Martins, and held a senior role in brand design and marketing for almost two decades. Burned out, she took a year away to recover her strength of spirit. ¶ *I rode horses, took Spanish lessons, did a carpentry course, and spent the winter in Spain. I concluded that I wanted to work for myself and shortlisted three traditional crafts: millinery, tailoring and saddlery.* At that stage, the effect it would have was more important than what she would be making. Retraining as a saddler won as it would get her out and about. ¶ She went for an interview at Capel Manor College and was offered a place on the two-year, full-time Saddlery Course for the following year. *I then received a call to say that one of the group about to start had broken their leg and I could enrol in three days' time; I had an hour over breakfast to decide my future.* Mia completed the syllabus at Capel Manor and signed up for a series of short courses with Mark Romain at The Saddlery Training Centre in Salisbury for the final two years required to become a Qualified Saddler. At this point, rules for apprenticeship funding changed and an age limit of 26 was imposed. *I was 42. A QEST Scholarship enabled me to complete my training in this way and augment my skillset in leather-related heritage crafts.* ¶ Mia launched a leatherwork repair service, but needed to diversify to make a living. *I founded a business based on the saddle stitch.* She now has a workshop in east London and trades as Sabel Saddlery, creating hand-stitched, hand-burnished leather products inspired by traditional saddlery techniques. *I love going to Clayton & Sons of Chesterfield and sifting through their leather stock to find interesting pieces.* They have supplied leather for cricket balls for 30 years and now make a fine leather goods version that she is experimenting with. Mia also has a roll of orange, bubbled leather, 'new old' stock from Pittards that was used for basketballs until around 15 years ago. ¶ One customer gave Mia a worn-out watch strap and asked her to make a replacement. The original had nine holes, so she made a nine-hole strap. *It was like making a miniature bridle.* Traditionally bridles have five holes, which she tried on the next strap, positioning the middle hole for the best fit, then went down to three. Mia now makes bespoke, fitted watch straps with a choice of leather, lining, thread and shape, and the elegance of a single hole and keeper (loop to hold it in place). ¶ In 2014, Mia was accepted onto Walpole's *Crafted* programme that helps small craft companies to develop their business skills. Her mentor was Robert Ettinger of British luxury leather goods company Ettinger; his advice was transformative. *Robert helped to focus my offering, improve quality and set pricing.* The watch strap service is now the core, alongside bespoke, corporate leather goods, and interiors projects (including wall mirrors for HOWE London). He also suggested that she moved from repairs to restoration: a subtle, but valuable shift. ¶ Mia has an arrangement with Bentleys, an antique luggage store near Sloane Square, where she meets customers for strap consultations and fittings. She also reconditions and repurposes Bentleys' vintage cases for watches. *I am a hoarder, so I have a ready supply of English vegetable tanned leather and moire silk.* The box she is holding is a cartridge case turned into a trove of fine watches with Sabel Saddlery straps for a regular customer. *Nothing I did as a creative director exists now; it was all digital. It is satisfying to make things that could last for generations.*

James Hamill

BEEKEEPER

'Purveyors of the finest honeys in the Kingdom' is painted above the door of QEST Scholar 1995 The Hive Honey Shop in Battersea, south-west London; inside are hundreds of honey products and, in the summer, around 20,000 bees in a glass-fronted hive. James Hamill is the founder and head beekeeper. *The craft has been in my family for the last three generations; it is a tradition at the age of five to be introduced to the queen and start helping to harvest the honey.* ¶ For James, it began as a hobby with a couple of hives. They grew in number and he sold honey on market stalls at weekends. One day he was asked 'where is your shop?'. *It was an innocent question, but a pivotal moment for me. I decided to open one.* He also set about clearing four acres of scrubland in Surrey where he planted hundreds of apple trees. *I chose 88 old English varieties. They were surrounded by wildflowers and neighbouring lime tree orchards; Bee Heaven Farm was ready for hives.* ¶ James joined a scheme at Hadlow Agriculture College to re-establish the British black bee that disappeared in the 1920s, travelled to Nepal to study the Himalayan cliff honey hunters and document their techniques, and collaborated with the Ministry of Agriculture bee units in Turkey and Egypt. In 1995, James applied for a QEST Scholarship to further his skills and research mechanised beekeeping methods. His trip to The Bee Institute in Kirchhain, Germany coincided with the Varroa mite being discovered in the UK. *It had already taken hold, wiping out more than half of the British bee population, and I wanted to be better informed to deal with the threat.* Having studied disease resistance, James changed his breed of bee to Buckfast, a cross of many strains developed by Brother Adam at Buckfast Abbey in Devon in the early 20th century. *These pedigree bees are strong yet gentle to work with.* ¶ James produces raw honey from Bee Heaven Farm and various locations around London and the rest of the UK. A few warm days in March or April will awaken a hive and the nectar starts flowing. *It is the beekeeper's job to help the colony stay healthy and on course. I know the weather forecast, they don't.* James likes to capture single floral varieties, for example watching closely to see when the bees switch from gathering bell heather nectar to ling heather from the Dorset moors. *It is labour intensive, but worth it.* The full frames are removed from the hives and the wax is placed into a traditional centrifugal extractor. *I avoid heat, so I can maintain the aromatic oils, body, texture and fine flavour.* The freshly spun honey is filtered through fine muslin and decanted into jars. ¶ In the winter, James deep cleans all the equipment and take the hives down to a single 'lift' (layer) to house the queen and her entourage for breeding. *The bees work so hard for us through the summer, I think of it as giving them a bath and fresh pyjamas.* ¶ The shop is busy throughout the year. Honey, pollen, propolis, beeswax and royal jelly have always been valued by the Hamills. *I have my grandmother's jottings for cosmetic and health products from rosemary hair wash to cough syrup, microbreweries are interested in the nuances of our honeys, and we work with chefs to find the right flavours for their recipes.* ¶ James is standing by a 1930s hive, designed for beekeeping in Scotland (it is double-walled for protection from cold, wet conditions). The gloves are coated in propolis, the antiseptic, glue-like substance that the bees use to fortify the hives. *I cannot bear to part with them even when they become unusable by the end of a season; I have a collection of around 70 pairs.* They are made of buffalo leather and the long gauntlets that go up over the elbow are essential for protection. *I am usually in my beekeeping suit, which has the luxury of built-in, waterproof knee pads. The Neal & Palmer bee waistcoat is for special occasions only!*

Gary Drostle

MOSAIC MAKER

QEST Scholar 2006 It is more than 30 years since Gary Drostle embarked on his first public art commission: murals at Alexandra Palace to depict the history of 'The People's Palace'. They were painted by the Haringey Mural Workshop, formed by Gary and fellow artist Ruth Priestly following his studies in fine art at three London institutions: Camberwell School of Art, Central Saint Martins and Hornsey College of Art. ¶ In 1990, he was asked by Islington Council to create a mural for a pedestrian underpass in north London. Longevity was one of the criteria, so Gary checked with the paint manufacturer; they would only guarantee the finish for five years. *Somebody suggested a mosaic. The closest I had come was studying classics at school, so it was time for some quick learning.* He read *The Technique of Mosaic* by Arthur Goodwin and went to visit a terrazzo company. *I spent the day with someone who had trained as a maker and spent his career in mosaics; he gave me sound advice on what to do – and what to avoid.* Gary made the vitreous glass *Sunburst Mosaic* in his parent's attic. It was a mission to get it out for installation, but the effect was superb and it became known as *The Light at the End of the Tunnel.* ¶ Gary has spent most of the last three decades specialising in site-specific floor and wall mosaics and mosaic sculptures. At first he worked as he would have approached a mural. *I still paint everything first, but I now think like a mosaic artist, continuing the design process through the making.* He adopted many of these skills on a QEST Scholarship to attend a school of mosaic and visit the studios of important mosaic artists in Italy. *The use of colour and flow they created was mind-blowing.* Gary's blending skills as a painter were not valid working with mosaic tiles; on the trip, he learned to introduce complementary colours, perhaps the odd block of pink or purple in a sea of blue, that would change the hue from a distance. They also made him more aware of texture and how the light falls across a mosaic. *Not everything has to be placed flat.* He continues to get glass from a bottega in Cannaregio in Venice where he studied for a couple of weeks. ¶ In the studio are two works in progress. On the table is a trompe l'oeil mosaic fishpond. The surface of water is continually moving: simultaneously there and not, reflecting, casting shadows and changing colour. *It is complex to capture, but there is something magical about working on a floor mosaic that represents water, and it offers the maker great freedom to create 'andamento', free-flowing, mosaic art.* ¶ The sculpture in the background is *Ozymandias for the 21st Century*, inspired by Shelley's poem about the discovery of the broken stone head of Ozymandias, 'king of kings', symbolising the return to nothingness, even for the mighty. *I have created a classical face, but on the reverse will be a mixed-media assortment of throw-away plastic and glass to convey the message that, if we are not careful, we will destroy the planet.* Gary is hoping to exhibit this work at *The International Festival of Contemporary Mosaic* in Chartres, France. ¶ Gary has developed a reputation for public mosaic works on a massive scale. He installed a 15-metre long ceramic floor mosaic based on the Iowa River as the focal feature for the atrium of Iowa University's state-of-the-art recreation and wellness centre. *A Walk Along The California Seashore* for a children's hospital in California took eight years from drawing to completion (two years of making alone). Gary has been a visiting lecturer at the Chicago Mosaic School for over 10 years teaching a practical course in the logistics of this type of work. ¶ As for Gary's first mosaic, it is buried firmly underground. Having wanted it to last forever, the underpass was filled in and replaced by a pedestrian crossing on the road above. *Maybe it will be uncovered by archaeologists in thousands of years!*

Mia Sarosi

CERAMICIST

Mia Sarosi rises with the lark. *I live in Oxfordshire, about as inland as you can get,* QEST Scholar 2004 *but I start every day swimming in a pool or in the lake near my studio.* ¶ She began working with ceramics in 1991 as an artist at an English Delftware studio. It was a useful grounding, but she craved the freedom to paint her own designs and make her own forms. Mia spent time with other potters to learn how to throw. One of her earthenware mugs was noticed by Fortnum & Mason. *This happy circumstance led to my first significant order: tea caddies, jam, honey and mustard pots for the store.* ¶ Mia wanted to move into porcelain, but it was harder to convince potteries to let her fire their kilns to the high temperatures required (because of the associated wear and tear). Intent on making the change, Mia set up her own workshop in 2003. *A QEST Scholarship gave me the chance to spend several months experimenting with clays and glazes.* She found a porcelain clay made in Stoke-on-Trent that gave her the 'whiteness' and translucency she sought as a canvas for her paintings, and a clear glaze that showed off these qualities. ¶ While commercially successful, Mia stepped back from her practice. *I have bipolar disorder and it was difficult to continue for a while when I was unwell.* A call from QEST, unknowingly at the time, helped her to find her way back. *They asked me to make some pottery dog bowls. I felt indebted to the charity for its support, so I got out my test kiln.* Everything felt aligned once more and Mia reassembled her studio. As well as blue and white brushwork motifs, one of the first new designs was *Fireworks*, bursts of colourful paint splatters. *Each piece is a one-off in celebration of the beauty of chance.* Mia presented the range at a trade show in 2015. Heal's, a champion of emerging design talent, selected *Fireworks* for its 'collectibles corner'; it was a sell-out success. Both *Fireworks* and *Mia Sarosi for Heal's* continue today. ¶ In 2016, to celebrate the centenary of its iconic Cecil Brewer staircase, Heal's invited ten of its favourite designers to decorate a cast of the *Heal's Cat* that has graced its steps from the beginning. Mia hand painted hers live in the flagship store with the swirling tentacles of *Octopus*, her signature design for Heal's. After a trip to West Africa, she produced another exclusive range. Mia sketched endangered Western Lowland gorillas and kayaked rivers to observe forest elephants, hippo, buffalo, birds and butterflies. *I found sources of inspiration as abundant as the flora and fauna I encountered.* Mia's designs for *The Rainforest Collection* include *Superb Sunbird & Ebony* and *Parrot & Raphia Palm.* There were hundreds of shards of pottery in the streams and swamps where the animals go to take the mineral deposits. *The guide told me they were from the extinct salt trade, so I included salt cellars in the my tableware.* ¶ Everything she makes is for everyday use, so Mia considers the multiple angles at which a piece will be viewed: displayed up on a shelf to being held in the hand whilst drinking. *I evolved form and surface design in harmony. My ostrich, for example, works best on tall mugs and long-necked vases.* She also likes to sketch from life. The Courtauld Gallery asked Mia to produce ceramics for its exhibition *Rodin and Dance: The Essence of Movement. I worked with an acrobat who went through poses in Rodin's drawings and sculptures.* ¶ Each ceramic is thrown on her potter's wheel and painted individually with freehand brushwork. As a result, every piece is unique, with its own tiny quirks and imperfections: the record of a time-consuming journey through over a dozen processes. This is where she finds balance. After her bracing and calming dawn swim, Mia's studio encourages craftsmanship. *I am completely seduced by the subtle properties of porcelain clay and brushwork and the depth of practice required to master them.*

Jane Fryers

MILLINER

QEST Scholar 2005

Standing on a shingle beach near her home in Hastings is Jane Fryers, milliner and master of the unusual. She is leaning against one of the historic net shops that protected the cotton nets and hemp ropes of the town's fishing fleet. The tar-varnished weatherboard provides a dramatic backdrop for Jane and her green tilapia fish leather hat with navy Icelandic cod and salmon flowers. Her route to this point has been no less uncommon or colourful. ¶ Jane's career began in television; she thrived on the technical challenge, but had no outlet for her creativity. Her weekday commute to the BBC took her past the London College of Fashion. She found her head turning more and more often until she took the plunge and signed up for Saturday classes. No consequences, purely for pleasure: millinery, silver jewellery making, then beadwork. After a term of millinery there was no turning back. ¶ Her tutor, Andrew Bristow, was an inspiration. *He could not have been more encouraging – although he did ask as I was vigorously blocking felt whether I was approaching this as millinery or therapy.* Over nine weeks she made six hats (most people made two). *I wanted to make the most of the teaching time, not to spend three hours tacking, so I sewed between classes.* ¶ Her hobby began to inhabit her London flat, the oven only ever used to dry silk petals, and the balance of her career tipped as she switched to freelance work on commercials to give her time to train as a millinery artist. ¶ Jane's good fortune in finding motivating, supportive teachers continued when she came across traditional millinery tutor Rose Cory MBE. Jane was obsessed with recycling. *I turned up one day with an old pair of Levi's jeans that I wanted to turn into a stetson. Thankfully Rose has a joyous sense of humour; she told me to put the kettle on, then we sat and figured it out. I made a lot of tea at Rose's over the years.* ¶ In 2005, Rose suggested that Jane should apply to QEST. *It came at the perfect moment and has had an amazing effect on my life.* Jane continued learning with Rose, and Kensington & Chelsea College let her dip into a two-year course to study the subjects that interested her most: block making and commercialism versus couture. ¶ A Paul Costelloe jacket soon met the same fate as the Levi's and Jane's *Réchauffé Collection* of hats with a past was born. A Russian client brought her five vintage jackets and a pair of python trousers to transform into six hats. *He rang me at dawn on his way home from a party to tell me how sensational his new black and gold top hat had been.* A lady in her 80s arrived with a clutch of silk scarves that she wanted made into turbans for a road trip around the south of France in an open top car with her niece. *I adored being part of their flights of fancy.* ¶ It was a picture of a salmon skin bikini in the *Evening Standard* that prompted her fascination with fish leather. The designer was Claudia Escobar, daughter of a Chilean fisherman, who had taken his discarded fish skins to a local tannery then used them to make clothing. She gave Jane a few pieces to experiment with. *I finally tracked down a supplier in Germany. They sent samples, colour charts and a price list. After that, I was unstoppable.* ¶ Jane's Indonesian supplier is less predictable, but no less inspiring. She asks for 50 skins at a time, pairs (both sides of the same fish) if possible. *The colours can be quite varied, but I have come to love the individuality. I start with an idea, but the hats tend to design themselves.* ¶ Everything about Jane is resourceful, imaginative and upbeat, epitomised by the 1920s wind-up gramophone she found at Portobello Road antiques market. After a few modifications to amplify the sound and finding three kindred spirits, The Shellac Sisters was formed. They DJ with their four gramophones (one wind plays one song) and vast collection of 78s, covering Charleston to rock 'n' roll, wearing vintage dresses and of course hats to match.

Deborah Carré

HAND SEWN SHOEMAKER

A hand sewn shoemaker at Tricker's inspired Deborah Carré to pursue the craft when the company sponsored the making of her degree collection. Her *Equus* boots were featured in *Vogue Hommes International* and Deborah received her first commission for actor Jaye Davidson on the film *The Crying Game. I knew then that I wanted to be a shoemaker.* For the next eight years she worked in public relations and took evening classes at Cordwainers College. Her tutor Claire O'Flaherty, one of the first QEST Scholars, suggested she apply. ¶ Deborah was awarded a QEST Scholarship to train with master shoemaker Paul Wilson; over four years, he taught her every stage of the hand sewn process. *I also learned to ride a motorbike for the 70-mile daily commute.* During her second year, James Ducker joined Paul as a John Lobb apprentice. James went on to work for John Lobb and Deborah worked as Atelier Carré until they founded Carréducker in 2004. ¶ From a studio in Cockpit Arts, decked with wooden lasts and leather hides, they specialise in the hand welted construction of London's renowned West End shoemakers. They also provide their bespoke service by appointment at Gieves & Hawkes on Savile Row and for country pursuits footwear at James Purdey & Sons. Brogued Oxford shoes to shearling-lined stalking boots, everything is made with tools and materials sourced from specialist businesses in Britain wherever possible. ¶ Their traditionally-made shoes are designed with a contemporary aesthetic. The simple loafers Deborah is wearing are made in Dashing Tweeds' *Red Raver* tweed, which is shot with reflective thread. *This is our summer resort shoe – understated for the day, but they catch the light at night, hence the name, 'Winkers'.* ¶ Deborah and James also work with artisanal manufacturers in the UK to create footwear for short run, ready-to-wear lines that are sold under their Carréducker London label. Launched via crowdfunding campaigns, they now have a range of *Barkan Desert Boots* from Suffolk, all-terrain Derbyshire *Tor Boots*, loafers made in Sheffield and slippers from Norfolk. ¶ In 2017, they were invited to be part of the first permanent exhibition at the Design Museum in Kensington, *Designer Maker User*, that explores modern design through these interconnected roles. A pair of Carréducker hand sewn Derby boots, *The Brunswick*, is displayed alongside the tools, materials and a film of the 200 plus steps that go into the construction. *It is gratifying to see our traditional craft in this dynamic environment.* ¶ Deborah has spent two decades listening to hand sewn shoemaking being described as a dying trade. *You know it is in trouble when US customs ask what you do, then say they didn't know people did that anymore. We beg to differ.* When Cordwainers stopped teaching the craft in 2006, James and Deborah took up the mantle and now offer a variety of pattern and shoemaking courses for beginners to professionals. ¶ Their students come from all over: Australia, Singapore, Japan, Malaysia, Ukraine, Brazil, USA and more. Some have set up their own shoe businesses or become lecturers; almost all continue making for friends and family. The blog that Deborah and James have written since 2005 and the shoemaking tools and materials that they sell on their website are used by people around the world too. *We're thrilled when we receive letters and emails with pictures of the shoes and boots they have made.* ¶ QEST Scholars Alistair Raphael, Frankey Pinnock and Maud van den Broecke are Carréducker alumni and Frankey is teaching with them too, running hand stitched leather goods courses at the Carréducker Shoe and Leather School that opened in Shoreditch in 2018. *We were outgrowing our studio. With this dedicated teaching space, we have reclaimed our original workbench exclusively for hand sewing shoes and boots for our growing coterie of loyal, bespoke customers.*

QEST Scholar 1997
QEST Thomas Fattorini Award for Excellence 2018

' *Turning my long-time hobby, of making armour for historical re-enactment, into a career would have been a fantasy without the QEST Scholarship. It enabled me to learn from a master armourer and establish my own workshop. I even had the chance to handle a 'sabaton' from one of Henry VIII's suits of armour along the way.* '

Graham Ashford

ARMOURER

On the left is Graham Ashford in workshop mode with his 1918 hammer in hand. On the right, he appears as a knight from 1360 AD, complete with visored bascinet and English gauntlets that he made in steel and decorated with brass. He is wearing his first attempt at sewing a reproduction Charles de Blois doublet (the only example to survive from the era) to which all the armour is attached. ¶ This is where Graham's second career began. He worked originally in IT and his antidote to sitting at a computer was indulging his passion for historical re-enactments. *My interest began before the internet. If you wanted equipment, you had to borrow a book from the library and figure out how to make it.* Graham started making for himself, then became the 'go-to' person for kit among his group. *I had a good job, but was aware that everything I was creating with an anvil and hammer in my shed was outlasting anything I was doing in the office.* ¶ In 2008, a redundancy package gave Graham the opportunity to see if he could create a business from his hobby. *I became full-time in my shed. When I look back at my early work I wince at the quality, but at the time I was chuffed to bits.* By then YouTube existed; there were a few metalworkers posting videos, but no armourers. He found a few bulletin boards that were useful to ask about metals and did a short course with an armourer (a gift from his wife), but it was a couple of chance encounters that changed the pace of his learning. ¶ Graham met Rupert Hammerton-Fraser in the beer tent at a re-enactment. *I was slowly turning myself from a blacksmith into an armourer and we chatted about it.* A couple of days later he received a call from Rupert, who had tracked him down to matchmake. *After meeting me, in another tent he had bumped into master armourer David Hewitt who had been bemoaning the fact that no-one wanted to learn the craft any longer.* The dots having been joined, Graham went to visit David in Chesterfield. *He offered to teach me at a reasonable rate, but with no income and anything I was making at that stage took me weeks instead of the days it was supposed to, I could only afford occasional tuition.* He made the decision to persevere. ¶ The Heritage Crafts Association suggested that Graham should apply to QEST. He took a bag of armour along to the interview and was awarded a Scholarship for the equivalent of 30 weeks of one-to-one tuition with David over three years, which they flexed according to what they were making. The level of skill required was bewildering to start with. *We worked in pairs, starting with a gauntlet each, as far as we could.* By the end, he had nine-tenths of the standard armour of a medieval fighter. *Early 14th century was my period as re-enactor so I could wear it; most people request 15th century.* ¶ Graham now works at his own forge, Greenleaf Workshop in Hampshire, making bespoke armour and iron goods for collectors, re-enactors, museums and living historians. He looks regularly at the hammer marks of original armour to check he is on track. The pair of steel 'poleyns' (knees) on the left are replicas for a customer from the *Effigy of Robert, Lord Hungerford* in Salisbury Cathedral, in Graham's view one of the greatest representations of 15th century armour in existence. ¶ He opens his doors to anyone wanting to try blacksmithing or armouring under his guidance and teaches helmet and gauntlet making regularly at West Dean College. Graham also has a mobile forge for public demonstrations, often visits schools, and once a year he can be found among many of Europe's best historical heritage craftspeople at the International Living History Festival in Essex. ¶ On the anvil in the centre is a replica of a Tudor child's breastplate that Graham is making for the Wallace Collection so young visitors can try on a replica of the original on display. *I would have been beside myself to wear this as a boy.*

Tom Sands

LUTHIER

QEST Garfield
Weston Foundation
Scholar 2014

A school friend of Tom Sands wanted to build an electric guitar for his A-Level design project. He had no idea how to go about it, but Tom was handy with a chisel and helped him in exchange for guitar lessons. They picked wood from a local yard and sacrificed a secondhand guitar for parts; it turned out surprisingly well. ¶ Tom continued to make instruments as a hobby during his Product Design degree at Glasgow School of Art and cabinetry apprenticeship with Wynn Bishop at Rupert McBain Studio in Durham. He was fulfilled working with wood and his hands, but could feel himself drifting more towards guitars than furniture. He wrote to makers and teachers to find out about training and Ervin Somogyi, father of the modern steel string acoustic guitar, offered him a two-year apprenticeship in Oakland, California. It was unpaid, but Tom was able to accept with the support of QEST. ¶ He worked with Ervin for six days a week, sometimes seven. *It was the most intense experience of my life, living and breathing as a luthier. I thought I was a perfectionist as a furniture maker, but he took my eye for detail to a level I didn't know existed.* Tom learned a deeper approach to design too by studying the lines, perspectives and proportions of Ervin's guitars. ¶ *We were also encouraged to make guitars to develop our own sound.* Tom built eight, all of which he sold. *I would like to have kept one, but QEST paid for my first year in California, the guitars my second; at least I know they are in the hands of people who play them all the time.* ¶ Tom now works in Ripon, North Yorkshire. He has converted his parents' garage, where he first picked up a plane with his grandfather, into a studio fully equipped for guitar making by commission. The most notable of the five currently under construction is for a leading collector using quilted mahogany from 'The Tree', which is legendary in the guitar world. Its remarkable pattern was discovered in a rainforest in Belize in the 1960s. Tom found a supplier who tracks down old furniture and boards of the timber and repurposes them as instrument grade wood. ¶ *I am taking this commission very slowly. The Tree is the rarest, most expensive wood on the planet and the grain is so highly figured, twisting through it like a concertina, that it needs a lot of gentle coaxing into shape.* Tom has selected master grade Swiss spruce for the soundboard (face of the guitar) and is preparing for the voicing, which gives the guitar its sound. This involves 'thicknessing' the soundboard and shaping the braces, the inner structure that withstands the pull of the strings and distributes their vibrational energy. *You are always on a knife-edge looking for the sweet spot, but I have learned from the best; the tone Ervin achieves is phenomenal.* ¶ Once this is complete and the glue is dry, Tom will slide the whole assembly out of the mould to add the neck, which is shaped to the client's hand. *It is the primary interface between player and guitar and has to fit like a glove.* After the decorative work, the guitar will be sent to a finisher in Northumberland for lacquering before Tom does the final set up: tuners, bridge, frets and strings. He likes to keep a guitar for a month after this to get a sense of how it is reacting as it opens up. *Adding the strings exerts 60 kilograms of tension and it takes a while for the wood to forget it is a tree, realise it is a guitar, and settle down.* ¶ Standing next to Tom is one of his speculative instruments in a mould. *These are my playground. I change one variable at a time to see how it impacts the sound, and experiment with aesthetics and ornamentation, which I like to keep understated.* Lending a hand on the next one will be Daisy Tempest, Tom's new assistant. *So many people helped me and let me shadow them, I feel it is important to do the same and am enjoying the progression from apprentice to maker and mentor.*

JoJo Wood

SPOON CARVER & CLOG MAKER

There is a photograph of JoJo Wood at four months old sitting on a shaving horse (a bench for green woodworking) with her mother, another aged ten on a junior version making wooden flowers at *Art in Action* in Ireland. Seven years later she turned her first wooden bowl (her father Robin is a founder of The Heritage Crafts Association and revived pole lathe bowl turning). By 22, she was teaching advanced spoon carving in the USA. ¶ *I grew up woodworking and was looking for a niche craft when the opportunity arose to learn clog making.* Clogs with hand-carved wooden soles and leather uppers were worn in Britain for hundreds of years. Today, there are only two expert traditional makers: Jeremy Atkinson and Geraint Parfitt. *My mother filmed Jeremy teaching Geraint for her PhD on passing on craft skills 10 years ago. He made a pair of clogs for her, which I started wearing and working on, teaching myself to re-sole.* ¶ QEST funded JoJo's apprenticeship with Jeremy. *I felt an instant connection handling the three stock knives, starting with the blocker, which I am holding here in my Birmingham workshop, Pathcarvers.* They can be remarkably delicate despite being a metre long. This first knife is used to block the soles in green wood (cutting to a manageable size like this would once have been done in the woods and the blocks transported to the city clog makers). *Jeremy uses mainly sycamore, but I work in alder and birch for now as they are softer and allow me to focus on technique.* Having dried in the cellar, the next stage is to rough carve the soles to a pattern made to an individual's feet. *Working to Jeremy's shapes was a good way to start; I am developing my own style too.* The top surface is then carved with the second knife, the hollower. Finally, the gripper, which has a v-shaped blade to cut rebates (where the upper is attached). *This was the most difficult tool I have come across. In the end, I set aside an entire day to practice on a pile of rejected soles; with constant feedback from Jeremy I got it under control.* ¶ The soles are tidied up with two small knives – one straight, one curved – in preparation for the leather upper. *Clog makers' lasts, the foot-shaped piece of wood that the leather is moulded over, are hard to come by, but I have been extremely fortunate.* JoJo has a set that belonged to Malcolm Huggett, who made beautiful dance clogs. His lasts and tools were packed away in a shed for more than 20 years until his wife Angela heard that JoJo was adopting the craft and gave her everything. ¶ The red clogs in the corner are the first pair she made completely. *The curve of the sole matches my gait perfectly, but as soon as I finished them I started to see flaws, which is as it should be. There was an awkward wrinkle on top, but I know how to prevent that from happening now; the making of every pair informs and improves the next.* She wants to learn leathercraft from shoemakers as well, so she can blend traditional wooden soles with a range of contemporary forms. ¶ JoJo has also been using the blocking knife for spoon making. *Although nothing beats the buzz of roughing out a pile of spoons with an axe, seeing each swing land exactly where I intend, wood chips peeling off under its razor-sharp edge and the form taking shape.* She has two favourite axes: one was an 18th birthday gift, the other is her own design as the perfect spoon carving axe for Wood Tools, a business she runs with her father. ¶ One of JoJo's dearest friends is another supremely talented spoon carver, Jane Mickelborough. JoJo was thrilled to discover that most of the clog making equipment that she inherited from Malcolm was given to him by Jane when he was starting out. *Taking a piece of wood and turning it into something useful for somebody is always a pleasure; it was extra special to carve a pair of bespoke clogs for Jane working with tools she had used herself many years ago.*

QEST Ernest Cook Trust Scholar 2015

Clare Pattinson

AUTOMATA MAKER

QEST Scholar 2015 The talents of illustrator, cartoonist and animator Clare Pattinson come together in the automata (mechanical figures constructed to move as if under their own steam) that she makes as Turner Handel Traditional Toys. ¶ Her first attempt was in 2011 for an exhibition, *What is Food?*. *How to configure the workings was a mystery initially, but I come from a 'make do and mend' family; if I wanted anything – stilts, rabbit hutch, go-kart, raft – I had to be resourceful and improvise.* She designed a combination of cams, cogs and levers to make *The Food Police*, three menu holders each with an officer chasing a thief escaping with their swag: steak, fish and baguette. On the reverse, she typed new verses to the song *Food Glorious Food*. ¶ Clare's artworks have a traditional British seaside feel and are constructed mostly from items she finds discarded on the streets of Margate or washed up onto the beaches of the Kent coast. Spokes and ball bearings from stray bicycle wheels come in handy, salvaging legs and spindles from broken chairs saves a lot of time turning wood, and the dowels from worn-out clothes horses provide a ready source of wooden shafts. *They're usually warped by the weight of damp laundry over the years, but I think this just adds to the quirkiness of a finished piece.* ¶ The source often inspires a design. A pool cue from a local pub became the shaft for operating the characters in *Cue Queue*: a line of people at a bus stop standing on grass made of green baize felt from a pool table. Clare likes observational humour too. The character in *Majors and Minors* (displayed on the right) is based on an old neighbour, Brigadier Lonsdale, who planted conifer saplings around the perimeter of his garden. *They stood in perfect lines as if on guard duty. I never saw him tend to them, yet there was never a branch out of place. I imagined an inspection by the Brigadier: when the figure salutes, the trees twitch and jump to attention.* ¶ In 2014, Clare launched a project on Kickstarter that generated 37 automata commissions from around the world. The final backer was an illustrator who wanted a gift for her husband to celebrate gaining his pilot's licence. She emulated her client's drawing style to create *Chocks Away!* with the couple taking off in a bright yellow propeller plane. *I enjoy being a co-conspirator and making mischief to surprise and delight the recipient.* ¶ Clare wanted to increase the interactivity of her 3D cartoons by devising more complex sequences and incorporating switches and sensors, so QEST funded a year at East Kent College. She took courses in mechanical and electrical engineering, by the end of which she could use a milling machine and turning lathe, and build a basic circuit board. *The welding course I wanted to do had closed, but the former tutor Frank White agreed to teach me privately how to do three types of welding and use a plasma cutter and grinders.* ¶ While studying, she wanted to continue making mechanical art, but nothing too complicated as she was absorbing so much technical information during the day. *I experimented with the humble clothes peg, which has a wonderful little spring mechanism.* On the table are Clare's peg-powered divers, bakers and a gardener: legs kick, cakes fly, pastry is rolled, hens peck and a wheelbarrow rocks. ¶ Clare has converted a camper van into a workshop: the bench running down the middle houses her chisels, mallet and manual pillar drill; there is a solar panel to power her fret saw; and the cupboards are packed with wood (lime for figures, scrap for cases), paints, springs, rivets, varnish and a supply of good coffee that she brews on the wood burning stove that she welded as a practice piece with Frank. ¶ *I can drive off and find a quiet spot to work or take Brook (the van) to shows around the country, as there is no substitute for letting people turn the handle and see the pieces crank and creak into life.*

Andrew Swinscoe

CHEESE MATURER & CHEESEMONGER

QEST Scholar 2010

When Andrew Swinscoe, a Culinary Arts & Hospitality graduate, was working in fine dining in the early 2000s, the cheeseboard in most British restaurants was almost entirely French. Whilst at the Michelin-starred restaurant at The Balmoral in Edinburgh, he asked their cheese supplier to arrange a research trip to France, which altered the course of his career. ¶ *I was offered an apprenticeship in the art of affinage (ageing cheese), which QEST supported to grow the craft in the UK.* Andrew spent eight months in Roanne learning about maturation from Hervé Mons, a 'Meilleur Ouvrier de France' (one of the country's best craftspeople). The Scholarship also covered an introduction to the science of cheesemaking at The School of Artisan Food in Nottinghamshire. The first maturation site he established was for a wholesale company in the West Country. *I was selecting Gruyère in Switzerland one day, helping to open a store in Qatar the next.* ¶ In 2012, Andrew and his wife Kathy opened their own shop to champion small, independent producers in the Yorkshire Dales. The Courtyard Dairy is now in its second location, near the market town of Settle, and employs 14 people. They stock washed rind, hard, soft and blue British farmhouse cheeses. The ageing is often finished in the shop so customers can see them whole; everything is cut fresh from these wheels. *On the shelf are Lancashire and Wensleydales, made originally to be eaten in the field; being Cumbria born, I grew up on their crumbly texture and gentle flavours.* ¶ The Swinscoes have four areas for maturation, with more to come. *I learned in caves, but our stone-walled barns and cool, slightly breezy climate work equally well.* More than 30 farmers have placed their trust in Andrew to age their cheeses. They tend to be made with unpasteurised milk from single herds of 70 cows at most. The rich, herbaceous Hebden Goats' Cheese comes from Gillian and Tim Clough, who farm just ten Anglo Nubian goats. ¶ The storage environment, day-to-day care such as turning, brushing and washing, and length of time vary according to each individual style, and even batch to batch. *Some are best sold young and fresh, cheeses like Cheshire are unlikely to improve after a few months – this is where my experience comes in.* Dutch-born Marion Roeleveld sells the floral Killeen Goats' Gouda that she makes in Galway from her 200-strong herd of Saanen goats at three months old. Andrew ages Killeen for another 11 months to develop the sweetness and bring through notes of roasted hazelnuts. *The results are interesting for us both.* ¶ There is a cheesemaking room and museum that connects visitors to the provenance of British farmhouse cheeses by showing how they are made, from raw milk to cloth binding. On display is a 19th century cheese press, cheese irons (used to take samples), and the 1912 notebook of Andrew's great-grandmother Mary Reid, a dairy maid. Her descriptions of starter cultures were discussed at their recent gathering of natural cheesemakers. *We are looking at ways for each maker to grow cultures that are specific to their locale rather than using generic, commercial varieties.* ¶ The Courtyard Dairy supplies top restaurants across the north of England (as this is the origin of most of their cheeses) and nearby pubs come in to buy local favourites. *It wasn't that people didn't want to offer British cheeses when I started; the quality and diversity didn't exist. You can now taste Britain at its finest, from the buttery tang of Hafod Welsh Cheddar to full-flavoured Vintage Sparkenhoe Red Leicester and creamy Stichelton, made to an old Stilton recipe.* ¶ Andrew and Kathy also help makers to find their place in the market. They might suggest something traditional or a new or hard-to-find cheese. *Either way, if we support the farmers at the beginning, we share the challenge and are all invested in making their cheese a success.*

Sally Mangum

CALLIGRAPHER & HERALDIC ARTIST

QEST Scholar 2007 Originally from Maine, calligrapher and heraldic artist Sally Mangum has lived in London for more than 30 years, since graduating with a degree in History of Art from Mount Holyoke College, Massachusetts. ¶ After nearly a decade of working with pen and ink, Sally was looking for a new specialist craft to expand the type of commissions she could take on. Browsing through the second-hand book stalls at Portobello Market one day she found the answer. *I reached for a well-worn copy of the 'Complete Guide to Heraldry' by A. C. Fox-Davies. Upon opening the cover, a stream of old handwritten letters and artist sketches tumbled out from between the pages. It was one of those serendipitous moments.* ¶ That same afternoon she searched and found a course at Reigate School of Art & Design where she could learn heraldic art and manuscript illumination, disciplines which have had a strong and colourful association with calligraphy for centuries. QEST supported her studies, during which she received prizes for calligraphy and illumination from the Worshipful Company of Scriveners and for heraldic painting from the Worshipful Company of Painter-Stainers. ¶ Sally has held a Royal Warrant as Calligrapher By Appointment to Her Majesty The Queen since 2006 and was recently made a Brother of The Art Workers' Guild, a body of around 350 artists, craftspeople and architects working at the highest levels of excellence in their creative professions. She focuses mainly on commissions for a handful of clients in London. These include calligraphy documents, illuminated vellum scrolls, pedigrees and heraldic work, as well as illustration and calligraphy for packaging and commemorative china. ¶ Sally has carved out a working space in the corner of her kitchen by the windows overlooking the garden to provide natural light. She perches on a stool at a tall, wooden workbench. *I tend to concentrate much better when my feet are off the ground.* If a deadline is not looming the work can become deeply meditative. *Sitting quietly at my desk, my breathing will slow to the rhythm of the pen or brush. Sometimes when I get lost in painting or thought, everything feels so still that I find myself wondering if my heart has stopped beating!* ¶ The materials and techniques that Sally uses are centuries old. She stretches calfskin vellum over a wooden panel, floats coloured pigments over its surface and mixes finely ground gold with water and gum arabic, burnishing to a shine with smooth agate – skills that date back to medieval times. *For calligraphy I use dip pens and have drawers full of bronze and steel nibs of all types and sizes – some manufactured recently, others around 100 years old.* Ink is ground on a stone daily by hand. For painting, there are fine sable brushes, gouache, watercolours and stacks of ceramic dishes and jars for mixing. Also to hand are tins of sharpened pencils, vintage drawing instruments and shelves crowded with reference books. ¶ Sally is deeply critical of her own work and always looking for things on which to improve. *Mastering a craft is a long journey. The further I go, the more there seems to be to learn and refine, but I hope this enables me to continue growing and improving as an artist.* In recent years Sally has begun expressing her creativity more freely in her spare time through oil painting (the ammonite fossils by her desk are a favourite subject). *Using large brushes is a welcome contrast from the fine detail of my commissions.* ¶ Whilst knowing it was an impossible task, Sally used to despair when seeking perfection. However, she has come to realise that one's work can be more beautiful for its slight flaws as they show the artist's hand. *Although I will probably always look at my work with an all too critical eye, sometimes, for a brief instant, I might appreciate the beauty in a single sweeping line or a delicately shaded leaf – and that brings joy.*

David Snoo Wilson

BELL FOUNDER

QEST Scholar 2016

Bells are one of the most significant and enduring instruments created. For centuries they have played a role in communication and ritual: markers of change from hours in the day to births, marriages and deaths and rung out to celebrate peace at the end of war. ¶ David Snoo Wilson used to live in an old pub. *When the time came to leave, I wanted to cast a bell to ring my final 'last orders'. The difficulty I experienced finding bell founders willing to share their knowledge made me determined to acquire the skills and make the craft more accessible for others.* ¶ David went on to establish Ore + Ingot, a Bristol-based travelling foundry, with Jo Lathwood. They run short courses teaching metal casting, make bells to commission around the world, and, when the foundry is at home, it is a hub for local artists. ¶ In 2014, David was awarded a Winston Churchill Memorial Trust Fellowship to visit central European bell foundries and witness the performance of international iron founders in Latvia. *This inspired 'Song of the Bell', a theatrical piece around folklore and myth with our foundry at the heart.* ¶ The more he found out, the more questions he had. *Bell bronze has been assumed to be the best alloy for the last three centuries, but I was curious to try as many variations as possible and experiment with variables in the casting process, from fuel type to cooling rate.* David's QEST Scholarship enabled him to conduct research with Marcus Vergette, one of the world's leading bell designers, into the harmonic consequences of adding new elements to the traditional bell mix. ¶ They created an archetypal pattern and played with different metal alloys and ways to temper the bells – heating to a rainbow of colours, cooling to discover the tonal changes in sound when struck. David, standing in a pair of old firefighter boots, welding leathers and a 1950s US Navy foul weather deck hat that he has appropriated for foundry work, is holding one of their experimental silicon bronze bells. ¶ The knowledge they gathered has had a major influence on David's bell founding. The metallurgical discoveries, bell founding rituals, and tales from the British Isles and beyond that describe the cultural importance of bells throughout European history come together in the Ore + Ingot live bell pours. ¶ At festivals including *Wilderness* and *Burning Man*, storyteller Nick Hunt narrates the process to the soundtrack of the roaring furnace as David and Jo make it happen. The temperature soars to 1100 degrees Celsius as the bronze is melted; alongside, the mould is heated. As the furnace is switched off, a moment of silence descends, laden with anticipation. The audience is asked to send good wishes as the red-hot crucible is carried to the mould for the final dramatic act: the pouring of the glowing, molten metal and the creation of the bell. ¶ Inspired by the reaction to the live pours, David launched Bespoke Wedding Bells. Guests are invited to add pieces of jewellery or metal with personal meaning to the bronze to create a bell and memories for the couple. This is based on a medieval custom of the travelling founder asking landowners for blessings and token gifts for the pot to give a new church bell a 'silvery ring'. ¶ In 2017, bell founding was identified as endangered on the Heritage Crafts Association Radcliffe Red List of Endangered Crafts. *This was a stark reminder of the obstacles I faced. I am working hard to ensure this traditional art endures in contemporary practice by creating new bells for new occasions, engaging as many audiences as I can, and by educating others in this magnificent craft.* ¶ David has taught bronze casting across Europe and at the City & Guilds of London Art School and Royal College of Art, where he introduced his students to making bells, and is a co-founder of the Bristol Bronze Club. With his strong survival instinct and fiery imagination, its future is in good hands.

Daniel Durnin

ARTIST MAKER

QEST Johnnie Walker
Scholar 2014

Artist maker Daniel Durnin is in his element standing in a field on the family farm in Oxfordshire with the Oxford Canal and River Cherwell in the distance. Off to his right, out of sight, is the barn he built with his father many years ago. In one half are the cows, in the other, Daniel's workshop with a curious collection of objects and tools squeezed around his grandfather's 1939 Austin 10. ¶ Daniel trained as a cabinetmaker at City of Oxford College's Rycotewood Furniture Centre and worked as a furniture maker before embarking on an MA at the Royal College of Art in Design Products. A QEST Scholarship funded his final year, which resulted in two projects that he continues to develop today. Daniel lived on a narrow boat while studying; walking along the towpath and stepping onto the water was his daily escape. He created *Water Bed: Mobile Architecture*, that can be towed along by a bicycle and floats like a rigid tent on water. *It is about the luxury of simplicity in an ever more pressured urban landscape; a chance to reconnect with nature by using the waterways often hidden in a city.* ¶ His other MA project uses a shotgun as a creative tool to make a unique piece of work and capture the instant of creation. The trace of the shot through insulation material can be used in reverse to fabricate objects: the stool next to Daniel is cast in aluminium and the glasses were blown in a clay mould. ¶ On completion of his course, Daniel was honoured to make a quaich with oak from Sandringham as a gift to mark Her Majesty The Queen's 90th birthday and patronage of QEST in 2016. *I had my visit to the Johnnie Walker cooperage in mind when I chose the oak, and thought about what the apprentices would be looking for when making a cask: no knots, no splits, nothing that would warp.* Daniel cut the wood to show the beauty of the end grain, charred the lugs, and mounted an engraved disc made of copper from an old Royal Lochnagar still onto the wooden box. ¶ In 2017, Daniel was invited to spend a month at the Venice Art Biennale as a British Council Fellow. The result was *Chandelier*, based on a Chinese-made inflated rubber tyre that he used as a vessel on the Venice canals, through which he examined the shifting dynamic between the trading and glass traditions of Venice and China as a manufacturing nation. This was exhibited in London alongside work made by the other 21 British Council Fellows. ¶ Back to the field...in the background are *Smokehouse* and *Stove*, which formed part of *Thought Beside Itself*, Daniel's installation for the Master of Fine Art collective show at the Ruskin School of Art in 2017. *'Smokehouse' was an investigation into preserving food and how we should engage with the environment, materials and natural resources around us and use craft skills to adapt these for the best way to survive.* For the cladding, Daniel split a fallen oak into ribbons with a 'froe' (the tall axe pictured) that he forged from an old lawnmower blade. This is the same method that the Vikings used to cut planks for shipbuilding, based on the desire of the wood to split and the froe deciding where. He used the bark chippings in the Stove to hot smoke cheese. Daniel employs the same wood-splitting process to make his vessels in the photograph, which he showed during London Craft Week. The inspiration came from Greek oil jars, but he allows the vessels to grow organically, the shape dictated by the wooden tiles. ¶ A little further up the hill in North Aston is the *Jubilee Bench* that Daniel was commissioned to make for his local village. Made in English oak, it is double-sided with a view across the valley from one seat and back towards the church from the other. The design of the divide evokes the distant wheat fields and long grass of the village green, which is left meadow-like for the local farmer's sheep as he has grazing rights. *I love to see people sitting chatting through the middle when I wander past.*

Imogen Woodings

UPHOLSTERER

Liverpool John Moores University Fine Art graduate Imogen Woodings worked in arts administration at Tate Liverpool and National Museums Liverpool, then for a mental health charity connecting people with community arts opportunities. She took evening classes in upholstery to keep her hands busy, satisfy her creativity and indulge her passion for fabric and interior design. ¶ *My day job was rewarding, but the opportunity to take voluntary redundancy gave me the time and money I had been looking for to start formal upholstery training.* This saw Imogen through the first stages of the Association of Master Upholsterers and Soft Furnishers (A M U S F) qualifications, for which she gained a distinction. At 35, there were no apprenticeship opportunities, so she volunteered with a local upholsterer to increase her knowledge of the trade. ¶ Imogen established Bluebird Upholstery in 2012. It was a steady start to self-employment, creating bespoke footstools and cushions and working on small upholstery commissions, but she knew that the A M U S F Level 3 Advanced Certificate in Upholstery, the gold standard, would enable her to offer a comprehensive, professional service. She studied on a Q E S T Scholarship at Kendal Upholstery (now the Oxford School of Upholstery). Over a minimum of seven weeks, Imogen had to undertake several compulsory tasks: a large, complex, traditional piece; a modern chair; and written project on the history of upholstery hide and textiles. ¶ Her traditional piece was a Victorian sofa, a family heirloom in need of attention. Imogen had to echo the curved, fluid shape of the frame with the upholstery to retain the elegance of the original design, change the configuration of the buttoning, and add lumbar supports. *I learned a great deal working on this under the guidance of tutor Blandine Bistoletti, especially the technical challenges of the sprung seat and deep-buttoned double back.* At seven weeks, Imogen had completed enough to be awarded a pass with distinction; it took another three to finish everything, including a detailed portfolio of notes and photographs to accompany her work. She maintains these records for every job and refers to them often. ¶ Imogen found premises hard to come by as they are being snapped up by developers, but discovered a shared space in the Georgian Quarter of the city. *I am lucky to have a light, airy, central location guaranteed for three years at a reasonable rent.* She is sitting outside her workshop in a 1960s Vono chair that she bought at auction and reupholstered from frame. It is covered in plain Havana by Warwick Fabrics, with hand printed linen on the outside back and arms from Rapture & Wright in the Cotswolds (the pattern, *Medina*, is inspired by a copper lamp brought back from North Africa). ¶ In the background is Liverpool Anglican Cathedral. This is the setting for the Winter Arts Market, an event that showcases original and handmade work from the 200 of the best artists, designers and makers in the North West. Imogen took a stall for the first time in 2017 to sell the soft furnishings she makes from her stockpile of vintage textiles. She tends to use these antique materials for decorative accessories rather than furniture, as durability is less of a consideration. *I made this blossom lampshade using a Japanese silk kimono remnant; I love the bold design and diaphanous effect with the light.* ¶ Traditional upholstery commissions often come with an interesting story. Last autumn, Imogen researched the maker's label, Heaton Tabb & Co., on a large wing chair that came in for a full rebuild. She discovered it was a quality furniture manufacturer in Liverpool, formerly known as A. Heaton & Co. Belfast shipbuilders Harland & Wolff had ordered furniture for the *Oceanic*, *Olympic* and *Titanic* before buying the company around 1930. *It was a nice piece of history to pass on to the customer with their restored piece.*

Q E S T Brian Mercer Charitable Trust Scholar 2014

[185]

Niki Simpson

DIGITAL BOTANICAL ARTIST

QEST Scholar 2003 Botanical illustration supports botanical science, which embraced computerisation long ago. Niki Simpson uses digital tools to create scientific images for 21st century botanists. ¶ She studied Environmental Science at Sheffield University before joining the Royal Horticultural Society at Wisley as a database administrator, then manager of the Herbarium image collection, which includes 3,300 watercolours and 30,000 transparencies. The paintings date back to the 1920s; from the 1940s, photography increasingly became the medium for recording the plants. *This led me to consider how today's technology could be used to create new descriptive data rather than simply digitising what already exists.* ¶ Niki was also establishing herself as a botanical artist with illustrations for *The New Plantsman* and received an RHS Gold Medal for her watercolour paintings. In 2004, wanting to keep pace with the academic side of her discipline, Niki presented her vision for digital botanical illustration to QEST. *It might have seemed futuristic, but they shared my enthusiasm for pushing my craft to achieve contemporary relevance.* ¶ Her main interest is in depicting British flora. Niki's innovative composite images are based on the traditions of botanical art from 'herbals' (the earliest record books) through lithographs, engraving and watercolours. Much remains the same, from finding, identifying and collecting a specimen to the measurement and observation of its colour and form. *Also in time-honoured fashion, I work with a botanist, Peter Barnes.* The evolution in her practice comes predominantly through the use of digital photography. She may also incorporate electron micrograph scans of pollen grains, computer drawings or scanned hand-drawn work. *It is still an artistic process: I work directly from life, there is a lot of hand-eye work, and composition is vitally important.* It can take months to build a picture of the diagnostic information and features shown by a plant throughout the year. ¶ Scientific images can convey complex botanical information to the viewer regardless of language, age or level of interest. Each illustration portrays the appearance of a plant, but to be truly useful, it also needs to tell a story: a botanical narrative of growth and reproduction. *Where pictures are inadequate for conveying features like smell or time of flowering, I include symbols, a time bar and minimal text.* ¶ The images have been developed primarily for on-screen use, where magnification can be used to explore micro-characters that would otherwise remain hidden. *I am working on how they can be viewed interactively so their dynamic potential can be fully realised.* There is also demand for her images in print. Niki was commissioned to illustrate *The Vegetative Key to the British Flora* and her briar rose was selected by experts as one of 300 outstanding botanical works of art for *Plant: Exploring the Botanical World*, published in 2016. Solo exhibitions include *PhotoSynthesis* at The Garden Museum in London and her work is held in major collections at the Royal Botanic Gardens Kew, RHS Lindley Library and The Linnean Society of London, the world's oldest active biological society. ¶ Niki has been a Fellow of the Linnean Society of London since 2005. In 2018, she was presented with the Society's Jill Smythies Award in recognition of excellence in published botanical illustrations in aid of plant identification. In the citation, she was described as 'a pioneer in the field of digital botanical art with an exquisite approach'. *I appreciate the open-mindedness of this traditional organisation in acknowledging the scientific relevance of my digitally-created work.* ¶ While her creative focus is on attractive detail and accuracy, the primary aim of these images is not beauty. *There is no place in my work for obscuring shadows or the charm of brushstrokes. I convey botanical truth.*

Jon Williams

CERAMIC SCULPTOR & ILLUSTRATOR

Art was everyday life for Jon Williams as a child (his father was an art teacher, his sister a sculptor). He would get up, switch on cartoons and make clay models. The figures he made of science fiction comic characters turned out to be his passport to art college. ¶It was there he got the chance to work with one of the *Spitting Image* puppet makers, realised his hobby could become something more, and discovered ceramics. A BA at Wolverhampton followed, then a postgraduate course in Derby, which included the opportunity to exhibit and hold a workshop at the City Gallery in Leicester. *I loved teaching and the ceramics I was making based on punk and skateboard subculture made it easier for me to connect with the younger attendees.* ¶Whilst self-employed running workshops at the City Gallery, Jon spent his spare time with the youth offending team at Charnwood Arts and Herbert Art Gallery in Coventry, which ran FIRE, a programme to engage children with a history of arson. *It was rewarding to see the turnaround, how firing their own ceramics became a source of pride.* ¶Keen to progress his own creativity, Jon applied to the Royal College of Art. This is where QEST came in, supporting his Masters in Ceramics & Glass. The most profound effect was one of scale. *I learned to create large figurative works and developed my anatomical knowledge through studying Italian sculpture at Biological & Medical Art in Belgium.* ¶Since graduating in 2014, Jon has established a ceramics practice, exhibited with fellow RCA alumni, and teaches ceramics at St Paul's School in Barnes. This enables him to live in London, which he documents in his work. ¶In the foreground of Jon's picture sits a dog made of oxide-glazed paper clay (the fibres make it better for modelling and create texture). This originates from *Kensington Mongrel*, a series of reflections on the London Borough in which he lived and studied for his MA. *On the streets I would see so many dogs: well-groomed pets of the wealthy and companions of the homeless. This black dog became a metaphor for the co-existence of affluence and poverty.* Jon revisited this idea after the Grenfell Tower fire in the area in 2017. *The two terracotta pieces are sketches I developed as my response to this devastating event, which brought back to me the social disparity in the area.* ¶Animals are a continual theme. *I get as much inspiration from city farms as I do the V&A.* He studies mannerisms – how a creature moves and eats – then tries to capture these qualities when sculpting to provide an inanimate figure with a sense of life. The fox in the photograph combines British urban wildlife with the concept of canopic jars, used by ancient Egyptians during mummification to protect organs for the afterlife. *I like the idea of works outliving a maker, how they can become a vessel in which their craft survives time.* Jon builds this sculpture by coiling terracotta, forming the skull then adding the muscle groups. Facial construction is the final step. *It's unusual to see my hand in the mirror here. I'm usually pulling faces to catch expressions. I'll then shape the clay until one glance says to me 'yes, this is true'.* ¶Comics, so influential in his early years, have become a meditation. Jon took a creative writing course at Imperial College, works on illustrations before the teaching day begins, and is pictured here modelling Evie, Hearth and Jan, the central figures in his comic book *Sum of Parts*. This stems from the autobiographical stories Jon wrote for his dissertation that look at his life in seven year cycles, based on philosopher Rudolf Steiner's theory of human development. The first issue combines fantasy with the adventures of his seven-year-old self through the eyes of his nieces and nephews. ¶Back to school: *It is a joy to teach. The children have wonderful imaginations and working with students with an interest in and affinity to ceramic sculpture is endlessly inspiring.*

QEST Garfield Weston Foundation Scholar 2012

[189]

Charlotte De Syllas

ARTIST JEWELLER

QEST Scholar 1992 *I steamed hats for Boo Field Reid, a 1960s milliner, and the radio was tuned to the cricket all summer. I knew nothing at the beginning, but listened avidly; proof that if you attend to something long enough, it gets interesting.* At Briglin Pottery, Charlotte De Syllas was combing the spines onto hedgehog figurines when a journeyman potter told her that to throw properly, you had to do it every day for three years, even on Christmas Day. Charlotte took these early lessons in sustained endeavour into her training and practice. ¶ In 1962, artist-jeweller Gerda Flöckinger C B E established a course in experimental jewellery at Hornsey School of Art. A year later, Charlotte, set to take up her place at Goldsmiths, changed her plans to be able to study under Gerda on this fledgling course. *There were only four of us and we just made and made; it was wonderful. She taught me, and so many others, to see jewellery as art.* Graham Hughes, Art Director at The Worshipful Company of Goldsmiths from 1951-1981, bought Charlotte's entire art school collection (there was a heart-stopping episode when she left it on a train in her mother's jewellery box, but it was returned safely). ¶ Charlotte attended evening classes in enamelling and engraving, but other than Gerda teaching her how to cut a cabochon, she is self-taught in stone carving. *Ultimately it comes down to practice and having the right tool for a job.* ¶ While lapidaries are solely interested in the cutting of gemstones, Charlotte has developed a signature approach of carving gemstones into ornamental jewels. This requires a deep understanding of the minerals and their crystalline form to ensure they remain intact. Charlotte also learned to hollow-cast glass on a QEST Scholarship to Wolverhampton University. She returned to stone as a medium, but the year in glass was invaluable as she had a chance to work with other people and gain from their expertise, as they did from hers. *Jewellers mostly work alone so this collaborative experience was wonderful.* ¶ Charlotte's work is made to commission with the personality of the wearer in mind; their stories are key to her vision for a piece. She first models in plaster or wood for the client's approval. Her colour palette comes from gemstones and hardstones and her distinctive carving reveals their natural beauty in organic forms: birds with wings widespread, flowers in bloom, sea creatures, and human heads in contemplation. *I am working here with a piece of chrysoprase, a bright green chalcedony that will slowly become a cactus-like necklace.* ¶ In 2016, Charlotte borrowed almost everything she has ever made for *Charlotte De Syllas: Jewellery in Carved Gemstones*, a retrospective exhibition of 74 pieces from over five decades held at Goldsmiths' Hall. These included the *V & A Shell Necklace* from the Jewellery Gallery at the Victoria and Albert Museum, and bespoke boxes made to hold her jewellery by lute maker, the late Steven Gottlieb. The poster piece for the exhibition was Charlotte's 1989 *Magpie Necklace* (pictured on her studio wall). It features two magpies flying in different directions, one in front, one behind, illustrating the folk rhyme: 'one for sorrow, two for joy.' It is made with black Wyoming nephrite jade, white Burmese jadeite, labradorite, silver and silk kumihimo braids. ¶ Students for her gemstone and hardstone carving summer courses in Norfolk are greeted by a studio full of grinders, carving spindles, micro-motors, files and polishing pastes. The house and studio was designed by Charlotte's late husband, architect Jasper Vaughan, and built with their sons Solly and Tom. Tom Vaughan, a furniture maker, was awarded a QEST Scholarship in 2018. *He designed the staircase; I love its simplicity.* Interestingly most of her major clients are architects. *They like modern jewellery and I think, being visually trained, they have the confidence to buy on artistic merit.*

Rodney Harris

SCULPTOR

Brick relief is an ancient art. The Louvre in Paris has a glazed terracotta brick panel QEST Scholar 1995 of a lion passant from the Processional Way at Babylon around 2,500 years ago and the British Library has early Persian Empire brick wall elements featuring archers and mythological creatures, excavated from the Palace of Darius I. ¶ These were uppermost in the mind of Rodney Harris when he returned to Bristol in the 1990s after an MA in ceramics at Cardiff University. He was looking to create work with a social purpose and to enhance the built environment. *If you live in the woods you use wood; I was living in the city, so bricks were the obvious choice.* Interest in this architectural craft was on the rise in the UK having fallen out of fashion in the 1960s, but most brick factories had destroyed their moulds and lost the skills. ¶ QEST funded six months of research on the factory floor at Ibstock Brick as they had a few workers nearing retirement who worked on reliefs early in their careers. They taught Rodney the old technique of hand pressing as well as modern manufacture with air-pressured tools to press the clay into the moulds, which is the method he uses as it removes air pockets so the bricks are more stable for firing. ¶ He likes the challenge of making engaging, public art that has historical relevance and stretches his imagination and technical ability. *The pleasure of relief sculptures is how they reveal themselves in different lights, appearing and disappearing throughout the day.* Rodney takes account of this in his studio. *I suggest the best elevation to a client then build an easel orientated to replicate the path of the sun while I carve.* ¶ Rodney continues to work with Ibstock on most projects and often collaborates with artist Valda Jackson. *Two minds are better than one and four hands divide the labour.* He is photographed by *The Washing Line*, a brick relief sculpture they created at the Shield Retail Centre in Bristol. This is their second commission at this former Victorian laundry after their glazed brick *Washing Machines* became a popular landmark. It is made using Ibstock *Cheddar Golden* bricks and modelled on Rodney's tennis kit (he had young hopes of playing professionally, but took up ceramics when he knew this would elude him). ¶ They are two years into a six-year project with the Peabody Trust in Clapham, London, documenting the social history of the 1930s estate in the brickwork of the redevelopment. They won the Marsh Award for Excellence in Public Sculpture for *Four Brick Reliefs* on the site, designed through consultation and clay workshops with the community: *Two Sinks* references the communal source of hot water; *Pinafores* the required dress to keep clothing clean; *Porter's Uniform* to remember the caretaker for every block; and *Garden Tools* for the allotments that sprang up during the Second World War. *We were proud when RIBA commented that these works were very moving and beautifully made.* ¶ Rodney is also a printmaker, using pigments and inks from dried clay and rock. His Leverhulme Trust residency at the University of Bristol in 2015 coincided with the bicentenary of the first geological map of Great Britain by William Smith. The original colours were arbitrary, so Rodney recreated it using pigments made with clay and rock samples from across England, Wales and Scotland, depicting exactly what lies beneath the surface. This led to *The Invisibility of the Sea*, a series of political, cultural and environmental maps based on bathymetry (the study of ocean floors) and pigments from seabed samples collected by scientists. *Their academic work is amazing and I love being able to communicate this in a visual, emotive way.* ¶ These naturally occurring pigments are often reflected in the vernacular of a place too – granite in Aberdeen, sandstone in the Cotswolds – which in turn informs the appearance of Rodney's poignant, contemporary, brick relief art.

Katherine Pogson

DESIGNER MAKER

QEST Scholar 2011 Trained as a designer in the theatre, Katherine Pogson enjoyed the costume research and hands-on making, and wanted to develop these elements into a studio practice. She specialised in leatherwork during an MA in Fashion & Textiles at the Royal College of Art and set up her own studio in 2000 to create limited edition accessories. *I was interested in exploring the tactile and sculptural qualities of my chosen material through a variety of techniques: moulding, gilding, stitching and print.* Clients included Mulberry Home and Hussein Chalayan and she published a book, *Complete Leatherwork.* ¶Losing a favourite emerald green leather glove was the catalyst for a journey of discovery. *I thought it would be complicated to make, but I had no idea how technical it would be until I started: which part of the skin for the palm; dealing with stretch; controlling the sewing machine in the tight space around the thumb.* A copy of *Practical Glove Making* (published in 1929) and a visit to the factory of Cornelia James helped Katherine to complete the pair. Making fitted leather gloves by hand is now a subject she teaches. ¶In 2005, Katherine set up Designer Courses to provide tuition in contemporary craft techniques and offer emerging designers bespoke training and consultancy on sourcing materials, range planning, working with manufacturers and pricing. *This is usually one-to-one and can be anything from helping someone to prototype an idea to supporting the creation of a small business.* ¶After a decade of hard work, Katherine felt like she was spending most of her time solving technical problems for clients. *I needed a creative fix.* She was awarded a QEST Scholarship for a series of short courses in skills that would enrich her handmade work and digital techniques to provide a fresh approach. *I spent months experimenting with decoration, laser cutting and screenprinting, which reignited my imagination.* ¶Part of this time was dedicated to rediscovering textiles, which have become the focus for Katherine today. She has embarked on a part-time PhD by practice at the Centre for Sustainable Fashion at University of the Arts London. Her research, 'The Companion Object', looks at how we connect with the environment through materials and making. *I wanted to think more deeply about the role of making at a time when human activities are increasingly impacting biodiversity.* ¶In 2016, Katherine completed a residency on the *NeedMakeUse* programme at the Pitt Rivers Museum in Oxford. She designed *Objects of Curious Construction* in response to the ethnographic collections and the lifecycles of moths and butterflies. Moths have become a motif within her doctoral research too. *People think of them as the enemy, but there are only four varieties that feast on our clothes; I want to turn the 'pest' idea on its head to highlight how many species are tumbling into extinction as we alter the environment that sustains them.* ¶Through light traps on the roof of her building in north London, Katherine has recorded the seasonal arrival of waves of different moths, their patterns influenced by the food they have eaten. *Last August, I opened one of the traps to be greeted by an array of bright, sunshine-coloured creatures; it was zinging. The photographs I took are the inspiration for the wall hanging I am working on here in my studio: 'The day everything was yellow'.* Katherine has hoarded fabric for years. She is working with these materials and threads – from her grandmother's saris and vintage silks from India to remnants from the cosmopolitan shops near her Finsbury Park home – to tell the symbolic stories of damage and resilience suggested by the lives of the moths. ¶Katherine continues to teach to earn the time in the studio to contemplate how re-thinking processes in craft can contribute to a narrative and set of alternative fashion practices that may help to reconnect us with nature.

Tomiwa Adeosun

CORDWAINER & FOOTWEAR DESIGNER

Photographer Irving Penn spent two years in the 1950s creating portraits of skilled tradespeople in London, Paris and New York, dressed in work clothes with markers of their occupation. This documentary work, *Small Trades*, inspired footwear designer Tomiwa Adeosun's MA show at the Royal College of Art in 2015. This was the culmination of four highly-pressured years. ¶ In 2011, Tomiwa completed his training to serve in the London Fire Brigade. This overlapped with the start of his footwear education at Cordwainers at London College of Fashion. The teaching at Cordwainers, originally an independent trade school, focused on design and technical skills with a link to London's historic manufacturing industry through related City livery companies. ¶ Tomiwa explored Northampton's shoemaking heritage too: he viewed the collections at the Northampton Museum & Art Gallery and Museum of Leathercraft, and took a short leatherwork course at the Institute for Creative Leather Technologies before enrolling at the Royal College of Art to study Fashion Menswear Footwear. ¶ In his second year at the RCA, adidas set a competition to redesign its *Forum* trainer, one of the most iconic styles from the 1980s. Tomiwa's design, with an asymmetric topline to bring to life the fluidity and 'flyness' of the breakdancing culture of the era, was one of five selected to be made. ¶ The idea for his final project was a bold combination of his traditional menswear footwear knowledge and cues from his occupation as a firefighter. *It was a huge relief when* QEST *agreed to part-fund my fees and enabled me to put the best quality into making my Masters collection.* ¶ Tomiwa studied the workwear in Penn's photographs, searched footwear archives in Northampton and at the Museum of London for archetypal work boots, and investigated the design and materials of firefighting equipment. He also worked with a fellow student to adapt and screenprint the texture of the non-slip, metal footplate of a fire engine onto leather as a motif to run throughout the collection. ¶ The eight boots surrounding Tomiwa form *Brother*, inspired by and named after the men on his watch at the Kings Road Fire Station: Coupe, Crowhurst (Spike), Epstein, Howe, Okoh, Renshaw, Simmons and Stephenson. *A big local character and historian, we called Stephenson 'Mr. Chelsea', so his had to be an edgy take on a Chelsea boot with burgundy fur replacing the elastic.* ¶ At the front are two conceptual galoshes with quick-release firefighter buckles. *Crowhurst*, on the left, represents Spike's 30 years of service protecting the public and has the Fire Brigade Union slogan 'Cuts Cost Lives' emblazoned on the sole. *Howe* on the right has a Velcro strap and clog sole for the younger upstart. ¶ Tomiwa is holding *Okoh*, the towering biker boot of the collection…and wearing adidas trainers. In 2016, Tomiwa was one of three footwear designers accepted into the adidas Design Academy. He has completed two years of rotations through the football, basketball, outdoor and 'originals' departments and visited the US design headquarters in Oregon, and factories in China. ¶ *I have a BSc in Sport Sciences that has been useful for understanding the biomechanical demands of each performance discipline and my traditional footwear training has helped to infuse craft elements into my designs.* Even with the reworked originals, the visual language might be familiar, but he has the chance to bring new vigour by exaggerating proportions, working with the materials team on new leather coatings and weaving with different yarns, and applying the innovative adidas concept of Futurecraft. ¶ Whilst the ethos of his firefighting career will always be an influence, Tomiwa has two major ambitions: to design a football boot that is worn at a FIFA World Cup and to establish his own men's lifestyle brand, perhaps with a reunion of his band of *Brothers*.

QEST Worshipful Company of Leathersellers Scholar 2015

[197]

Nick Gill

TYPEFOUNDER

QEST Garfield Weston Foundation Scholar 2013

As a musician, Nick Gill was simply looking to find a way of making sleeves for a CD being released by his eight-piece instrumental group when he discovered an interest in type. *We bought a second-hand tabletop press and, as I went about the process of typesetting and printing, I wondered if anyone was still practising this as a trade.* ¶ Phil Abel at Hand & Eye Letterpress was only a bus ride away from where Nick was living at the time in south London. Phil had started out in 1985, equipped with an Adana 8x5 press and an Arab treadle platen, a passion for good printing and a pile of typographic journals. Phil offered Nick two weeks' work experience. A few months later, a couple of big jobs came in and Nick went back to help. A year later, Phil acquired Monotype Composition and Super Casters, with the intention of being able to cast type under the same roof as a useful support to the letterpress work. *Running the casters is a complex skill; it used to require a seven-year apprenticeship, but I had to start by getting some actual jobs cast, and by asking retired Monotype instructor Gerry Drayton whenever I ran into trouble.* ¶ The Type Archive in London has a collection spanning the nearly 600-year period when foundries cut letters in steel, drove them into copper blanks, and cast metal type from them in an alloy of lead, tin and antimony. Thanks to the tuition of Parminder Kumar Rajput, Nick is one of two people in the world capable of making Monotype composition matrices from Monotype punches, and has worked at The Type Archive (on and off) for many years. ¶ The last English punchcutter, Edward Philip Prince, died in 1923. With the aim of supporting someone in the UK who could work to revive these lost skills, QEST provided the funding for Nick to travel to the United States to study with Stan Nelson, Museum Specialist Emeritus in the Graphic Arts Collection at The Smithsonian Institution. *Stan is a specialist in early printing methods, and he spent two weeks teaching me to cut punches by hand.* ¶ Nick returned to working at Hand & Eye and set up a computerised system to control the Monotype caster. His initial two-week stint stretched to seven years in total: setting type, making up pages, proofing, comping, printing and running the Monotype casters under Phil's expert eye. ¶ While working at Hand & Eye, Nick printed at home as Effra Press, named after the underground river flowing through south-east London. When his wife was offered a position at York University in 2016, he bought the typefounding machinery from Phil and moved to a village in North Yorkshire. Under the renamed Effra Press & Typefoundry, Nick continues to cast and sell letterpress type, leads and rules, provide hot metal typesetting to other printers, cut typographic punches, experiment with making paper by hand, as well as print broadsides, ephemera and books. ¶ Letterpress is undergoing a revival. *Those doing it as a hobby craft tend to be more interested in the look and character of old wooden type, but interest in new type is growing and Instagram is proving a good shop window.* Nick often announces what he is casting for people who are looking to build collections, and requests vary from the vague 'I am looking for something big and blocky for a poster' to the precise 'I need more 10 point Joanna'. He also casts large ranges of type for a number of universities and fine letterpress printers. ¶ Plans for the future include casting from historic matrices on restored pivotal casters, making wood type from new and existing designs, and cutting new typefaces and casting them as metal type. Nick continues to make music too, and while anyone can access the entire history of recorded music with no more than a few clicks of a mouse, his group's next LP will be housed in packaging made in the press, just as he started out.

Wayne Meeten

DESIGNER GOLDSMITH & SILVERSMITH

Having left school at 16 years old, Wayne Meeten started work renovating antique jewellery in the Brighton Lanes. He spent his mid-twenties travelling solo around Canada, Australia, New Zealand and Asia. On his return, Wayne returned to the fundamentals of his craft and enrolled at The Sir John Cass School of Art. ¶ *Intent on making the most of it, I waited at the classroom door every day to make sure I got the best seat.* In his sixth year, he began to experiment with the ancient Japanese technique of 'mokume gane' to blend his own metal. *The first sheet went like a dream, the next 20 split!* Wayne persevered with this technical challenge and won the top awards across all categories from The Goldsmiths Company, Jerwood and British Jewellers Association for his degree show and sold all his works. ¶ The Goldsmiths' Company provided Wayne with a grant to progress his mokume gane work through postgraduate study. *A Japanese tutor said I should go to Japan and meet Professor Tamagawa.* Wayne wrote to him and applied to several art colleges. *One response said I had applied to an all-girls school! They suggested I should contact Tokyo University of Fine Arts & Music (Tokyo Geidai).* He was accepted as a visiting professor, on the condition that he could speak Japanese. Two years later, he felt able to make a passable claim. After a year in Japan, he found out that Tamagawa had asked the tutors to send progress reports and was now ready to meet him. *I boarded the train to Niigata and arrived to several feet of snow…and a sign in the garden saying 'Welcome Wayne'. I was in awe holding his work in my hands; it was out of this world.* ¶ Tamagawa told him to save up, then come and spend a week with him. They started work at seven every morning and Wayne would sand sheets of mokume gane late into the night. *I mentioned that there must be an easier way and was told 'the metal will tell you when it is flat'.* Wayne was learning Tai Chi to aid his recovery from an accident. The soft, flowing movements of the martial art also had an effect on the expressive qualities of his work. Back in the UK, Wayne raised the sheets in the way he had been shown to create a collection for his first Goldsmiths' Fair. ¶ In 2014, he noticed that others were adopting a similar process and form; he decided that he needed to master another technique. Wayne got in touch with a contemporary from his studies in Japan, now living in Melbourne. *He emailed the Tokyo Geidai on my behalf and received a reply saying that they had been watching my work for 15 years and I was ready to come back.* ¶ Wayne has returned multiple times over the last four years on a QEST Scholarship sponsored by Pamela de Tristan (a conserver and restorer of Japanese prints and drawings) to learn uchi-dashi (a form of repousse, raising the metal with steel and wooden chisels) and inlay with Living National Treasure Katsuri Morohito and his assistant Naoko Tamura. They have requested that he should enter competitions in Japan, as they feel his work provides an exciting and different perspective on their techniques. ¶ Wayne has developed a wonderfully fluid style and is a master of the emotive qualities of silver. *Stillness in Flight*, a Japanese hammer-chased, silver vessel, was selected by The Goldsmiths' Company for its contemporary Buffet Plate, the first to be created in 700 years, and in 2018, Wayne received Gold at the Goldsmiths' Craft & Design Council Awards for his *Spirit of Energy* centrepiece that reflected the wonders of the sun. His originality, artistry and skill were all evident in the sunrise, sunrays, sunset and aurora borealis. ¶ Wayne is pictured at his studio in Devon with his work balanced on a piece of magnolia from the garden. *It is the perfect height and stops the energy going into the floor.* He is about to return to a university in Japan for a lecture, although this time Wayne will be the lecturer, presenting in Japanese.

QEST Pamela de Tristan Scholar 2014

Jonathon Kelly

CLOCKMAKER

QEST J Paul Getty
Jr Charitable Trust
Scholar 2014

As a production engineer on a factory floor, Jonathon Kelly was used to sorting out technical issues, but stepping up the career ladder meant he was becoming less hands on. He took the opportunity of redundancy to get back to using his hands. ¶ Like many engineers, Jonathon was interested in the workings of mechanical watches and the history of timepieces. In 2009, he enrolled on the three-year course at Birmingham City University's School of Jewellery that follows the syllabus and examinations set by the British Horological Institute. The first year was a general introduction to watches and clocks. *This is when I discovered an appreciation of clocks and realised I would prefer the working environment this would lead to; this settled my second-year specialism.* On completion of his studies, having learned many essential skills and processes such as bushing, turning on a watchmakers' lathe and soldering, he started taking on repair work. ¶ A year later, Jonathon saw that West Dean College near Chichester was looking for a recently-qualified clockmaker to assist lead conservator Malcolm Archer with the restoration of the *George Pyke Organ Clock* (dated 1765) from Temple Newsam House in Leeds. The near eight-foot-high clock had an automaton dial with layers of painted, moving scenery and an organ barrel, believed to have been re-pinned by Jos Gurk (an associate of Haydn) in 1817 to play eight new tunes; the only way to identify them was to return the clock to working order. Jonathon undertook some of the repair work and documented every step of the five-month project. ¶ Whilst working at West Dean College, Jonathon applied for a place on the Postgraduate Diploma in the Conservation of Clocks & Related Objects, on which the emphasis is teaching through practical conservation over theory. He was accepted and awarded a QEST Scholarship for the year-long course. *It was an intense period, but I found the work to be greatly rewarding and it led ultimately to my current job at Carter Marsh & Co. in Winchester.'* ¶ Jonathon is standing in the shop of this antique clock and watch specialist. In the background are longcase clocks in ebony by Thomas Tompion and burr walnut by Daniel Quare and in front are table clocks by George Graham and Henry Jones. There are five craftsmen in the workshop. Gerald Marsh still comes in a couple of days a week (he started in 1950), and Jonathon is mentored by Roger Still, one of the most skilled restorers in the country with more than 50 years' experience. ¶ *There is a lot of variety to my work: from the most humble and simple to complicated clocks; some very valuable, others not worth repairing from a financial point of view, but their sentimental value makes them priceless to the owner and worth every minute.* Jonathon has worked on three by Restoration-era English clockmaker Joseph Knibb: a lantern clock; longcase regular striking clock; and a Roman striking longcase clock, which was the first on his bench at Carter Marsh & Co. Knibb is known as the inventor of Roman striking. *A small bell is struck for 'I' and a larger bell with a lower tone represents 'V': for example, four o'clock (IV) is struck by a high note followed by a low note; 11 o'clock is two low notes followed by a high note.* ¶ Another stand-out commission was a Victorian-era, German clock. The movement had an unusual calendar mechanism. It could keep track of the day, date and month throughout the year, but had stopped working because the original date ribbon had perished. *I had to research the old font, match the colour and find somebody who could custom-make a short length of ribbon. Replacing it and returning it to the owners in working order was very satisfying.* ¶ Jonathon also feels privileged to see some of the rarest clocks that come through the shop, such as a 17th century lantern clock by William Bowyer, even if he is not working on them…yet.

Christabel Helena Anderson

ICONOGRAPHER

QEST Scholar 2011

Christabel Helena Anderson is an iconographer who creates holy icons painted in egg tempera on wood panels, illuminated miniatures on vellum, and vitreous enamels. Her first encounter with iconography came in her late teens when her family moved to France, settling near an Orthodox Christian monastery high in the mountains. It was a tiny, closed community, but their profound humility, gentleness, dedicated work, and collection of icons (some rescued from the Russian Revolution) made a lasting impression. ¶ Searching for her true artistic path, Christabel took a degree in History of Art & Archaeology at the School of Oriental & African Studies in London. She then spent time in Canada as an artist and working with a traditional animator who drew every frame by hand. *I learned to execute rapid studies of people and was encouraged to draw and paint in all places.* This led to a focus on portraiture, which continued when she moved to Italy in 2001. Surrounded by the art of the Etruscans, Romans and multitude of forms of Christian and Byzantine art, she began to reflect on the disjunct between these earlier arts and European and British culture today. She read about the destruction caused by iconoclasm during the Reformation, which resulted in a new artistic culture from the 18th century. *I wanted to learn more, although this was a difficult task with no living artists and a scarcity of objects to study.* ¶ Christabel went in search of primary source material in UK churches, ruined monasteries and museums, and also studied the theological and art historical background. The realisation grew that she must dedicate her time fully to this work for God, and this led to her conversion to Orthodox Christianity. In 2008, she was accepted to study for an MA at The Prince's School of Traditional Arts (now part of The Prince's Foundation), which offers the most in-depth training in icon painting to be found west of Greece, and from which she graduated with distinction in 2010. ¶ She then established a studio where she works principally as an iconographer. The designs and methods of the work are inspired by the glorious treasury of Orthodox iconography and the sacred art of Britain and Ireland from the late antique and early medieval periods. The images are stylized, the deified persons contemplating divine reality, wearing appropriate garments and, if they founded a church or monastery, holding an architectural object. *I painted St Moluag, a sixth century Saint of Scotland, holding a 'beehive' monastic cell and his crozier (still owned by his ancestors).* ¶ Christabel uses exactingly prepared materials. *I make paints according to ancient methods: grinding stones such as malachite, cinnabar and lapis lazuli on the mulling slab in front of me.* In addition, she is a specialist in gilding, early quill written letterforms and handmade inks. She also incorporates 24 carat gold leaf and gemstones such as rubies, sapphires and pearls. To increase her knowledge in this area, in 2011 she was awarded a QEST Scholarship to study for the Accredited Jewellery Professional Diploma at the Gemological Institute of America. ¶ Her teaching is primarily in the subjects of gilding and manuscript illumination. In early 2018, she taught at The Queen's Gallery in Buckingham Palace during *The Charles II: Art & Power exhibition.* People came from around the world, including Doha and Hong Kong, to learn gilding on stone, paper, vellum and moulded plasterwork, exploring the theme of the ceiling as a luminous and Heavenly space. In the photograph, she is grinding minium, an ancient pigment used to make watercolour paint, which will be transferred into a seashell (there is an assortment in the corner) for a lesson in illumination. ¶ Icons, however, remain the focus of her practice, each one prayerfully researched, designed and created in the tradition of the Holy Orthodox Church.

Hayley Gibbs

STONE CARVER & SCULPTOR

QEST Kirby Laing
Foundation Scholar
2016

Stone carving has a powerful draw; I felt like the craft found me. Visiting friends at The City & Guilds of London Art School, Hayley Gibbs knew that she needed to train there. She had studied Fine Art Sculpture at the University of Brighton and was making props and sets for theatre and high-end retail installations. *This involved casting and sculpting on a large scale, but the more successful the business became, the more removed I was from the making.* ¶ The artistic and manual skill of stone carving and the permanence of the result contributed to the allure for Hayley. She spent time with artist Corin Johnson to see if the reality of working in stone suited her; there was no doubt. In 2014, she began the City & Guilds Architectural Stone Carving Diploma, funded by continuing to work around the course. *I was fully occupied mentally and physically: from anatomy and geology classes to creating giant Rubik's Cubes for a client.* QEST paid her final-year fees to relieve the pressure so Hayley could commit fully to the course. ¶ *The relief was coupled with an intense feeling that I needed to learn as much as possible from my final project. This was not the time to play it safe.* She made a list of things she wanted to incorporate: historical research, figurative work, drapery, ornamental detail, masonry and engineering to handle the logistics of working at scale in stone. The risk paid off. After three months of designing and five months of hand carving, she assembled the three sections of a two-metre, 19th-century-inspired column featuring Telamon (a character in Greek mythology). ¶ The School also provided exposure to live commissions and encouraged the building of a professional network. Sculptor Raphael Maklouf, who runs one of the leading private mints in the UK and is best known for his effigy of Her Majesty The Queen on many Commonwealth coins, visited in search of craftspeople with the carving skills. *After looking around The Tower Mint I asked immediately if I could work on a relief.* Hayley was soon pouring a circle of plaster to create a replica of James I for the Janvier machine, which scales the cast to coin-size for stamping. *I loved the combination of art, craft and trade.* ¶ Hayley was delighted when Raphael asked her to collaborate on a life-size, bronze sculpture of William Shakespeare for the site of The Theatre in Shoreditch, which opened in 1576 and is where the playwright and actor learned his craft. The salvaged timber from its deliberate destruction (the owner fell out with the landlord) was moved to Bankside where it was used to build Shakespeare's Globe. ¶ Hayley and Raphael visited The Royal Shakespeare Company to select an historically accurate, Elizabethan outfit for their life model. *Shakespeare would have been in his thirties when he was at The Theatre, so we are making him appear younger than the familiar Droeshout engraving of 1622 in the background, but still capturing its essence.* On the advice of experts Carolyn Addelman and Ella Hawkins, they made the ruff based on a small, soft fabric design he is likely to have worn at the time. ¶ Craftspeople are physical by nature; verbalising what they are doing does not always come naturally, but Hayley and Raphael found a way of working and rhythm that was rewarding for them both. *Working clay is very different to the subtractive nature of stone and there is room for experimentation as it is applied and manipulated.* The armature to hold the clay was designed to provide stability at the core, but flexible enough to reposition the limbs as they finalised the composition. Her City & Guilds training came into play throughout, from life drawing considering the all-round view to making the fabric appear as if reacting to the anatomy beneath. While overseeing Shakespeare being cast in bronze at the foundry, Hayley is returning to her architectural carving practice with a new string to her bow.

Tom Adams

ORCHARDIST

The apple varieties of the once great orchards around the Welsh borderlands are QEST Scholar 2009 undergoing a revival; orchardist Tom Adams is part of this rescue mission. His first job as a gardener made him see the fruit trees on his cousin's Shropshire farm, which he had been visiting all his life, in a different light. ¶ *I was interested in pruning methods, which made me look more closely one day. There were several varieties I couldn't place, so I sent samples to Mike Porter, a botanist for the Marcher Apple Network that identifies and propagates rare apples and pears in the area.* Three of Tom's family's apples had not been seen for over a century: *Gipsy King, Round Winter Nonesuch* and *Bringewood Pippin*. This was in 2004. *We propagated from these trees, they grew well and are now sold from my nursery.* ¶ Tom established his one-acre fruit tree nursery in Oswestry, Shropshire in 2010 after a QEST Scholarship to learn from horticulturist Tony Gentil at his Cheshire orchard and nursery. They covered a range of practices: propagating rootstock, budding and grafting, winter and summer pruning, pest and disease management, soil analysis, plant physiology, orchard surveys, and fruit storage. *It was a particularly good year for plums and damsons, but these trees have a weak branch structure and snap easily when fully laden, so we propped them up with canes, known as 'May polling'.* It was not quite long enough to see all the results (for example, from sewing mistletoe seeds onto the branches of unproductive pear trees to encourage them to bear fruit), but having this all-round experience through every season was excellent preparation for Tom to set up on his own. *It also affirmed my view: biodiversity rules! Aphids love fresh, sappy growth, so applying high nitrogen fertilisers can be counterproductive; planting wild flowers among the trees and providing a habitat for lacewings, earwigs, ladybirds and hoverflies is a much friendlier and more effective way to protect an orchard.* ¶ Tom continues to work with the Marcher Apple Network, which has invested a lot of time and money sending leaves for DNA testing. When they find a unique variety, it is saved from extinction by Tom and another nurseryman, who propagate two copies for five different orchards, including ones belonging to the National Trust and HRH The Prince of Wales, to ensure a healthy spread. Another of these locations will be Tom's six-and-a-half-acre plot of land that he is cultivating for the Welsh Marcher Collection and to give more space to the heritage and modern varieties of apple, pear, plum, damson and cherry that he sells as bare root trees for traditional orchards, small holdings and home gardens. ¶ *I have always followed organic practices and plan to apply for official certification as an organic producer at this new site.* To this end, Tom is planting to attract natural pollinators and predators. High on the list is an evergreen shrub, *Elaeagnus*: it fixes nitrogen into the soil; bees love its flowers; the dense foliage can form a windbreak to create a better microclimate; and it produces small, edible berries. The increased acreage will allow for proper rotation (beds should be dormant for seven years before replanting). *I am also going to establish a field laboratory to work with forward-thinking farmers on experiments such as willow wood chip for the prevention of scab, a fungus that can spore in bark and fallen leaves.* ¶ In the winter, Tom runs sessions on pruning and grafting at his nursery, local community orchards and schools, and for allotment societies. He also teaches a day on pruning restricted forms – espaliers, fans and cordons – for The Orchard Project, a national charity for the creation, restoration and celebration of community orchards. Through the summer, he holds occasional green woodworking workshops, including a handy project for anyone buying his apple trees: how to make a cider press.

Jenny Pickford

ARTIST BLACKSMITH

QEST Scholar 2010 *Steel can be a sewing needle or a skyscraper and so much in between.* Originally a fine art student, Jenny Pickford was in awe of the material from day one of a blacksmithing workshop at The Rural Crafts Centre of Herefordshire & Ludlow College (despite her first attempt – a terribly made toasting fork). ¶ She took a two-year course at Hereford College of Arts to explore its artistic potential. *Running steel through the forge, heating the bar and manipulating it under the power hammer or on the anvil, I felt the metal wanted to come alive and take on beautiful organic shapes.* A taster session in glassblowing completed the picture for Jenny. *I could visualise large-scale sculptures of flowers and plants combining galvanised steel with spectacular blown glass.* ¶ QEST funded a three-week summer course at the Pilchuck Glass School. Artists from all over the world gather at this campus in the foothills of the Cascade mountains in a remote corner of Washington State. *It was the perfect setting in which to investigate ways to harness the beauty of nature in my chosen materials.* Jenny got to understand the process thoroughly so she could brief studio glass artist Stuart Fletcher to make to her specifications back in the UK. ¶ She is standing in her forge in Herefordshire with 'Goliath', a power hammer that exerts six tonnes of pressure per square inch. It came from blacksmith Ivan Smith, a legendary tool-maker for the glass industry. *If you mention his name to any glassmaker of note, they show you at least one piece by Ivan; I often wonder how many careers his tools have made over the years.* The hammers and tongs are her own handiwork, made during her training. ¶ Jenny creates installations that have dramatic impact, yet are in harmony with and have a meaningful attachment to their location. A Hong Kong art consultant contacted her about a public art commission for Chengdu, the capital of Sichuan province in China. She made and installed a four-metre sculpture, *Hibiscus City*, in response to the story of King Mengchang ordering hibiscus to be planted on the walls in the 10th century. At the Chelsea Flower Show, Jenny met visitors from a garden centre near Melbourne who invited her to create a sculpture for their exhibition *Eden Unearthed. I flew to Australia with a flat-pack, giant agapanthus to assemble.* Her work has graced the grounds of The All England Lawn Tennis Club during The Championship for the last few years; in 2018, they ordered a custom-made, three-metre allium in classic Wimbledon purple that is now on permanent display. ¶ A year ago, Jenny was asked by the Nightingale Macmillan Unit in the Royal Derby Hospital to create a sculpture that would act as a 'signpost' to the entrance. She worked with the palliative care team and patients, who decided that bluebells would be a soothing choice. *I received a letter to say the sculpture had also been a beacon of hope for a suicidal patient, who commissioned a painting of it as a positive reminder when they got home.* ¶ Jenny loves the simplicity of wild flowers and says even dandelions, one of the most common weeds, can create a stand-out piece. *The natural world, particularly in spring, is an endless source of creativity.* Waterperry Gardens in Oxfordshire, home to the School of Horticulture for Ladies from 1932 to 1971, was the inspirational setting for *Supernature III*, her solo exhibition in 2018. Jenny made 20 striking works that were set through the eight acres of formal gardens, meadow, woodland paths, water lily canal and arboretum. Her sculptures are not designed to be in galleries; the cold, industrial steel comes into its own outside with sunlight pouring through the glass, pooling colours on the ground and reflecting the surroundings. *The light changes the effect all day and there is often a dramatic moment when the sun dips in the sky, but as an artist, I try to make people look up into the light.*

Rebecca Hellen

PAINTINGS CONSERVATOR

Rebecca Hellen started her career at art college, but it was during her BA in History of Art at the University of Bristol that she had a lightbulb moment. She spent the second year studying Titian; and her research led her to technical bulletins published by the Conservation Department at The National Gallery. *The more I read, the more I could envisage myself in that world.* Rebecca chose 'conservation controversies' as the subject for her dissertation and, after graduation, took classes in Chemistry for Conservators while working for a restorer in private practice. ¶ She was accepted onto the Postgraduate Diploma in Conservation at The Courtauld Institute of Art. *I saved enough for the first year, at the end of which I had a strong enough portfolio to apply to QEST; they agreed to cover the remaining fees.* There were four tutors and only five students in each year, ensuring a high level of scholarship and craftsmanship was passed on. Rebecca inherited a project: *Dream of the Virgin,* the pinnacle panel of an altarpiece by Simone Dei Crocefissi from 1380. X-radiography analysis showed the background, tooled in gold to depict Christ on the tree of life, had been overpainted in 'gesso', a preparation layer for a new composition of Christ on the cross. *I removed the 19th century scheme and conserved the original to restore the iconography with the late Caroline Villiers, a brilliant tutor, as my mentor. The panel is now at the National Gallery; I pop in occasionally to have a look.* ¶ The Leverhulme Trust sponsored Rebecca's next post at the Liverpool Conservation Centre before she joined Tate in 2002. The senior team at the time were key innovators. *They had made some of the biggest ethical leaps of the previous decades; I am fortunate that my career overlapped with them.* Their concepts are everyday practice for Rebecca: preventative conservation, secure packing for travel, and the artist interview. *This sounds obvious, but they were the first to talk to artists to find out the details of their studio practice and feelings about intervention.* ¶ On the microscope table, for examination under normal and ultra-violet light to identify varnishes, pigments and technique, is a painting by John Singer Sargent. *He trained in Paris, but moved to London when his painting of Madame X scandalised the city.* The artist was the subject of a six-year study by Rebecca and Tate conservation scientist Dr Joyce Townsend, exploring evidence such as mark making and sequences of painting. Their essay, *The Way In Which He Does It: The Making of Sargent's Oils,* was published in Volume IX of the *Catalogue Raisonné.* ¶ Rebecca and Joyce also conducted a study of Turner. *One area that fascinates everybody, but had not been looked at from a technical point of view, is his 'Varnishing Day' practice at the Royal Academy of Arts.* After a work was selected for the Summer Exhibition, it was hung by committee. Varnishing Days were an acknowledgement that its position would affect how the artist wanted to finish their painting. *We looked at Turner's exhibited artworks and historical records to understand the physical evidence behind the embellished stories about Turner using this time to alter his work.* ¶ For Rebecca, Tate remains a forward-thinking environment. *I have opportunities to navigate research into new methods of cleaning, such as the use of gels and even lasers. Our aim is always to establish the least invasive treatments for the original surfaces we treasure.* ¶ My instinct at Bristol was right; it is a fascinating craft with global reach. The Getty Conservation Institute runs COOL, a busy online forum, conferences by industry bodies such as ICON (Rebecca is a trustee) are well-attended, and in the museum world, conservators often act as couriers. *This provides an opportunity to engage with international colleagues and, given the shared appreciation of art, can also be an act of soft diplomacy.*

QEST Spink & Son Scholar 1996

Steve Tomlin

WOODWORKER

QEST Adam Connolly
Memorial Fund
Scholar 2013

The Steve Tomlin way has always been to find something that interests him (invariably a woodland craft), fathom how to do it, and hand on the knowledge. ¶ Take scything. He first mowed while working in the Pyrenees in 2001. He was given a scythe, but not a word of instruction. *I made a start, mesmerised by the effortless rhythm of the old French farmers, moving as if they were simply strolling along.* He volunteered for meadow conservation projects in the Czech Republic and Transylvania, visited factories in Austria that were importing scythes into the UK, and is now one of this country's leading experts and instructors. ¶ Steve has taught for the National Trust, The Wildlife Trusts, Natural England and at Highgrove, and written a manual, *Learn to Scythe*. He spends May to September running classes in fields, allotments and community orchards across England and Scotland. It takes a little time to master, but a scythe is cheaper, lighter and safer than a strimmer – and quieter too, just the swish of the blade and birdsong. *People arrive in the morning not knowing which way up it goes; we end the day mowing a meadow together.* Every June, Steve can be found teaching at the Green Scythe Fair in Somerset. *Nowhere else will you hear the word 'snath' (handle) quite so many times or the music of dozens of people hammering on tiny anvils to sharpen their blades.* ¶ Steve is also fascinated by crafts that originate from the properties of different trees. Having grasped the fundamentals of green wood carving for kitchenware, he applied for a QEST Scholarship to further his use of this skill. *I spent three weeks studying and working in Sweden with Fritiof Runhall, who has been an inspiration since I attended one of his spoon carving masterclasses in 2011.* Steve also visited the Skansen open-air museum and Nordic Museum in Stockholm for their woodenware collections and spent a day with Ramon Persson, a maker of birch bark boxes. The trip honed Steve's carving, design and decorative techniques that he displayed in a new range of carved bowls. ¶ *I also love how the ash tree lends itself to a style of making.* It grows two layers each year, one more porous than the other. Steve hammers the logs to separate these annual rings into ribbons of wood, known as ash splints, that he uses for basketmaking. Greta Bertram, compiler of the Heritage Crafts Association (HCA) Radcliffe Red List of Endangered Crafts, was given one of Steve's creations on completion of the research in 2017. This drew his attention to the report; he read down the crafts categorised as most at risk of extinction as though they were a to do list. *I spotted the name of a former colleague, Mark Snellgrove, as the only remaining maker of Devon stave baskets.* Steve contacted him to find out more and a year later received the HCA Marsh Endangered Crafts Award to learn to make this agricultural basket from Mark. ¶ Steve is pictured constructing his fourth Devon stave basket. They are unusual in being built from solid wood rather than woven: the side staves are individually cut, shaped and fitted with copper nails to a curved rim of bent ash and wooden base. *It says something about the precarious nature of the craft that, only three-and-a-half baskets in, I am the second most experienced maker in the country, the first being my tutor.* He is getting a feel for how to hold the basket as he builds and starting to think a stave or two ahead of the one he is fixing. *I think this one will be good enough to sell. Next on my mind is getting to the stage where I am sufficiently practiced to teach others.* ¶ This approach has stood him in good stead, as has the outdoor-indoor nature of his year. *After a summer of scything, my workshop in Manchester provides shelter for a winter of spoon, bowl and basketmaking. It is also a quieter time, in tune with the season, to explore techniques and look for my next challenge.*

Alan Floyd

COACH BUILDER

Keeping cars in immaculate condition has been an obsession of Alan Floyd's for as long as he can recall. *I have around 70 toy models from my childhood that look box-fresh, even though they left the Corgi factory more than 50 years ago.* His father repaired cars as a hobby and Alan would sit on the workbench, goggles on, taking it all in. *I watched him work on a pre-war Bentley. It was used as a runaround then; it would be worth a fortune now.* ¶ When Alan left school in the 1970s, the north of England was dominated by heavy industry. Having been taught to weld at an early age by his father, he did his first official welding course with the Coal Board, worked there as a heavy metal fabricator by day, and restored classic cars at the weekends. Coach building was a rare craft even then and he could not find anyone nearby to teach him what he needed to know. ¶ By 1985, he had accumulated sufficient knowledge to set up his own business in Worksop, Nottinghamshire, taking on single panel repairs, historic race and rally car preparation, and entire body rebuilds using traditional techniques: panel beating, wheeling, oxy-acetylene welding and riveting. Whenever he could afford it, Alan would spend a week with Geoff Moss at MPH Motor Panels to refresh and advance his skills. In 2015, 30 years on, Alan felt he needed to invest in a block of instruction to consolidate his decades of experience and be confident that he was offering a first-class service. *Geoff is a former Aston Martin panel beater and one of the best coach builders in the world. It made such a difference being there day in, day out on a QEST Scholarship – the finer points of his technique are so instinctive and subconscious that the only way to pick them up is to work alongside him.* ¶ Alan now specialises in the manufacture and repair of hard-to-find or non-existent panels and complete body shells. Good hammers with a hard, perfectly smooth face are important. Alan's first job every morning is to clean and polish them, as any little nick will show on the body. *You also need your hands to feel for any dimples or bumps when making panels, as your eyes can deceive you.* Some hand tools are difficult to get hold of, particularly the wheeling machine (used to turn sheet metal into compound curves). *I drove all the way to Cornwall to buy one for my workshop; it probably dates from the 1950s.* ¶ On the right of the picture is his new, British-built, portable wheeling machine that he takes to customers' premises. Alan is standing in the workshop of Andy King, who he works with on pre-1955 MG restorations. *This is the limit of my era; anything later doesn't inspire me as much.* He also recently started the restoration of a 1939 Daimler DB18 Drop Head Coupe that was built for King George VI. *I am preserving as much of the original as possible for the current owner, but am having to make new wings and running boards.* ¶ Another customer, in his seventies, wanted a more drastic change to his 1930s Lagonda. Alan removed the shell and, based on lines and measurements taken from other vehicles, transformed the car into a convertible. *He drove away happy and the original body has been put into storage for future generations if they wish to convert it back.* ¶ Often when he removes panels he finds the names of people who worked on them long ago and old theatre tickets and all sorts fall out. *These cars have a wealth of stories to tell, it is reassuring to know they are owned by people who appreciate their connection with the past and take care of them.* Alan worked on a beautiful Jaguar XK120 for a client who did not have enough space at home for his collection, so found someone with a spare garage for the winter. The owner covered it in blankets and said farewell; when he returned in the spring he found it in a perfectly tailored jacket. *It turned out he had unwittingly left it with a retired seamstress.*

QEST Iliffe Family Charitable Foundation Scholar 2015

[217]

Joey Richardson

WOOD TURNER & MIXED-MEDIA SCULPTOR

QEST Worshipful
Company of Carpenters
Scholar 2012
QEST Thomas
Fattorini Award for
Excellence 2015

Turner and sculptor Joey Richardson was born in Lincolnshire and grew up on a small farm in Twigmoor Woods surrounded by magnificent trees. *Wood warms and restores the soul. It shaped me and in turn, I shape it.* ¶ She is known for her delicate, richly hued wood forms, made predominantly with reclaimed local timber. Each piece is sculpted on a lathe, cut, shaped and sanded by eye and decorated by piercing, pyrography (wood burning) and spray painting. Her sculptures are held in museum collections around the world and she passes on her knowledge through international masterclasses and demonstrations. ¶ Joey is holding a teapot called *Tea of Peace* that she made in honour of her mentor and friend Binh Pho who died in 2017. She first met Binh, an artist working in wood and glass, when she received a bursary in 2005 from the Worshipful Company of Turners to study wood turning in the USA. She spent three days at his studio in Chicago; they hit it off and began to collaborate on pieces when she returned the following year. In 2012, Joey received a QEST Scholarship in glass casting to add a new dimension to her work in wood. Binh was one of the three experts she studied under. ¶ The teapot is laden with symbolism that depicts their relationship through woodcraft. It is made from reclaimed English sycamore from Joey's childhood home. The butterfly is Joey's trademark, there is one on everything she makes. *I used to tell my children that the butterfly's struggle to get out of its cocoon gives it the strength in its wings to fly.* Binh is Vietnamese for 'peace' (he was born during the Vietnam War) and he is represented by the dragonfly. *After the fall of Saigon he was in the queue at the American Embassy awaiting evacuation by the helicopters, which he thought looked like dragonflies hovering in the sky. Binh was left behind, but later escaped to safety as one of the 'boat people'; the dragonfly remained his emblem of hope.* ¶ Joey is continuing her wood turning alongside part-time study for a Masters in Fine Art at the University of Lincoln. She is sitting in her *Tree House*, a studio that she created for a module of her MFA (the tutors had to visit to mark it). *I had the idea after a symposium on 'Doing Deceleration'. In true Joey fashion I was trying to squeeze in too much: I missed my train, had to drive to Nottingham and rushed in, out of breath, five minutes late.* The next few hours were spent listening to artists talking about the creative importance of pacing yourself. This made her stop and think. *I got home and picked a spot above a tangle of ash and sycamore trunks to build this sanctuary. It is a fabulous space for contemplation. I can focus entirely on my work – writing, sketching and carving – and if I pull up the bottom four steps of the ladder, my family knows not to disturb me.* ¶ The course is bringing a theoretical depth to Joey's work. *I am using my craft skills to investigate the symbiotic relationships that humans have with trees and nature and how we must appreciate what we have before it is too late.* The axe in the picture is carved in wood from an avenue of lime trees felled in Sheffield. *They were ignored for years until they were about to be cut down, then everyone was up in arms.* It will be exhibited at her final degree show along with a wooden chainsaw and ice logs, all material transpositions that blunt the effectiveness of the object. She is also making a shed, *Distillation of Experiences*. It comprises 110 panels of pierced wood that cast patterns outside when the light is on inside to reflect the fragility of nature. ¶ For someone who is constantly seeking deeper meaning through her craft, Joey doesn't need to look far to find a metaphor for the wisdom of her current work on the veracity of nature. The owl box on the trunk next to her tree house has been empty for the 15 years; she recently caught sight of a mother and fledgling chick.

Mila Chielman

SPECTACLE MAKER

Mila Chielman grew up in a Buddhist community near York. There was a workshop full of equipment and tools with which the homes were built. Over time, it filled with craftspeople: masons, carvers, woodworkers and more. *I was back recently and someone told me that I was always in there asking questions, obsessing over a skill, then moving onto the next.* Spectacle making is the one he could not put down. ¶ Mila's grandfather has been hand making spectacles for 63 years: bespoke frames for opticians; contemporary styles for London Fashion Week; and specially-fitted glasses for children at Great Ormond Street Hospital. *I used to sort hinges into drawers when I went to stay with him in Kent.* Mila discovered that his grandfather had been holding off taking on an apprentice in the hope that Mila would want to pick up his tools. *He didn't say a word, but it happened naturally. I was able to learn from him, but he is not accredited, so the training would not be formally recognised.* ¶ Cubitts, founded by Tom Broughton in 2012 with a mission to revive the craft of hand making spectacles in the UK, welcomed Mila as a QEST Apprentice. He is pictured in the Cubitts Optical Workshop in London's King's Cross. The green instrument on the bench is his grandfather's 'bridge bumper'. *Manual ones are almost impossible to get hold of now.* Mila is working with Cubitts' expert maker Mat Havercroft to learn the 50 stages of production. ¶ Each frame begins with quality materials, including Italian cellulose acetate, sustainably-farmed water buffalo horn from India and Scotland and 18 carat gold. For the first year, he worked mostly in acetate, the most forgiving. Mila is shaping his second pair in horn. *It requires constant oiling to make the fibres less likely to split.* He has also experimented with a wool composite. It is soft to carve, yet durable, and during polishing, ends of the strands emerge to create interesting texture. Progress is checked against a design drawing throughout. *Precision is essential: we work to within a tenth of a millimetre.* ¶ The set up brings everything together and distinguishes a skilled frame maker. Attaching the arms to the front is a complex process with lots of judgement calls to make to get the right pantoscopic tilt, the angle at which the lens is level with the line of sight and at the right distance from each eye. *Nobody's ears are level! I have to consider how they will fold too.* All Cubitts spectacles have mitred joints to create a strong bond and superior fit, and most are secured by pin drilling Cubitts' custom rivets. This traditional process requires more time and skill, but the elegant join is worth it. ¶ *Working with my grandfather gave me a head start, but that was entirely using hand skills.* At Cubitts, technology is used in an interesting way to revive and refine some elements. Mila is learning to cut on a CNC (Computer Numeric Control) machine, and studying optics (how lenses work has implications for the frame) and cephalometry (taking measurements of the face and head) for bespoke frames. Cubitts is using this principle to develop a method of using smartphones to take images of a customer's face. They are meshed into a 3D scan from which a frame is designed to fit to the individual and made from scratch in the workshop. ¶ Mila shares Cubitts' obsession with tradition and progress and is full of ideas. In the meantime, he is dedicated to making immaculate spectacles at professional pace. While Mat tends to work on a single frame from start to finish, Mila usually has six or seven pairs on the go. *I am equally focused, but don't think I have lost my butterfly mind entirely; this keeps me engaged.* Mat sums up perfectly the ethos of the QEST Apprenticeship. *Mila is only 20; I wish I had discovered spectacle making at his age. He has so much natural talent and decades ahead of him to make his mark in the craft.*

QEST Garfield Weston Foundation Apprentice 2017

Roll of Honour

SCHOLARS WHO APPEAR IN THIS BOOK ARE HIGHLIGHTED IN RED

1991 SCHOLARS

RUPERT CHRISTIE *Equicentre, Farriery*

DEBORAH FIETTE *Sir Nevil Macready CBE, Tapestry Conservation*

STEVEN GRAVESTOCK *Findlater Mackie Todd & Co Ltd, Stonemasonry*

TIMOTHY HARRIS *R. Twining & Company Ltd, Glassmaking* page 13

CLAIRE O'FLAHERTY *John Lobb Ltd, Shoemaking*

MARLIESE SYMONS *Ainsworths Homeopathic Pharmacy, Homeopathy*

1992 SCHOLARS

DAVINA CHAPMAN *Mobil Oil Company Ltd, Calligraphy*

SANDIE ENNIS *Sir Nevil Macready CBE, Rugmaking*

MARTIN ENOCH *Wilkinson PLC, Glassmaking*

JUDITH GARDNER JONES *M Leslie CVO, Opera Singing*

SONJA NUTTALL *Stephens Brothers, Haute Couture*

FRANCES PLOWDEN *Blacksmithing* page 53

DAVID SAX *Moët & Chandon, Winemaking*

GRAHAM WILLIAMS *H P Bulmer PLC, Antique Furniture Restoration*

1993 SCHOLARS

SPIKE BUCKLOW *Hamilton Kerr Institute, Painting Conservation*

MARY BUTCHER *Basketmakers' Company, Basketmaking*

JONATHAN DARRACOTT *Crafts Magazine, Watchmaking & Repair*

DENISE DURHAM *Procter & Gamble Ltd, Chairmaking*

SARAH GOODWIN *J Dege & Sons Ltd, Gold Embroidery*

PHILIPPA HUNT *Camberwell College of Arts, Paper Conservation*

BISI OSINDERO *House of Fraser, Millinery*

1994 SCHOLARS

RUTH BODDINGTON *Calligraphy*

GRAHAM COLLIS *Ironbridge Gorge Museum, Blacksmithing*

RICHARD FAULKNER *Clockmakers' Company, Horology*

JANET WICKS *Rhône-Poulenc Agriculture Ltd, Quilting*

CATHERINE WOODFORDE *Carvers & Gilders Ltd, Gilding*

1995 SCHOLARS

ROS CONWAY *Pâte de Verre Glassmaking*

ANGELA CRAFT *Bookbinding*

NICOLA DUNN *West Dean College, Antique Metal Conservation*

JONATHAN FRASER *Probiotics Ltd, Garden Design*

JAMES HAMILL *Beekeeping* page 157

RODNEY HARRIS *Brick Sculpture* page 193

VERONICA MAIN *Straw Work*

STEPHEN MILLS *Albert E. Chapman Ltd, Upholstery*

LISA SHEKEDE *Domestic Wall Painting Conservation*

1996 SCHOLARS

RUPERT ALEXANDER *Austin Reed Group PLC, Portrait Painting*

LEE COLLINS *Farriery*

RICHARD DRAYTON *Boatbuilding*

REBECCA HELLEN *Spink & Son Ltd, Easel Painting Conservation* page 213

BEX MARRIOTT *Ms Jen Lindsay, Bookbinding*

PETER NORRINGTON *Cordwainers' College, Western Saddle Making*

RACHEL FOSTER *Confectionery*

TIM WADE *Professor Pennell, Woodcarving*

1997 SCHOLARS

SEAN ATHOW *Michael Oswald CVO, Farriery*

DEBORAH CARRÉ *Hand Sewn Shoemaking* page 165

ALAN GRAYSTOCK *UK Skills, Scagliola*

SUE HUDSWELL *Henry Maxwell & Co Ltd, Shoemaking*

ANTHEA LAING *Upholstery*

HEATHER SPROAT *Harvey Nichols Ltd, Haute Couture*

PETER TING *Thomas Goode & Co Ltd, Ceramics & 3D Printing* page 66

1998 SCHOLARS

CLAUDIA CLARE *Ceramics* page 45

JONATHAN HARRIS *UK Skills, Woodcarving*

BARBARA JONES *Living Earth, Exeter, Lime Plastering & Cob Building*

STEPHEN LEWIS *Fenland Laundries Ltd, Stained Glass Conservation*

SHEM MACKEY *Luthiery* page 98

JAMES SHOULDER *UK Skills, Geometrical Staircase Building*

LUCINDA TURNER *Puppet Carving*

1999 SCHOLARS

JULIET BANKES *Gilbertson & Page Ltd, Wood Engraving*

MATTHEW CAINES *Classical Figure Carving*

CHARLOTTE DE SYLLAS *Jewellery* page 190

MARTIN HASWELL *Digital Photography*

DEIRDRE HAWKEN *Millinery* page 74

SALLY HAYES *Woodturning*

SARAH HOCOMBE *Fresco Painting* page 146

CHRIS MELLOY *Royal National College for the Blind, Piano Tuning*

JOHN POOLE *Gilding*

DUNSTAN RICKHUSS *Paint Effects*

JOHN ROGERS *Farriery*

EDWARD SCHARER *Conservation & Restoration*

2000 SCHOLARS

RICHARD BALL *Stone Carving*

SARAH BERRY *Architectural Woodcarving*

GABRIELA DENNY *Portrait Painting*

DANIEL DORMAN *Boatbuilding*

STEVEN GARRETT *UK Skills, Ecclesiastical Joinery*

ROD KELLY *Goldsmithing & Silversmithing* page 82

CHRISTOPHER MCBETH *Farriery*

ROBERT OGBORN *Decorative Paint Effects*

MICHAEL RHYS JONES *Farriery*

SHARON SMITH *Interior Design*

LAI SYMES *Millinery* page 102

LAURA WEST *Bookbinding*

LOUISA WOOD *Hemp Weaving*

ROY YOUDALE *Basketmaking*

2001 SCHOLARS

MARCIA BENNETT MALE *Stone Carving & Lettering*

CHRISTOPHER CHESHER *Clock Restoration*

WALLY GILBERT *Silversmithing*

PAMELA HOWLETT *Millinery*

ADELAIDE IZAT *Conservation of Easel Paintings*

ANNA KETTLE *Pargeting* page 145

AMANDA LANE *Photography*

JON LETCHER *Harp & Dulcimer Making* page 138
STEVEN NEWELL *Glassmaking*
MARK UPTON *Bronze Casting*

2002 SCHOLARS

TERRY ADAMS *Winterborne Zelston Fencing, Cleaving*
ROSANNA BANKES *Decorative Arts*
JON BEER *Furniture Making & Design*
PIERS CONWAY *Stonemasonry*
JESSIE HIGGINSON *Ceramics*
SHIRLEY JUSTICE-VOSE *Side Saddle Design & Manufacture*
ELIZABETH MONK *Craft Pottery*
SANNA PALOSAARI *John Lobb Ltd, Shoemaking*
CHRIS ROBINSON *Clock Restoration*
JILL SMALLCOMBE *Cob Building & Sculpture*

2003 SCHOLARS

ZOË CULL *Stone Lettercutting*
ELIZABETH CHEADLE *Polychromed Timber Conservation*
DR BRIAN COLES *Clock Restoration*
CORDAELIA CRAINE *Leather Moulding*
MATTHIAS GARN *Stonemasonry*
ADAM GREENWELL *Blacksmithing & Forged Ironwork*
DAVID GUNDRY *Stonemasonry*
SARAH PENNAL *Stonemasonry*
ELIZABETH MEEK *Bookbinding & Book Conservation*
KAYE NELSON *Farriery*
MARTIN PENNING *Double Bass Making*
NIKI SIMPSON *Digital Botanical Illustration* page 186

2004 SCHOLARS

LAURA COWLING *Stonemasonry*
JACQUELINE CULLEN *Whitby Jet Jewellery*
SIÂN EVANS *Coppersmithing*
GILLIAN FORBES *Stone Carving & Lettercutting*
ZOË HARDING *Goldsmithing & Jewellery* page 137
BOB JOHNSTON *Basketmaking & Willow Sculpture* page 130
FIONA JONES *A G Joy & Sons, Plasterwork Conservation*

JILL JONES *Botanical Illustration*

PETE LAMBERT *Hedgelaying*

CLIVE LEE *Bowed Instrument Making*

DEBORAH MITCHELL *Wood Fired Pottery*

BEN MURPHY *Bronze Sculpture Conservation*

ADAM PEIRSON *Cookery*

MALCOLM RUFFELL *Ladder Back Chair Making*

MIA SAROSI *Ceramics* page 161

JULIAN STAIR *Monumental Thrown Pots* page 29

GEOFFREY WALKER *Clock Restoration*

LOUISE WILDE *Animation*

2005 SCHOLARS

CHERYL BRANFORD-PEERS *Textile Design*

JACQUI CAREY *Braidmaking* page 85

EDWARD CHEESE *Book Conservation*

JANE FRYERS *Millinery* page 162

REBECCA HARVEY *Ceramics*

ANTONIA HOCKTON *Stone Carving*

JUNG-JI KIM *Jewellery*

SUZY MERRIFIELD *Wendy Keith Designs, Knitwear Design*

ADAM NASH *Thatching* page 106

RUTH PARTINGTON *Paper Conservation*

ANNETTE PRICE *Photography*

BRENT QUILLIAM *Stonemasonry*

JANET STOYEL *Wire Weaving*

TOM WAUGH *Architectural Stone Carving*

2006 SCHOLARS

PAUL ALLISON *Buttons Saddlery, Side Saddle Making*

GARY DROSTLE *Mosaic Art* page 158

PAUL GRAY *Farriery*

RACHAEL HODGSON *Intaglio Printing*

TRACY HOLMES *Stained Glass Conservation*

BERNARD JOHNSON *Stone Carving*

JACKIE KING *Digital Fine Art Photography*

GARRY LEWIS *Winterborne Zelston Fencing, Forestry & Cleaving*

AIDAN MCEVOY *Furniture Design & Making* page 70

TIMOTHY PHIPPS *Thatching*

CAMILLA SKOVGAARD *Women's Footwear Design*
RHIAN SOLOMON *Textile & Print Design*
HANNAH TAYLOR *Costume Design*

2007 SCHOLARS
JOSEPHINE BENEY *Conservation*
WILLIAM DAVIES *CWO Ltd, Stone Carving*
EUGENIE DEGAN *Hedley Foundation, Luthiery* page 34
KATE HETHERINGTON *Collar & Harness Making* page 149
KATHERINE HOWLETT *Printed Textile Design & Making*
KERRY LEMON *Illustration* page 30
SALLY MANGUM *Calligraphy & Heraldic Art* page 178
GILES MORGAN *Woodcarving*
ALAN PARTRIDGE *Organ Shallot Making*
ANNA ROLLS *Metal Conservation*
SIMON SAGGERS *Hedge Laying & Hurdle Making*
FELIX THORNTON-JONES *Sculpture & Decorative Arts Conservation*
CAROLE WALLER *Glass Painting & Enamelling*
MELISSA WHITE *Decorative Arts* page 18

2008 SCHOLARS
RUTH ANTHONY *Hand Engraving* page 122
SU BLACKWELL *3D Paper Artistry*
ELEANOR BIRD *Stained Glass Painting*
CAI JIA ENG *3D Paper Artistry*
JIM FLEETING *Luthiery*
SIMON FOULSER *Carpentry & Joinery*
MEL HOWSE *Vitreous Art* page 46
LAURA HOMER *Easel Painting Conservation*
MARINA HUGHES *Mural & Decorative Artistry*
BEN MARKS *Historical Keyboard Intrument Conservation* page 37
RICHARD MCGUINNESS *Classic Wooden Car Body Restoration*
ANDRIAN MELKA *Sculpture & Stone Carving* page 49
RACHEL SAWICKI *Book Conservation*
MARTINA SCOTT *Calligraphy & Illumination*
SUSANNAH SILVER *Artisan Baking*
KATIE ROSE WHITING *Hedley Foundation, Shoe Design*
BETHAN LLOYD WORTHINGTON *Ceramics*

2009 SCHOLARS

TOM ADAMS *Orcharding* page 209

SAM BAKEWELL *Ceramics*

TOM BROWN *Stone Carving* page 87

CHARLES COLLIS *Double Bass Making*

CATHERINE DAND *Archive Conservation*

ROSE FORSHALL *Illustration*

HANNAH GRIFFITHS *Mosaic Art* page 81

MARIA HAGGLUND *RWHA, Gilding Restoration*

GAIL MCGARVA *Traditional Wooden Boatbuilding* page 129

GRANT MCCAIG *Silversmithing*

DANIEL MEEK *Stonemasonry & Lettercutting*

EYIZERA PHOENIX *Hedley Foundation, Children's Book Illustration*

JESSICA POOLE *Jewellery Making & Design*

JENNY SAUNT *Stucco Duro*

ANN-SOFIE WIDEGREN *RWHA, Gilding Restoration*

JASON WILLIAMS *Classic Car Restoration & Welding*

ELIZABETH WOOLLEY *Wall Painting Conservation*

2010 SCHOLARS

GRAHAM ASHFORD *Blacksmithing & Armoury* page 167

TRISTRAM BAINBRIDGE *Furniture Conservation*

POLLY BELL *Textile Design*

GRACE BRENNAN *Scenic Painting for Theatre*

TREVOR CAIN *Dolls House Conservation & Restoration*

SOPHIE D'SOUZA *Stained Glass Painting* page 78

TOBY GOUGH *Paper & Book Conservation*

JENNIFER GRAY *Hedley Foundation, Silversmithing & Jewellery*

JAY HERYET *Woodturning & Lathe Artistry*

WILL KEMP *Portrait Painting*

JAMES KIRBY *Stone Carving*

GABRIELLA MACARO *Easel Painting Conservation*

REUBEN MARSH *Stone Carving*

JENNY PICKFORD *Blacksmithing & Glassblowing* page 210

MIA SABEL *Saddlery & Leather Design* page 154

ANDREW SWINSCOE *Cheese Maturing* page 177

MAKIKO TSUNODA *Paper & Book Conservation*

ANJA VON KALINOWSKI *Haute Couture Dressmaking & Embroidery*

2011 SCHOLARS

CHRISTABEL HELENA ANDERSON *Iconography* page 205

SHELLEY ANDERSON *Hedley Foundation, Metalwork* page 17

TERESA DYBISZ *Stone Carving*

JESSICA EDWARDS *Textile Design & Embroidery*

SARAH FREEMAN *Easel Painting Conservation*

CHRISTOPHER GRANSBURY *Saddlery & Harness Making*

WAYNE HART *Lettercarving & Sculpture* page 41

JOSEPH LOTITO *Violin Making*

DANIEL MAIER *Fine Cabinetmaking & Engraving*

NICOLA MATHEWS *Upholstery & Embroidery*

CATRIN MORGAN *Illustration*

RICHARD MOSSMAN *Stone Carving & Sculpture* page 33

TOM NICHOLLS *Stone Carving* page 87

KATHERINE POGSON *Bespoke Leatherwork* page 194

CAMERON SHORT *Hand Block-Printing* page 94

HAZEL THORN *Silversmithing* page 26

2012 SCHOLARS

ANNELIESE APPLEBY *Printmaking* page 113

ALASTAIR BARFORD *Drawing & Painting* page 109

NIGEL BENNET *Photographic Art & Printmaking*

EFFIE BURNS *Glass Engraving* page 134

JESSICA COLEMAN *Garfield Weston Foundation, Mixed-media Textile Design*

STEVEN COOK *Carpenters' Company, Diamond Jubilee Bog Oak Project*

JAMIE CORETH *Garfield Weston Foundation, Portrait Painting* page 125

SUSAN EARLY *Garfield Weston Foundation, Basketmaking*

CAREY ELLIS *Textile Design*

MARY FRENCH *Clothworkers' Company, Book Conservation*

ANTHONY GRIFFIN *Garfield Weston Foundation, Diamond Optical Setting*

RUTH HEENAN *Cordwaining*

TIMOTHY HUGHES *J Paul Getty Jr Charitable Trust, Conservation & Restoration of Clocks*

BEATRICE LARKIN *Iliffe Family Charitable Trust, Woven Textiles*

ANNA LORENZ *Garfield Weston Foundation, Jewellery, Silversmithing & Metalwork*

MANDEEP MANN *Garfield Weston Foundation, Textile Design*

NATASHA MANN *Radcliffe Trust, Zouaq Art* page 38

ROSANNA MARTIN *Bendicks (Mayfair) Ltd, Ceramics*

EMMA NICHOLS *Clothworkers' Company, Conservation*

TIFFANY PARKINSON *Saddlers' Company, Saddlery*

EMMA PAYNE *J Paul Getty Jr Charitable Trust, Archaeological & Museum Conservation*

JOEY RICHARDSON *Carpenters' Company, Woodturning & Glass Artistry* page 218

LEWIS ROBINS-GRACE *Tallow Chandlers' Company & J Paul Getty Jr Charitable Trust, Conservation of Historic Objects & Buildings*

MEERA SLEIGHT *Radcliffe Trust, Hand Embroidery*

MEGAN STACEY *Hedley Foundation, Stained Glass Conservation*

NINA THOMAS *Radcliffe Trust, Farriery* page 142

SARAI VARDI *Clothworkers' Company, Book Conservation*

MATTHEW WARNER *Eranda Foundation, Pottery & Ceramics*

JON WILLIAMS *Garfield Weston Foundation, Ceramics & Illustration* page 189

MARY WING TO *Leathersellers' Company, Whip Making* page 50

SOPHIE ZAJICEK *Weave Design & Making*

2013 SCHOLARS

MARK ANGELO-GIZZI *Leathersellers' Company, Leatherwork* page 93

BENJAMIN ARNOLD *Hiscox Fine Art Insurance, Fine Art*

JULIET BAILEY *Woven Textile Design & Weaving* page 119

CLARE BARNETT *Saddlers' Company, Saddlery* page 141

SCOTT BENEFIELD *Eranda Foundation, Glassmaking* page 58

FLETT BERTRAM *Hedley Foundation, Embroidery & Textile Design*

FRANKI BREWER *Woven Textile Design & Weaving* page 119

GAYLE COOPER *Wig Making* page 65

HELENA CURRY *Sculpture*

JOCELYN DANBY *Garfield Weston Foundation, Saddlery*

RUTH EMILY DAVEY *Leathersellers' Company, Cordwaining*

KATE EARLAM *Silversmithing*

MARTIN EARLE *Radcliffe Trust, Iconography*

SARAH EDWARDS *Leathersellers' Company, Leather Goods Design & Making*

NICK GILL *Garfield Weston Foundation, Typefounding* page 198

EMILY GOODAKER *Garfield Weston Foundation, Jewellery Design & Making*

LUCIE GRAHAM *J Paul Getty Jr Charitable Trust, Natural History Conservation*

MERLYN GRIFFITHS *NADFAS, Stained Glass Conservation*

CHARLOTTE HETHERIDGE *Garfield Weston Foundation, Textile Design & Making*

LAURA JEARY *Garfield Weston Foundation, Stonemasonry & Building Conservation*

AALIA KAMAL *J Paul Getty Jr Charitable Trust, Easel Painting Conservation*

CHRISTOPHER MADLIN *Stained Glass Design & Making*

LIDA MARINKOVA *Garfield Weston Foundation, Mixed-media Textile Design*

ROBIN MATHER *Garfield Weston Foundation, Bicycle Design & Making*

RYAN MCCLEAN *Silversmithing*

KATE MONTAGNE-MACDONALD *Andrew Lloyd Webber Foundation, Architectural Sculpture*

TARA OSBOROUGH *Bendicks (Mayfair) Ltd, Textile Design & Making*

ELIZABETH PEERS *Silversmithing*

ALEX PENGELLY *Iliffe Family Charitable Trust, Textile Design & Knitwear* page 97

BENJAMIN POINTER *Clothworkers' Company, Book & Paper Conservation*

JAY PRICE *Garfield Weston Foundation, Fine Art Printmaking*

GORDON W. ROBERTSON *Pewterers' Company, Metalsmithing* page 73

JACK ROW *Goldsmithing & Pen Making* page 21

STEPHEN SHOEBRIDGE *Bespoke Tailoring*

BEN SHORT *Ernest Cook Trust, Charcoal Burning & Coppicing* page 77

THOMAS SKEENS *Rumi Foundation, Pottery & Ceramics*

SOPHIE STAMP *Silversmithing*

OLUWASEYI SOSANYA *Design Engineering* page 117

LAUREN ELIZABETH TIDD *Garfield Weston Foundation, Jewellery Design & Making*

STEVE TOMLIN *Adam Connolly Memorial Fund, Greenwood Carving* page 214

TOM VOWDEN *Eranda Foundation, Stained Glass Conservation*

KATE WALLWORK *Garfield Weston Foundation, Stonemasonry*

KIRSTEN WALSH *Tallow Chandlers' Company, Wood & Stone Conservation*

SARAH WARSOP *Garfield Weston Foundation, Jewellery Design & Making*

NICOLA WATSON *Saddlers' Company, Side Saddle Making & Restoration*

HOLLIE WHITE *Cordwaining*

2014 SCHOLARS

JAMES ADAIR *Saddlers' Company, Saddlery* page 105

ZOE BARNETT *NADFAS, Stonemasonry*

ELOISE CAISLEY *Saddlers' Company, Saddlery & Leatherwork*

SUSAN CATCHER *Paper Conservation*

SAMANTHA CAWSON *Almary Green Awards, Paper Conservation*

STEVEN CUGNONI *Tallow Chandlers' Company, Bricklaying & Building Conservation*

LAUREN DAY *Bendicks (Mayfair) Ltd, Textiles*

AMY DIX *Eranda Foundation, Stained Glass Conservation*

DANIEL DURNIN *Johnnie Walker, Artist Maker* page 182

SAMUEL FLINTHAM *Garfield Weston Foundation, Stone*

EDDIE GLEW *Garfield Weston Foundation, Rural Crafts*

FELIX HANDLEY *Garfield Weston Foundation, Stone Carving & Sculpture*

ALISON HEATH *Clothworkers' Company & Radcliffe Trust, Bookbinding*

JORUNN HUSTOFT *Garfield Weston Foundation, Knitted Textiles*

MARGARET JONES *Garfield Weston Foundation, Tapestry Weaving* page 61

JONATHON KELLY *J Paul Getty Jr Charitable Trust, Clockmaking* page 202

BILLY LLOYD *Eranda Foundation, Ceramic Tableware*

LISA MCCONNIFFE *Iliffe Family Charitable Trust, Textiles*

WAYNE MEETEN *Pamela de Tristan, Goldsmithing & Silversmithing* page 201

THOMAS MERRETT *Garfield Weston Foundation, Stone Carving & Sculpture* page 62

ALAN MOORE *Garfield Weston Foundation, Textiles*

GILLIAN MURPHY *John Smedley Ltd, Knitted Textiles*

KIM NORRIE *Johnstons of Elgin, Textiles*

ANNE PETTERS *Garfield Weston Foundation, Glassmaking* page 133

ALEXANDRA PYE *Carpenters' Company, Woodwork & Classical Guitar Making*

TOM SANDS *Garfield Weston Foundation, Luthiery* page 170

HANNAH SUTHERLAND *J Paul Getty Jr Charitable Trust, Historical Costume Conservation*

JOSEPH WARD *Garfield Weston Foundation, Stone & Wood Conservation*

IMOGEN WOODINGS *Brian Mercer Charitable Trust, Upholstery* page 185

2014 APPRENTICES

PARHAM ALIZADEH *Shoemaking*

CURTIS CHIPPERFIELD *Hedley Foundation, Building Conservation*

ISATU HYDE *Heritage Crafts Association, Ceramics*

PAUL KIRKOS *Andrew Lloyd Webber Foundation, Silversmithing*

WILLIAM POWELL *Hedley Foundation, Shoemaking*

ALISTAIR RAPHAEL *Radcliffe Trust, Cordwaining & Shoemaking*

2015 SCHOLARS

TOMIWA ADEOSUN *Leathersellers' Company, Cordwaining & Footwear Design* page 197

CLAIRE BARRETT *Heraldic Drafting*

FIONA ROSE BATEY *Rumi Foundation, Children's Book Illustration*

KATE BOUCHER *Radcliffe Trust, Mixed-media Art*

JADE CROMPTON *Rumi Foundation, Ceramics & Digital Design*

AMELIA CROWLEY-ROTH *Radcliffe Trust, Woodcarving* page 69

CAITLIN DOWSE *D'Oyly Carte Charitable Trust, Painting Conservation*

SAM ELGAR *Kirby Laing Foundation, Stonemasonry*

ALAN FLOYD *Iliffe Family Charitable Foundation, Coachbuilding* page 217

EMILY JUNIPER *Clothworkers' Company, Bookbinding*

JESSICA LECLERE *John Smedley Ltd, Knitwear Design*

MELANIE LEWISTON *Leathersellers' Company, Millinery*

MANUEL MAZZOTTI *Clothworkers' Company, Bookbinding* page 42

CLARE PATTINSON *Automata & Mechanical Art* page 174

MARTIN PRESHAW *Carpenters' Company, Irish Union (Uilleann) Pipes*
HELEN READER *Leathersellers' Company, Saddlery*
ANOUSH WADDINGTON *Bendicks (Mayfair) Ltd, Jewellery & Fashion Accessories*
JESSICA WETHERLY *NADFAS, Figurative Sculpture*
JOJO WOOD *Ernest Cook Trust, Clog Making* page 173

2015 APPRENTICES

JUSTINE BONENFANT *Heritage Crafts Association, Broderers' Company (Associated Liveries), Embroidery*
SEAN HENDERSON *Andrew Lloyd Webber Foundation, Stonemasonry*
BETHAN HORN *Heritage Crafts Association, Cordwaining*
SARAH JARMAN *Heritage Crafts Association, Brain Mercer & Radcliffe Trust, Traditional Signwriting*
LIBBY KATES *Heritage Crafts Association, Drapers' Company, Textile Design* page 119
SHANNON KNIGHT *Cambridge Satchel Company, Jewellery*
JOHN KYNASTON *David Blackburn, Farriery*
CHARLOTTE MCGRATH *Cooks' Company (Associated Liveries), Culinary Arts*
SAMUEL MCMAHON *Hedley Foundation, Jewellery*
SOPHIE MICHAEL *Glen Dimplex, Analogue Film Conservation*
THOMAS SARGEANT *Heritage Crafts Association, Masons' Company (Associated Liveries), Stonemasonry*
OSCAR WHAPHAM *Made in Britain, Woodcarving*

2016 SCHOLARS

JENNIE ADAMSON *Johnnie Walker, Bespoke Tailoring* page 110
LORA AVEDIAN *John Smedley Ltd, Embroidery & Textile Design*
CORALIE CHUNG *Heritage Crafts Association, Leathersellers' Company, Saddlery*
AMY ROSE COLLINS *Radcliffe Trust, Printed Textile Design*
JACK DARACH *Turners' Company, Woodwind Instrument Making*
POPPY FIELD *Finnis Scott Foundation, Sculpture*
HAYLEY GIBBS *Kirby Laing Foundation, Stone Carving* page 206
AMY GOODWIN *Traditional Sign Painting* page 90
DANIEL HARRISON *Howdens, Furniture Design & Making* page 114
NICK HOBBS *Bendicks (Mayfair) Ltd, Trompe l'oeil & Mural Artist*
FRANCESCA LEVEY *J Paul Getty Jr Charitable Trust, Metals Conservation*
AUBURN CLAIRE LUCAS *Traditional Hand Embroidery*
ROWAN MCONEGAL *Stained Glass & Printmaking*
NAOMI NEVILL *Dengie Crops Ltd, Enamelling & Jewellery Design*
ANNEMARIE O'SULLIVAN *D'Oyly Carte Charitable Trust, Basketmaking* page 153
LOUISE PARRY *Silversmithing & Timepiece Making*
AURORA PETTINARI YORK *Radcliffe Trust, Hand Embroidery* page 14
MANASI DEPALA *Clarins, Silversmithing* page 82

KAYO SAITO *Gem Carving* page 126

MARIO SIERRA *Rokill Ltd, Handloom Weaving* page 23

BEN LAUGHTON SMITH *Sir Siegmund Warburg's Voluntary Settlement, Fine Art* page 150

SABINA WEISS *Cambridge Satchel Company, Product Design & Furniture Making*

DAVID SNOO WILSON *Bell Founding* page 181

2016 APPRENTICES

GIOVANNI COLAPIETRO *Highgrove Enterprise, Horticulture*

POLLY COLLINS *Bespoke Shoemaking*

ROBERT DEAN *Jewellery Making*

SARAH HOBBS *Pewterers' Company, Engraving*

DEAN HOMER *Gosling Foundation, Classic Car Restoration*

MATTHEW JACQUES *Allchurches Trust, Architectural Leatherwork*

DAMIEN MCKEOWN *Pilgrim Trust, Handloom Weaving* page 23

RICKY TELFORD *Radcliffe Trust, Diamond Setting*

HANNAH VICKERS *Associated Liveries, Textile Conservation*

ADELE WILLIAMSON *Radcliffe Trust, Bespoke Shoemaking*

NICHOLAS WILLS *Gamekeeping*

SAM WOOLHAM *Pewterers' Company, Farriery*

NICK SMITH *Ice Sculpture*

2017 SCHOLARS

JAMES BANHAM *Cabinetmaking*

MATTHEW BRIGGS *House of Fraser, Knitted Textiles*

HEIDI BROAD *Ana, Fine Art*

ANTON CATALDO *Charlotte Bonham-Carter Charitable Trust, Fine Art*

MATTHEW COOK *Architectural Stonemasonry Conservation*

PHOEBE CORKER-MARIN *Garfield Weston Foundation, Doll Making*

MARIE DOINNE *Ernest Cook Trust, Bookbinding*

CELIA DOWSON *Tom Helme, Ceramics*

HARRY FORSTER-STRINGER *Bendicks (Mayfair) Ltd, Enamelling* page 101

CANDICE LAU *Heritage Crafts Association, Leathersellers' Company, Leatherwork*

LILY MARSH *Howdens, Stonemasonry*

FRANKEY PINNOCK *Garfield Weston Foundation, Cordwaining*

THEA SANDERS *Knitted Textiles & Upholstery*

HANNAH TOUNSEND *Howdens, Ceramics*

CRAIG STRUTHERS *Johnnie Walker, Watch Case Making* page 55

JOHN SUTCLIFFE *Kirby Laing Foundation, Stonemasonry & Sculpture*

CARA LOUISE WALKER *Penhaligon's, Glassblowing, Casting & Silversmithing*

2017 APPRENTICES

MILA CHIELMAN *Garfield Weston Foundation, Spectacle Making* page 221

BEN FAIRGRIEVE *Robertson Trust, Stonemasonry*

PAUL FALLOWS *Pilgrim Trust, Thatching* page 106

MATTHEW FOSTER *Stanley Picker Trust, Ceramics*

BLUEBELL HILL *Garfield Weston Foundation, Ceramics*

JACK MCGONIGLE *Ceramics*

HENRY MIDDLETON *Dulverton Trust, Farriery*

JOANNA MURPHY *Alborada Trust, Saddlery*

GABRIEL NOBLE *Bee Farming*

OLIVER PONT *29th May 1961 Charitable Trust, Bee Farming*

2018 SCHOLARS

LAURA ADBURGHAM *D'Oyly Carte Charitable Trust, Textiles*

ROSANNA BISHOP *Garfield Weston Foundation, Printed Textiles*

KENDALL FRANCIS *Finnis Scott Foundation, Easel Painting Conservation & Restoration*

JÉNNIFER GONZÁLEZ CORUJO *London Art History Society, Easel Painting Conservation & Restoration*

JEMMA GUNNING *Johnnie Walker, Printmaking*

OTIS INGRAMS *Leathersellers' Company, Leatherwork*

PAUL JEFFERIES *Edith Murphy Foundation, Percussion Instrument Making*

JOE MILNE *Heritage Crafts Association, Hedley Foundation, Stonemasonry*

JASON MOSSERI *Windsor Chair Making*

GILLIAN STEWART *Jenifer Emery, Bookbinding*

KAJA UPELJ *Glassmaking*

MAUD VAN DEN BROECKE *Cordwainers' Company, Hand Sewn Shoemaking*

THOMAS VAUGHAN *Howdens, Wood & Metalwork*

ALICE WALTON *Carole Bamford, Ceramics*

ZOE WATTS *Company of Arts Scholars, Silversmithing*

JACK WAYGOOD *Axe Forging*

2018 APPRENTICES

ENNA COATES *PF Charitable Trust, Windsor Chair Making*

ZOE COLLIS *Drapers' Company, Paper Making*

PATRICK WOODWARD *Garfield Weston Foundation, Horology*

Photo by Emma Loughton, Dash & Miller

In 2012, I photographed *Keepers*, a book of one hundred portraits of the ancient offices of Britain. This book for QEST, *A Celebration of British Craftsmanship*, is another serious project. Commissions like this are so rare that they are highlights of one's career. ¶ I liked the QEST team enormously from the moment I met them and am thankful for the trust they placed in me. On day one, I met Natasha Mann, Christabel Anderson, Deborah Carré and Jennie Adamson. I realised I was going to be spending the next four months in the company of extraordinary people and my photography had to do them justice. The camera guarantees a likeness, but a portrait has to be more. Jennie said she was nervously excited; I felt the same! ¶ The thrill of being a professional photographer is walking into a location, 'finding' the picture then 'making' it; I have to leave with the shot or I am no more than a camera owner. There was a challenge. Creative people love their workspaces, but this could not be a book of photographs of a hundred workshops. Lateral thinking was needed. I am grateful to those who went along with me and ventured to other places. I discussed the portraits of Rod Kelly and Manasi Depala, Graham Ashford and Niki Simpson with them for weeks beforehand. Other Scholars made pieces especially for their shoot. ¶ On the day, it was immensely satisfying to have several hours with each person. While we talked, my mind processed their words and the surroundings to find the essence of their craft before taking control to apply the technical process: composition, lens, lighting…and some coaxing patter to get a performance. Most of the portraits chosen for the book came from the last 15 frames, testament to the fact that we built them together. ¶ It has been a pleasure driving from Zennor in Cornwall, to the Shetlands, Newry in Northern Ireland and everywhere in between. I have seen the country at its finest and met QEST Scholars of all ages and at different stages of their careers sustaining its creative spirit. ¶ To show the craftsmanship, I photographed the Scholars' hands. The beautiful shapes they made while engaged in their skills are a wonderful photographic subject. ¶ However good a picture, it is better with text. Working with Karen has been a joy. I hope we have captured everyone's character and story and that I have shown my craft of photography to be a worthy companion to those of the QEST Alumni.

Acknowledgements

QEST would like to thank the following individuals and organisations for their generosity, time, patience, passion and support in helping to bring to life this magnificent book of British Craftsmanship.

Mark Van Oss, who had the idea and initiated the book, the first featuring QEST Scholars.

Karen Bennett, *writer*
Chantal Bristow, *researcher*
Julian Calder, *photographer*
Prof. Phil Cleaver, *creative director*

Guineviere Nicholas, *alumni liaison*
Jennifer Penny, *designer*
Joe Thomas, *picture preparation*
Minna Rossi & Nico Wills, *assistants*

An Anonymous Donor *and* R W Armstrong & Sons Ltd

Donors, Supporters & Sponsors – Past, Present & Future

Thank you to the Royal Warrant holders, livery companies, trusts, foundations, organisations and individuals who have generously supported QEST over the years. And, to those future supporters who have been inspired by this book.

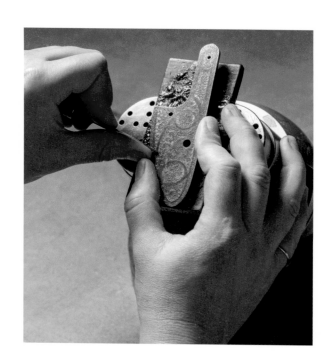